Aubrey De Vere

May carols

Or, Ancilla Domini, Legends of the Saxon Saints

Aubrey De Vere

May carols
Or, Ancilla Domini, Legends of the Saxon Saints

ISBN/EAN: 9783337231774

Printed in Europe, USA, Canada, Australia, Japan

Cover: Foto ©ninafisch / pixelio.de

More available books at **www.hansebooks.com**

MAY CAROLS

OR

ANCILLA DOMINI

LEGENDS OF THE SAXON SAINTS

BY

AUBREY DE VERE

NEW EDITION

London
MACMILLAN AND CO., Limited
NEW YORK: THE MACMILLAN COMPANY
1897

CONTENTS.

	PAGE
Preface	xiii
PROLOGUE	3

MAY CAROLS (Part I.)

I.—Who feels not, when the Spring once more	7
II.—Upon Thy Face, O God, Thy world ...	8
III.—All but unutterable Name! ...	9
IV.—How came there Sin to world so fair ...	9
V.—Sancta Maria	10
VI.—Fest. Nativitatis B. V. M.	10
VII.—Ab Angelo Salutata ...	11
VIII.—Nihil respondit	12
IX.—St. Joseph's Doubt ...	13
X.—Fest. Visitationis	14
XI.—Amor Innocentium ...	15
XII.—Fest. Nativitatis ...	16
XIII.—Protevangelion	17
XIV.—Dei Genitrix	18
XV.—Adolescentulae amaverunt te nimis ...	19
XVI.—The infant year with infant freak	20
XVII.—Fest. Epiphaniæ	21
XVIII.—Fest. Epiphaniæ ...	22
XIX.—Mater Dei ...	23
XX.—Gaudium Angelorum ...	24
XXI.—Legenda	25
XXII.—Fest. Presentationis	26
XXIII.—The First Dolour	27
XXIV.—The golden rains are dashed against	27
XXV.—Legenda	28
XXVI.—The Second Dolour ...	29
XXVII.—Saint Joseph	30
XXVIII.—'Joseph, her Husband'	31
XXIX.—Saint Joseph's Patronage	32
XXX.—Mater Christi ...	33

XXXI.—Mater Christi ... 33
XXXII.—Mater Creatoris ... 34
XXXIII.—Mater Salvatoris 35
XXXIV.—Her Foundations are on the Holy Hills 36
XXXV.—Mater Admirabilis 36
XXXVI.—Mater Amabilis ... 37
XXXVII.—The Third Dolour 38
XXXVIII.—Mater Filii 39
XXXIX.—When April's sudden sunset cold 40
XL.—Not yet, not yet ! the Season sings ... 40
XLI.—The moon, ascending o'er a mass 41
XLII.—Nazareth 42
XLIII.—Fœderis Arca 43
XLIV.—Spiritus Sponsa ... 44
XLV.—Orante 45
XLVI.—Respexit Humilitatem 46
XLVII.—Mulier Fortis ... 47

MAY CAROLS (Part II.)

I.—Agios Athanatos 51
II.—Pastor Eternus 52
III.—Jesum Ostende 53
IV.—Turris Eburnea ... 53
V.—Conservabat in Corde ... 54
VI.—The Kindly Transience ... 55
VII.—Stronger and steadier every hour 56
VIII.—Mariæ Cliens 57
IX.—In morte Tutamen ... 58
X.—Speculum Justitiæ 58
XI.—Auxilium Christianorum ... 59
XII.—O Cowslips sweetening lawn and vale 60
XIII.—Ab Eterno Ordinata 61
XIV.—Three worlds there are—the first of Sense 62
XV.—Alas ! not only loveliest eyes 63
XVI.—Idolatria 64
XVII.—'In Him we have our being' ... 65
XVIII.—Tota Pulchra 66
XIX.—'Ad Nives' ... 66
XX.—Fest. Puritatis 67
XXI.—The night through yonder cloudy cleft 69
XXII.—Stella Matutina 70
XXIII.—The Flesh and the Spirit 71
XXIV.—' Made subject to Vanity ' ... 72
XXV.—Mater Divinæ Gratiæ ... 72
XXVI.—Mater Divinæ Gratiæ 73
XXVII.—Detachment 74
XXVIII.—The Beginning of Miracles ... 75
XXIX.—Filia Mariæ ... 76

CONTENTS.

	PAGE
XXX.—Expectatio	77
XXXI.—Whitens the green field, daisy-strewn	78
XXXII.—'Jesus and His Mother were there'	79
XXXIII.—Lumen Nuptiarum ...	80
XXXIV.—The golden day is dead at last ...	81
XXXV.—If God for each fair action wrought	81
XXXVI.—'When Thou hast set my heart at liberty'	82
XXXVII.—Gratiæ Plena	83
XXXVIII. Vas Insigne Devotionis	84
XXXIX.—The Letter and the Spirit ...	85
XL.—The 'Single Eye' ...	86
XLI.—Mystica	87
XLII.—Beati qui audiunt verbum Dei	88
XLIII.—Authentic Theism	89
XLIV.—'Teste David cum Sibylla' ...	90
XLV.—'Teste David cum Sibylla'	91
XLVI.—'Teste David cum Sibylla' ...	92
XLVII.—Deus Absconditus	93
XLVIII.—The Veil	94
XLIX.—'The Secret of God is with them that fear Him'	95
L.—Janua Cœli	95
LI.—If sense of Man's unworthiness	96
LII.—Causa Nostræ Lætitiæ ...	97
LIII.—Stella Maris	98
LIV.—Aaronis Virga	99
LV.—Unica ...	99
LVI.—Regina Prophetarum	100
LVII.—Still on the gracious work proceeds	101
LVIII.—Turris Davidica	102
LIX.—'Tu sola interemisti omnes Hæreses' ...	103
LX.—Ut Acies Ordinata	104
LXI.—As children when, with heavy tread ...	104
LXII.—Sedes Sapientiæ	105
LXIII.—Truth	106
LXIV.—Implicit Faith ...	107
LXV.—Mater Viventium ...	108
LXVI.—Gens non Sancta ...	109
LXVII.—Mater Venerabilis	110
LXVIII.—The sunless day is sweeter yet	111
LXIX.—The Fourth Dolour	112
LXX.—Refugium Peccatorum ...	113
LXXI.—The Fifth Dolour ...	114
LXXII.—Stabat Mater	115
LXXIII.—Regina Martyrum	115
LXXIV.—The Sixth Dolour	116
LXXV.—The Seventh Dolour	117
LXXVI.—Mater Dolorosa ...	118

CONTENTS.

MAY CAROLS (Part III.)

	PAGE
I.—The 'Unknown God'	121
II.—Ascensio Domini	122
III.—Ascensio Domini	123
IV.—A sudden sun-burst in the woods	124
V.—Dominica Pentecostes	125
VI.—Dominica Pentecostes	126
VII.—Here, in this paradise of light	127
VIII.—Regina Cœli	128
IX.—Fest. SS. Trinitatis	129
X.—Festum SS. Trinitatis	130
XI.—Thronus Trinitatis	131
XII.—Regina Sanctorum Omnium	131
XIII.—Advocata	132
XIV.—Exaltavit Humiles	133
XV.—Where is the crocus now that first	134
XVI.—A low ground-mist, the hills between	135
XVII.—In Civitate Sanctificata Requievi	136
XVIII.—Quasi Cedrus exaltata sum in Libano	137
XIX.—Sapientia	138
XX.—Beati mites	138
XXI.—Sine Labe originali Concepta	139
XXII.—Sine Labe originali Concepta	140
XXIII.—Sine Labe originali Concepta	141
XXIV.—Sine Labe originali Concepta	142
XXV.—Sine Labe originali Concepta	142
XXVI.—Fremuerunt Gentes	143
XXVII.—The Rainbow	144
XXVIII.—Ancilla Domini	145
XXIX.—Brow-bound with myrtle and with gold	146
XXX.—Corpus Christi	147
XXXI.—Corpus Christi	148
XXXII.—The Two Last Gifts	149
XXXIII.—Domus Aurea	149
XXXIV.—Pleasant the swarm about the bough	150
XXXV.—Fest. Assumptionis	151
XXXVI.—Elias and Enoch	152
XXXVII.—Fest. de Monte Carmelo	153
XXXVIII.—Vas Spirituale	154
XXXIX.—Sing on, wide winds, your anthem vast!	154
XL.—Cœli enarrant	155
XLI.—Caro factus est	156
XLII.—Condescensio	157
XLIII.—The Created Wisdom	158
XLIV.—Regina Angelorum	159
XLV.—Regina Angelorum	160
XLVI.—Regina Angelorum	161
XLVII.—Mulier Amicta Sole	162

CONTENTS.

	PAGE
XLVIII.—Regent of Change, thou waning Moon	163
XLIX.—Other Sheep I have	164
L.—Is this, indeed, our ancient earth?	164
LI.—No ray of all their silken sheen	165
Epilogue: The Son of Man ...	166

LEGENDS OF THE SAXON SAINTS ... 169

Odin the Man	203
King Ethelbert of Kent and St. Augustine	213
The Consecration of Westminster Abbey ...	228
The Penance of St. Laurence	239
King Sigebert of East Anglia, and Heida the Prophetess	253
King Sigebert of Essex, or a Friend at Need ...	267
King Oswald of Northumbria, or the Briton's Revenge	279
Ceadmon the Cowherd, the First English Poet	292
King Oswy of Northumbria, or the Wife's Victory	311
The Vengeance of the Monks of Bardeney ...	326
How Saint Cuthbert kept his Pentecost at Carlisle	337
Saint Frideswida, or the Foundations of Oxford	362
The Banquet Hall of Wessex, or the King who could see	373
Epilogue: Bede's Last May	401
Notes	419

TO

THE MEMORY OF

CARDINAL MANNING

This Poem

IS DEDICATED

WITH

AFFECTION AND RESPECT

1881

PREFACE

TO

MAY CAROLS.

To be rightly understood, this work must be regarded, not as a collection of Hymns, but as a poem on the Incarnation, a poem dedicated to the honour of the Virgin Mother, and preserving ever, as the most appropriate mode of honouring her, a single aim, that of illustrating Christianity, at once as a Theological Truth, and as a living Power, reigning among the Humanities, and renewing the affections and imagination of man. Theism was God's primal Revelation of Himself to the Patriarchal world; and it included the promise of the Messiah. Christianity was that Authentic Theism with the Promises fulfilled. In it the One God revealed Himself in the Trinity, and gave Himself to man in the Incarnation. Of these two mysteries, the latter, comprising the more palpable aspect of Christianity, is the least beyond the range of the Poetic Art. But in Religion, the palpable, and the transcendent, although distinct, are never separated, except where Religion has been materialised. If the Three Parts of the present Poem begin and end with pieces which relate to 'The

Unknown God,' or to the Blessed Trinity, the intermediate portions have ever a reference not the less constant for being indirect to those all-embracing Verities.

We are alike meditating the Incarnation, whether our *direct* theme be Incarnate God, or that Virgin Mother through whom it pleased Him to become incarnate. In either case, our point of view is placed at the centre of Christianity. In the former case, the higher elevation commands a wider field of vision, and one 'sun-clad' with the glory of a stronger light. Yet, for some purposes, the lesser elevation and the fainter light are not without their advantages. We are not thus so much brought face to face with matter too awful for poetry. But in the Incarnation, the Atonement is, of course, included—the sacred Death in the assumption of that Life which subjected the Lord of Life to Death. The blood that trickles from the wound is the same blood that mantles also in the cheek of health. Christian Poetry must ever be a 'Rosa Mystica,' the palest leaf of which has a suffusion from Calvary.

But this is not all; the Incarnation contains within itself all the mysteries of our Lord's Life on earth, His hidden life, His ministering life, His Sacramental life in His Church. That one mystery, 'The Word was made Flesh,' is, as St. John tells us, the test by which we are to 'try the Spirits.' Around it, all doctrines group themselves, and each of them has a special relation with her through whom He became Flesh. Some years ago, this truth could hardly have been illustrated for English readers of Poetry without controversy; and Poetry, though it may be Theological as well as Philosophical, can never be polemical.

But that higher Teaching, of which Wilberforce's work on the Incarnation was an eminent and influential specimen in earlier days, and Keble's 'Eucharistic Adoration' the most striking in later, has left but a narrow field for discussion on this subject among those who are capable of comprehending it. Few would now risk the assertion that the Angel might equally have been missioned to any other Hebrew Maiden as to Mary—that her Sacred Motherhood was but a material Instrumentality—that there was no connection between the Function assigned to her, and that Grace which made her, more perfectly than any beside, hear the words of God and do them. The Consent—'Be it done unto me, according to Thy Word'—the Beatitude—'Blessed is she who believed,' are now well understood: and the contrast drawn by antiquity between the Disobedience of the First Eve and the Obedience of the Second is commonly appreciated. So again, as regards Mary's place in Holy Scripture. Few would now fail to see that she has a part in that first of Prophecies respecting the 'Woman' and her 'Seed,' and in St. John's Vision of the Woman 'clothed with the Sun,' whose Son was ruling on high (whatever else may be referred to also in those passages), or scruple to confess with the Fathers, that from His Cross, our Lord consigned all His brethren to His Mother, in St. John, to be her sons. Apart from other Types or Prophecies, she has thus a place at the beginning, at the close, and at the mid point of the Scriptural Scheme. Among the learned, it is now understood that there is as good reason for the fainter utterances of Holy Scripture, and for its occasional silences, as for its louder voice: —and that the meaning which each man can snatch for himself from the surface of the Written Word is, compared to its full contents, no more than what Sense without Science can snatch from Nature, when it has cast aside Telescope and Microscope.

Wordsworth, in one of his later Sonnets, measuring the claims on our reverence possessed by Scientific Discovery, makes this the Test of its worth—'Help to Virtue does it give?' This is a test the force of which relatively to other subjects also few would dispute. If Mary holds indeed a peculiar office, relatively to Christian Truth, and the Christian Life, as she held, and ever retains one, relatively to Him Who is the Truth and the Life, this is matter in which virtue is concerned, and therefore the whole Intellect of Man, including his Imagination—that Imagination which, when it works lawlessly or in subjection to Sense, not Truth—is among man's most fatal seductions. Let us cast a glance round these two fields of thought; and first, as to Revealed Truth.

I. Mary's place in Theology reminds us then of the Fall, in the most pointed way, because, as the Mother of the Incarnate God, she had an *Instrumental* part in that great Restoration, whereof the Second Adam was the sole *meritorious* cause. In Predestination, her part was also special: for in that original Decree, respecting the Incarnation, the base, as it were, of all subordinate Decrees, He Who 'became Flesh,' and she who clothed Him in Flesh, were both included. Redemption she preaches to us specially, because she was its first-fruits, being redeemed, not only from the punishment of sin, but from sin itself through the foreseen merits of her Son. She tells us of Grace, because it was only in consequence of being 'full of grace' that her soul was so strengthened as to exclude all corruption from first to last. So again of Mediation. God, Who might have conferred all His Gifts on us *immediately*, has conferred them all through the One Mediator. Throughout the whole economy of Redemption, a vast system of 'Mediation' is carried out, deriving its whole virtue from the one great Mediator, but binding together all His family on earth in offices of Supernatural Love and mutual good, as the domestic and social Ties bind them in offices of natural love and help. In this great System, Mary, assisting us as she does relatively to every part of our being, and as a Mother, has an office that belongs to her alone among the saints, and yet remains wholly distinct from that of the King of Saints. In mediation, regarded as Atonement, even the Mother of the Atoner has no part; in Intercession, another form of mediation, she has incomparably the highest part among all those who are commanded to make intercession one for another. And yet even the highest of creatures has no more a part than the lowest in that which constitutes the incommunicable Intercession of her Son, viz. His perpetual Presence in Heaven, the Regal Presence of that Divine Priest, Who offers there for ever that Human Body which suffered on earth. What else can bring home to us so vividly the remembrance that the Atonement was a Divine Act, and that prayer, too, rests upon a mystery that is more than human? The chief of creatures stood beside her Son's Cross, and offered Him to His Eternal Father:—but this her Offering was not the Atonement. They prayed together on earth. He Who in His unimaginable Humility condescended to be ever learning, in one way of knowledge, what in a higher way He already knew, had learned from her to pray : yet, even then, between the might of her prayer and of His, there lay an Infinity.

Everywhere we find that the clear conception and familiar contemplation of the highest *Created* Greatness are the preconditions for worthy thoughts respecting that Greatness which is *Uncreated*. This is most felt the higher that Mystery in connection with which we contemplate Created Excellence. It cannot eclipse what is immeasurably above itself :— it can assist in defining it to our intelligence, as the straight line measures the curve. Thus, as to the Mystery of the Blessed Trinity. It is simply impossible, as history has proved, to question that doctrine where Mary is reverenced at every hearth as Mother of God the Son—Who is given to man by the Eternal Father, in the Love and Power of the Holy Spirit. The Title, 'Mother of God,' was accorded to Mary at the General Council of Ephesus, not because there was then any question relatively to her, but solely because when all other Tests had failed, that Title was found the surest vindication of her Son's Divinity against Nestorian prevarication. So, again, as Cardinal Newman has remarked, her position in Theology obviously excludes the Arian Heresy, which, denying our Lord's Divinity, leaves Him no place but that of chief among creatures, the exact place which she fills. In any system not *identified with* the doctrine of the Trinity, as well as admitting it, there could be no more room for Mary than there could be room for a colossal statue in a low-roofed cave.

And so of Theism. There is a true, and there is a false, Theism. No one can fail to feel the distinction between the Authentic Idea of God, and an arbitrary abstraction made by Man's Intelligence, if he has always known that between Him Who is the Infinite, and her who is the highest of creatures, the interval still remains infinite—that, compared with Him Who is Absolute Being, she who is the crown of all created excellence, remains but a crowned Dependance, the most creaturely of all creatures, the Handmaiden to whose *lowliness* He had regard. We may go farther. The place divinely assigned to Mary is the protection not so much of any doctrine in Religion, however fundamental, as of Religion itself in its essence. Mary is the guardian of all those mysteries which relate to the Sacred Infancy: through her Holy Church keeps a perpetual Christmas; through her the childlike heart lives on in the maturer knowledge, rejoicing in mysteries which thus can never lose their objective character and historical attestation. Through Mary the Palpable is preserved in the Spiritual, and the Truth of Fact holds its own against that subjective habit of the modern mind, which, 'with error opposite to that of Narcissus,' to quote Dante, wastes away because it imagines that it sees but its own face in all things, believing in no other reality. This form of Philosophic Hypochondria makes religion itself but a type of good things, not the living bond by which fallen man is bound again (*re-ligatus*) to his Creator through that Truth which alone is Freedom. This is the most dangerous form of unbelief, because the most plausible. It leaves sacred names unchanged. By a sort of evil transubstantiation, it changes into itself the *substance* of Religion, leaving its accidents unaltered. The 'Species' remain to give speciousness to a Philosophy whose ambition it is, not to overthrow this or that Religion, but itself to take the place of all Religion. If such a Philosophy were accepted, it would speedily be worked up into newer forms of thought. 'The earth hath bubbles as the water hath:' but this dusky bubble would soon break. It is not a question as to the best of Religions, but as to Religion, the Last and the Sole, together with all its gifts and bequests—so often insidiously turned against itself.

The chief intellectual dangers are often those of a gradual character. The human mind, insensibly shrivelling up and dwarfing itself, reduces to pettiness its loftiest subjects of thought, without perceiving the change. It is thus with Theism. Nations have believed in a God, and yet come to believe that He created Man without Free-will, although with responsibility. Schools of Philosophy have exulted in that supposed discovery of modern times—a God in whom Sanctity has little part—the Philanthropist, the Mechanist, and Contriver. But conceptions of God more ambitious, are at least as spurious. Thus, there are some who think the system of Reward and Punishment, of Heaven and Hell, unworthy of a Divine Revelation;—not knowing that God is Himself Heaven; and that Hell is the exile from God, self-inflicted by persistent hate of Him. As well might they quarrel with Virtue for being 'its own *Reward*.' Others would subordinate to His own Creation that Being, Whose Attributes, of which we know so few, exceed in number all the possible combinations of notes on all the harps that praise Him, and Whose Essence stretches illimitably beyond Angelic ken. They have never really taken in the difference between the Creator and the Creature, and their short-comings have arisen, in part, from their having never fixed their attention on a sufficiently great exemplar of creaturely excellence. The diversity between different grades of being becomes most marked when we contemplate the nobler specimens of each grade. It is easy to confound the lower forms of vegetable, with the lower forms of animal life; but when we rise to the higher forms of each, their diversities are unmistakable. In reaching towards the Idea of Divinity, we are not helped, and we may be much hindered, by comparisons taken from Pagan Divinities; for these last were often spurious and arbitrary conceptions, as where Purity is embodied in the same Divinity as Pride. Such creations have no place in the truth of things. The highest idea of the creature, aids us to think worthily of the Creator, because it is a Truth; and it helps us in the same way as Nature helps us to conceive of the Supernatural; viz. on the one hand, by analogies, and on the other, by contrasts. Let us illustrate these remarks by an example. Ambitious thinkers often exclaim against the theological statement, that God has made all things for Himself, and for His own glory, on the ground that it attributes to Him selfishness and vanity. This is more than mere confusion of mind. A man that makes himself his own object, doubtless defrauds his neighbour, who is of equal worth with himself; but, above all, he sins against that true Centre towards Whom all things should gravitate by building up in self a false centre, and so deifying himself. But such statements have not even a meaning when applied to God. He alone is Absolute Being: suns and systems are but as motes in His beam. He is Himself the true Universe; and the created universe, material and immaterial, was but an overflowing of that Eternal Love which had ever its infinite Operations and unmeasured Blessedness in the internal universe of the Blessed Trinity, and the relations of the Three Persons, One in the Unity of Godhead. These pretentious negations are but a clumsy attempt to assert in exclusiveness what has always been included in the authentic Confession of God, viz. that the Creator delights in creating the Good of His creatures. But He more than creates that Good. He *is* that Good; and this He could not be, were He not the Term and End of all things, as well as their Origin and their Life. God is all Love: and God is also His own Divine End. To evade the difficulty in reconciling these two statements—a difficulty which exists for 'the Mind of the Sense' alone, and neither for Faith nor for the higher Reason—our 'advanced thinkers' substitute, for the vast and manifold Idea of God, a notion alike arbitrary and false. They implicitly assert either that God is not the end of all things—that is, that He is not the Infinite, or else that what He is, He does not know Himself to be—in other words, that He is not the Truth. Their aspiration is to outsoar the anthropomorphism of the vulgar; their achievement is to create for themselves a God in their own image. They say, '*our* God shall not resemble a selfish and vain-glorious man;'—and say it because their notion of God is but man, magnified and modified.

The humblest peasant's idea of Mary would of itself preserve him from such debased conceptions. He venerates her more than all other Saints, as he venerates Saints more than Kings; but he knows that to offer to her the great Christian Sacrifice, would be, at once, as blasphemous and as preposterous as to offer it to the lowest of creatures, since the oblation ever presented, alike in Heaven and on earth, being Divine, and offered by a Divine Priest, can only be offered to the Holy Trinity. When the child just taught to pray, sees his parents kneel down to pray also, the greatness of the unseen Being, Who also permits Himself to be called Father, comes more closely in upon him than it could come if he only saw other children at their prayers. To witness the adorations of the angels would exalt our own. It is thus that they are exalted also by the thought, and by the daily footsteps in our hearts and lives, of one who, while venerated by the angels themselves as their Queen, bows herself down before God in an adoration, by so much deeper than theirs, by how much that Vision of His Glory accorded to her is higher than theirs—esteeming herself to be a nothing, and Him to be the Fullness of all. Is this, her estimate, an Illusion or a Truth? If it be a Truth, that first and last of Truths must set its seal upon the Idea of God prevalent among those who revere her.

These are but a few illustrations of the mode in which Mary ministers at the Table of her Son, for the solace of His Guests, like the Queenly matron sung of by the best among the Anglican Religious Poets since the days of George Herbert.* She is qualified thus to give help in the Church by a special characteristic— her resemblance to the Church. Few things can be said of the Mystic Bride which are not applicable to the Mother. Like Mary, the Church is Virgin and Mother; and her fruitfulness is, not in spite of, but in necessary association with her purity. If the Church is ever offering up her Divine Lord, so Mary offered Him at the Presentation, at His death, and at

* See Archbishop Trench's *Gertrude of Saxony*.

every moment of His Life. If the Church is ever pleading for her children, so is Mary; and the earliest pictorial representation of her is the 'Orante' of the Catacombs, who stands, with outstretched arms, in endless intercession, among tombs still red with the martyrs' blood. If the 'Sword' passed through her heart, the Church, too, has to suffer. If it was a hidden life that our Lord lived with His Mother for thirty years, it is a Sacramental Life that He leads with His Church. If Mary could be suspected, cannot the Church be reviled? The Church is a Teacher, and so is Mary: 'Wisdom doth sit with children round her knees.' Nor is it only as a Mother that Mary has a place at every hearth. Mr. Longfellow's 'Golden Legend' has a passage of rare discernment, which illustrates the confidence reposed in Mary by that of little children in the intercession of an elder Sister. Mary has the elder Sister's teaching office no less. As Faith 'comes by hearing,' and as it is 'with the heart man believeth,' so the best part of what belongs to Religion is learned by us, not like the irksome school-lore of our boyhood, but like our native tongue, that is through sympathy and unconscious imitation. It is here that the elder sister is helpful. We all know how the younger children see through her eyes, and hear through her ears, and how the feeling, ere yet completely revealed in her face, is mirrored in the smile or blush upon theirs. She initiates not their thoughts only, but their perceptions: and out of a thousand germs latent in their minds, her influence vivifies such as are destined to emerge into reality. Mary has such an office among the Children of Adoption. She moves besides us:

she goes in before us. It has been well remarked, that the Hymn 'Stabat Mater' penetrates our hearts because it makes us gaze on the Cross, not so much with our own eyes, as through those of the chief of the Bereft. But Mary assists equally in summing out every other Christian Affection. In her 'Magnificat' she daily leads forth the triumph of the Meek; and annually her Paschal Anthem, 'Lætare Regina,' helps those that wept to rejoice. To this day the 'Ausonian Shepherds' leave their flocks on the mountains, as Christmas draws near, take their stand beneath the pictures of the Madonna at the corner of every Roman street, and, with those reedpipes that once but made boast of sheepfold or orchard store, gratulate her through whom 'to us a Child is given.' There are lessons without sermons —a lore that calls the sage away from his lamp. Who would not advance more bravely if an Angel held his hand? In our earthly pilgrimage we are given these helps because we have been given instincts which demand them; and the Supernatural does not despise the Natural. To us, too, is extended a hand, all light; and it loosens itself from ours but to beckon to us from the heavenly shore. The thought of Mary amid the heavenly Court, is the thought of our own pilgrimage accomplished, and our rest completed. The Church is ever 'stepping westward,' and her endless evening does not lack its Evening Star. The remoter and full-orbed glory of Mary shines in the eyes of the Militant Church beyond this vale of tears—an image of the Church Triumphant.

Few things are more wonderful than the difference between the relations in which Mary stands to Christian Science, and to the Teaching of that Science.

Her mere position strengthens the Church as with a fortified citadel; yet her Teaching is of all Teaching the most unpolemical. It leaves a blessing even at the door that will not open to it; but with the franker natures it leaves the heritage of that Truth which is one with Love. It is in the heart that it lodges Truth —that heart which it 'penetrates without a wound,' knowing that thence it must ascend into the higher Intellect, and diffuse itself through the being. It conquers the Controversial Spirit, that Fury of the Schools, without a battle, by leaving for it no place: and thus Religion remains the soft but mighty Mother of Man, and Truth retains her placid seat in a Temple which attack alone can convert into a Fortress. When the Faith is associated from early days with those unhappy contentions, which are but its accidents, there Religion may either live on as a boast, protected by the Institutes it protects, or it may be trampled out as a cause of offence; but in either case its essence is ignored. It gives little glory to God, and no peace to men. It bickers on every hearth, sows the Dragon's teeth in every field, inflames every youthful presumption, and envenoms every sore of age. There is no greatness which the Spirit of Controversy cannot reduce to littleness. We deal with God's Word as we do with His Works. Half-a-dozen obtrusive white houses, scattered along a range of hills, so arrest the eye, and force it to draw imaginary lines connecting house with house, that in the invisible net-work of this luckless geometry, all the grace and the might of mountain outlines is lost. So fares it with the sacred Scriptures, when favourite Texts have become the entrenched camps of amateur Controversialists: — they may know the Bible by heart; but for them the Word of God exists not. Never once can they wander through its infinitudes with the reverent eye of the Seer, with the simple wonder, the loving delight, the blameless curiosity of the child. For the love of Truth they have substituted the love of *Knowledge discovered*, and the joy of contention.

But the remedy? Does it lie in disparaging Doctrine? Certainly not; for Revelation not setting forth a Truth would be no Revelation. Does it lie in substituting Love for Truth, as the soul of Christianity? Certainly not; for Christian Love is inseparable from Christian Truth. To love a Divine Redeemer, we must know that He *is* Divine; and all the Councils for successive Centuries were needed but to refute the Errors that assailed that Truth. Such warfare must always be going on. On some far border of the Christian Empire, there will be always eruptions of new Barbarians; and they must ever be repelled, lest they should reach hearth and home. The battle of Truth must last till its last foe is destroyed. The Luminary that lights that battle-field is the Mystery of 'The Word made Flesh:'—a sister orb reflects its light:—and to the end the prayer of the Prophet-Chief will ascend—'Sun, stand thou still upon Gibeon, and thou, Moon, in the Valley of Ajalon.' Relatively to Christian Science, Mary has a place, so inextricably interwoven with it throughout that she cannot but add force to its most stringent affirmations, and a severer exactitude to its most refined definitions. Religion *is* not a Science; but it *has* its Science, and can never discard it. If, relatively to that Science, as well as to the teaching of it, Mary is a help to the

Christian Church, here, again, we find that she helps her because she resembles her. Mary 'pondered all these things in her heart.' This is what the Church is ever doing in her Theological processes. She remembers and she witnesses. Her Science is based upon her profound and secure heart-appreciation of that Truth originally committed to her; and consists in following onward that changeless Truth into clearer light, from Definition to Definition, as the Providence of God suggests, and His Grace permits, through the aid of that Spirit Who was sent to the Apostles, both that He might call all things to their minds, and also that He might lead them on into all Truth. With a method chiefly Deductive, she deals with the great Truths committed to her, as the Mathematician deduces corollary from proposition. Thus, only, could a method of Thought exist in connection with a subject matter to which Induction and Experiment are as obviously inapplicable as a priori reasoning is to Natural Philosophy. But such Theological Thought, what is it? It is a *long Meditation*. It is to 'ponder all these things in her heart.' Relatively to our intellects, Mary is thus a Type of the Christian Church's Unity; and the Type again is a bond, moral, not governmental, which cements that Unity. She is not 'Rock of the Rock'; but she is a smile from Him who is 'Light of Light.'

II. We have considered, though most inadequately, Mary's Office in connection with Christian Truth: let us now turn to the second subject, her office relatively to the Christian Life. It consists largely in ennobling human Affections by elevating our conception of human Ties. If we do not exercise our Affections as Theologians say, '*in God*,' they must be Idolatries; since, in that case, the stronger they are, the more they must lead us from God, binding us, not to heaven, but to earth. They must thus become the prisons of Love, or its sepulchral vaults, not its temples or its palaces. But in Mary we have a Love at once the strongest, as a human love, and the most obviously a deliverer from the Idolatries of human love. To her Son, in His Human Nature, Mary stood in the relation, not of a Parent alone, but of Sole Parent; yet her love for Him not only was consistent with a sovereign love for God, but lived in, and advanced with, her love of God; for her Son was God. The Affection corresponded with the Tie. All human Ties met in her, in their essential Unity. We venerate the Virginal estate, and we venerate the maternal; but in Mary these two glories were united, in a union only less wonderful than that of the Two Natures in her Son. It is a revelation of Woman, such as she was created—not as the mere Female of an animal-intellectual Race; but as one of those two forms in which Humanity, made in the Divine Image, was permitted to mirror its manifold and Infinite Creator. Mary has a peculiar office also relatively to her Son's human character. Parallel mountain ranges help us far more to conceive height, than a single range could do, although the highest: and thus the spotless Humanity of Mary, when duly pondered, is a great assistance to us in conceiving the Human Character of our Lord, the altitudes of which we cannot always measure with entire reverence, and our endeavours fully to realise which, in what seems nearest to ourselves, sometimes fails, to the extent of an implicit, though not explicit, denial of His Divinity. The Redeemed Humanity, like the Unfallen, has been set forth before us in a twofold Type. The Virgin Maternity has fixed in the heart of that Humanity an Idea never to be dislodged. There it sits, enthroned; and thence it diffuses blessing over those who but dimly apprehend it, and tenfold blessing over those who 'discern' it. This Idea has done for human Life what the most authentic Theism could not by itself have done. Amongst its many gifts, it has lifted to an immeasurable height the Institute of Marriage, which received its first benediction in Paradise; it has consecrated it into a Sacrament, and rendered it irrevocable. It has done this, in no small measure, by giving it the counterweight of the Conventual Life. It was impossible for the married Sister to remember the Sister beneath the veil, without remembering also that the home brightened with children, and the convent home on its lonely height, must alike, though in different fashions, be homes of Reverence and of Worship, of Purity and of Peace. From these two Homes went forth Christian Civilisation. There moved over the earth a conception of Human Character such as the Greek had never dreamed of. It was that of Womanhood. It had not the strut of the Pagan Hero or Demigod; but it was greater than all the gods. And yet how few elements made up that greatness!—only Humility, Purity, and Love. And with how few franchises it was endowed! Only with the joy of one who from childhood had panted for Divinity, as the hart pants for the waterbrooks, and had found Him; and again, with the sorrow inseparable from Love in a world of sin—the Sorrow of a Heart transfixed at the moment of its most sacred triumph. Mary had entered into the Temple. She had made—she first—the Church's everlasting Offering; and with it she had offered up the tribute of a gratitude such as the earth had never offered before. But she had offered up herself no less, and the answer was that predicted Sword by which her Heart also was to be pierced. From that Heart it never departed. Thenceforth there dawned upon man's thought the Christian Idea of Womanhood. It came from Mary. It stood the Image at once of Lowliness and of Greatness, of Innocence and of Majesty, of Gladness and Holy Sorrow; for to it ever remained the bleeding Heart. It took its place beside that Image of Man associated with the 'Ecce Homo'—the purple robe of regal dignity, and the ensanguined Head crowned with a crown of thorns.

That fair and fruitful Idea which set free the intelligence and the heart of man, raised his Imagination proportionately, and created the Art of the Ages of Faith. It re-revealed Beauty—no longer the Syren's smile, but the radiance on the face of Truth—the sweetness and graciousness of Virtue itself. Everywhere throughout the worlds of Painting, Sculpture, and Architecture, shone out that nobler Beauty, severe at once and tender, mystic yet simple, gladsome yet pathetic. It was a Spirit, but a Spirit ever embodying itself in sensible form, for the redemption of Sense. Compared with Classic Art, its insight was deep, and its flight was high: but it had one fixed home, the 'Holy Family'—a limit apparently narrow, yet found to be inexhaustible. Again and again the mighty Masters returned to it, and gathered strength from the touch of their native soil. Art grew neither more heroic nor more beautiful when it abandoned that early Eden, and exchanged the higher for the lower knowledge. Religion, in keeping it central, had kept it human. The Holy Family was the centre at once of things earthly and things heavenly; and Art, when it first saw that Vision, wisely desired to build Tabernacles in its light, and whispered, 'it is good for us to be here.' This was the true preaching of the Incarnation. The Pictured Prophet or Apostle might be honoured though only for the word spoken, or the deed done; but that Infant on His Mother's knee could have significance for one cause alone, viz. because He was God.

These, then, are some of the moral influences which are connected with the love and reverence of Mary, rightly understood, and which are not the less precious, because, like the Bible, the Sacraments, and all else that is good and helpful, they are capable of being abused instead of used. To say depreciatingly, 'But Mary could not but love her Child in God, and as God, since He was God,' leaves the marvel undiminished. That marvel is, that God should have made the creation of a being such as Mary a part of the Redemptive Scheme. The Divine Redeemer might have taken to Himself a human form out of the dust of the earth, as Adam's body was taken; or He might have been born, as Mary was, of earthly marriage, and yet have remained wholly exempt from earthly taint. But He willed it otherwise. He made both the Divine Maternity, and the Virginal Maternity, the means of the Incarnation:— and thus, by necessity, shone out this wondrous Sign in the face of Creation. The Sign grew clearer as it grew nearer. In the earlier dawn of prophecy it was said, 'The

Seed of the *Woman;*' in its later announcements, 'A *Virgin* shall conceive.' Those who understand the Incarnation will not imagine that to gaze in appreciation, as well as in glad affection upon this Sign, has no tendency to draw us nearer to Incarnate God.

There exists a very sublime doctrine respecting the Incarnation, which, though not a matter of defined Faith, has a peculiar interest in our own day. Scientific discovery has made the universe so vast a thing, that the modern Imagination, overpowered by its grandeur, and not weighing in the scales of Faith the comparative worth of Spirit and Matter, sometimes finds a difficulty in the statement that, merely for the sake of a Fallen Race on this petty planet, such an event as the Incarnation took place. Centuries before this difficulty had been felt or fancied, some of the Theological Schools had answered it. They had maintained, as a probable opinion, that, though the Fall doubtless imparted to the Incarnation its *Expiatory* character, and made the God-man, the 'Man of Sorrows,' yet that Incarnation itself would have taken place even if there had been no Fall, and taken place for the exaltation of the whole Creation, not merely for the Redemption of a part of it. According to this opinion, the Creation, without the Incarnation, must ever have been an imperfect work. A *finite* Universe must have remained at an infinite distance from its Infinite Creator, buried far away, as it were, in a perpetual Exile—a Harp without a Harper—a robe with none to wear it. It was part of the Eternal Purpose that the Creator should Himself become a Creature, and thus *assume*

His own Creation. That Creation is twofold, spiritual and material; and Incarnate God therefore assumed it most fitly in assuming the nature of Man, who is made up of soul and body, his soul being the lowest link in the scale of the Spiritual Creation, while his body occupies the highest grade in that of material Nature, as she works up successively through her mineral, vegetable, and animal kingdoms, to her highest work, the frame of man. The 'Good Shepherd' had ever decreed to go forth into the lonely desert of finite things, and bring back Creation, like a lost sheep on His Shoulder, to His Father's Throne. Creation, thus assumed, was at last to find a Divine King to rule it in equity, and a Divine Priest to offer up its Adorations, till then voiceless and dumb. From its Head in heaven to its remotest depths, the Universe, thus taken into alliance with God, was destined to become flooded with His grace. The unction of the great Priest must needs flow down 'to the skirts of His clothing.'

This opinion involves nothing opposed to existing analogies. The visible world exists for the sake of Him Who made it, and stands to Him in manifold relations of which we as yet know but a few. There is, therefore, no difficulty in the thought that, by the Incarnation of its Creator, it may have been indefinitely raised, and drawn closer to Him. It interprets between Him and His Intelligent Creation; and the medium of communication may have been thus rendered fitter for its purpose—a more translucent and musical exponent. A World, once but God's outer Court, may have become His Temple, and may be destined to become His Holy of Holies. The earth was 'cursed for man's sake;'—consequently the whole material Universe is *capable*, at least, of very different degrees of Blessedness, received by it and by it communicated, in connection with some Act, not human but divine. According to this teaching, the Spiritual part of Creation has had its full part in the Gift. In a Vision of the Divine Infant, and the all-blessed Mother, the Incarnation was presented to the reverence of the Angelic Hierarchies, the First-born of the Creative Love. It was a *Revelation* of God in His Infinite Condescension— nay, in the Humiliation of a Hypostatic union not contracted with the Angelic, but with the later, and humbler, human and material Creation; and this Revelation was made to those who had hitherto but known God in the splendours of His Power, and known Him through their own resplendent Faculties irradiated by His light. Those who turned away in Pride from the 'enigma,' and refused to adore with Supreme Worship their God 'made Flesh,' fell. Those who stood the test, and welcomed the Revelation, advanced instantaneously into a nearness with God commensurate with their profounder Knowledge of Him, and with that Love which Obedience alone ripens to its Perfection, and so passed at once into the state of Indefectibility. According to this teaching, the Incarnation had three distinct effects, apart from those wholly beyond our ken. To Fallen Man it gave his Restoration—to the Unfallen Angels their Instauration in Glory, endless and complete—to the material Universe, explored by us or unexplored, some more sacred and intimate relation with God, which elevated what had before been the Type of His Being into the Sacrament of His Presence, after a sort that we shall only fully comprehend when we fully comprehend the Resurrection of our own Bodies, and have ourselves become consummated, alike in Body and Soul.*

This view of the Incarnation is referred to in many of the following poems, especially in 'Caro factus est,' p. 156, and 'Regina Angelorum,' p. 159; and by it were in no small degree suggested the descriptive pieces interspersed among the meditative. These last are an attempt towards a Christian rendering of external nature. Nature, like Art, needs to be spiritualised, unless it is to remain a fortress in the hands of an adverse Power. The visible world is a passive thing, which ever takes its meaning from something above itself. In Pagan times, it drew its interpretation from Pantheism; and to Pantheism—nay, to that Idolatry which is the popular application of Pantheism—it has still a secret, though restrained tendency, largely betrayed by modern Imaginative Literature, which is constantly dallying with Pagan Myths, though it is too cold to adore them—*our* Idolatries being chiefly those of 'covetousness,' lawless affection, and self-love. A World without Divinity, Matter without Mind, is intolerable to human instincts. Yet, on the other hand, there is much in fallen human nature which shrinks from the sublime thought of a Creator, and rests on that of a sheathed Divinity diffused throughout the universe, its life, not its maker. Mere personified elements, the Wood-God and River-Nymph, captivate the fancy and do not over-awe the soul. For a bias so seductive no cure is to be found, save in authentic Christianity. The whole truth, in

---

* This subject is illustrated with depth and eloquence in Father Ventura's Conferences delivered at Paris, in the Rev. A. Hewit's *Problems of the Age*, and in M. Nicolas' profound and beautiful work, *La Vierge Marie*.

the long run, holds its own better than the half truth; and minds repelled by the thought of a God who stands afar off, and created the universe but to abandon it to general laws, fling themselves at the feet of a God made Man. When the 'Word was made Flesh,' a bridge was thrown across that gulf which had else for ever separated the Finite from the Infinite. The same high Truth which brings home to us the doctrine of a Creation consecrates that Creation, reconstituting it into an Eden meet for an unfallen Adam and an unfallen Eve; nay, exalting it into a heavenly Jerusalem, the dwelling-place of the Lamb and of the Bride. It does this, in part, through symbols and associations founded on the all-cleansing Blood and the all-sanctifying Spirit—symbols and associations the reverse of those in which an Epicurean mythology took delight.

One word on the *form* of this Poem. Religion is not, as has been proved by a few great examples among many failures, incapable of a treatment poetical, as well as metrical; but Religious Poetry can never be dialectic, especially when lyrical, much less controversial. Poetry—an ideal art—is most ideal in this its most meditative vein. It presents Ideas; but it only suggests their coarser intermediate links, as the early Greek Sculptor but suggested the bridle of his brazen horse. Poetry has habitually a wide-handed synthesis, and can sharpen itself no less to a very keen analysis; but its logic is the inner logic of imaginative Thought. It detects the remote analogy; but it is not careful to point out the obvious connection. It elicits Truths; but it forces them on none. It wings them with image and allusion; and bids them fare forth as they may: but they have to fare forth separately; and the complete Poem must often appear to consist of but detached fragments, except so far as it possesses the interior unity of Truth, and the harmony of a common sentiment. This Poem therefore, as regards its form, belongs, by necessity, to that of serial poems, a species of compositions once common in Italy and among our Elizabethan poets, and most happily revived in England in the present century. Its three parts are in some respects dissimilar. Part the First was intended to illustrate chiefly what have been named the 'Joyful mysteries,' and Part the Third the 'Glorious mysteries'; while Part the Second, while including the 'Sorrowful mysteries,' ventures also to indicate a few of those manifold relations, so helpful and so healing, in which the predicted 'Woman' of primeval Prophecy, in the great 'Protevangelion,' stands to the Human Race, to Human Life, to Visible Nature, and most of all to Christian Theology.

ADVERTISEMENT TO THE FOURTH EDITION OF 'MAY CAROLS; OR, ANCILLA DOMINI.'

The gratitude of Christians has long since dedicated the month of May to the Mother of our Lord, a circumstance to which the present Volume owes its Title of 'May Carols'—for the Carols of Shepherds were accepted at the Bethlehem Crib not less than the tribute of the 'Wise Men' and Kings. I have been told that that Title is not sufficiently characteristic of the Volume's main scope, and that to some persons it may prove misleading. But any such misconception ought to be precluded by the explanatory words added to the last edition, viz. 'Ancilla Domini,' words anticipated indeed by the original Preface. That Preface begins with a remark that the main scope of the Poem can only be comprehended where the work is distinctly understood to be, not a collection of short poems, but a single poem, one 'on the Incarnation, dedicated to the Virgin Mother, and preserving ever, as the most appropriate mode of honouring her, a single aim, that of illustrating Christianity at once as

"The Lord and Mighty Paramount of Truths," *

and also as a living Power, reigning among the Humanities, and renewing the affections and imagination of men.'

* Wordsworth.

PROLOGUE.

PROLOGUE.

Religion, she that stands sublime
    Upon the rock that crowns our globe,
Her foot on all the spoils of time,
    With light eternal on her robe;

She, sovereign of the orb she guides,
    On Truth's broad sun may root a gaze
That deepens onward as she rides,
    And shrinks not from the fontal blaze:

But they—her daughter Arts—must hide
    Within the cleft, content to see
Dim skirts of glory waving wide
    And steps of parting Deity.

'Tis theirs to watch the Vision break
    In gleams from Nature's frown or smile
The legend rise from out the lake
    The relic consecrate the isle.

'Tis theirs to adumbrate and suggest;
    To point toward founts of buried lore,
Leaving, in type alone expressed,
    What Man must know not, yet adore.

For where her court true Wisdom keeps,
   'Mid loftier handmaids one there stands
Dark as the midnight's starry deeps,
   A Slave, gem-crowned, from Nubia's sands—

O thou whose light is in thy heart,
   Reverence, love's mother! without thee
Science may soar awhile; but Art
   Drifts barren o'er a shoreless sea.

MAY CAROLS.

PART I.

THE DIVINE CHILDHOOD.

'I will put enmities between thee and the woman, and thy seed, and her seed.'—GEN. iii. 15.

MAY CAROLS.

I.

Who feels not, when the Spring once more,
    Stepping o'er Winter's grave forlorn
With winged feet, retreads the shore
    Of widowed Earth, his bosom burn?

As ordered flower succeeds to flower,
    And May the ladder of her sweets
Ascends, advancing hour by hour
    From step to step, what heart but beats?

Some Presence veiled in fields and groves
    That mingles rapture with remorse,
Some buried joy beside us moves,
    And thrills the soul with such discourse

As they, perchance, that wondering pair
    Who to Emmaus bent their way,
Hearing, heard not. Like them our prayer
    We make:—'The night is near us . . Stay!'

With Paschal chants the churches ring;
    Their echoes strike along the tombs;
The birds their Hallelujahs sing;
    Each flower with nature's incense fumes.

Our long-lost Eden seems restored—
   As on we move with tearful eyes
We feel through all the illumined sward
   Some upward-working Paradise.

II.

Upon Thy Face, O God, Thy world
   Looks ever up in love and awe;
Thy stars in circles onward hurled
   Sustain the steadying yoke of Law.

In alternating antiphons
   Stream sings to stream and sea to sea;
And moons that set and sinking suns
   Obeisance make, O God, to Thee.

The swallow, winter's rage o'erblown,
   Again on warm Spring breezes borne
Revisiteth her haunts well-known;
   The lark is faithful to the morn.

The whirlwind, missioned with its wings
   To drown the fleet or fell the tower,
Obeys Thee as the bird that sings
   Her love-chant in a fleeting shower.

Amid an ordered universe
   Man's spirit only dares rebel:—
With light, O God, its darkness pierce!
   With love its raging chaos quell!

III.

All but unutterable Name!
    Adorable, yet awful, sound!
Thee can the sinful nations frame
    Save with their foreheads to the ground?

Soul-searching and all-cleansing Fire!
    To see Thy Countenance were to die:
Yet how beyond the bound retire
    Of Thy serene immensity?

Thou mov'st beside us, if the spot
    We change, a noteless, wandering tribe:
The planets of our Life and Thought
    In Thee their little arcs describe.

In the dead calm, at cool of day,
    We hear Thy voice, and turn, and flee:
Thy love outstrips us on our way:
    From Thee, O God, we fly—to Thee.

IV.

How came there Sin to world so fair,
    Where all things seem to bask in God,
Where breathes His Love in every air,
    His life ascends from every sod?

O happy birds and happy bees,
    And flowers that flash through matin gems!
O happy trees, and happier breeze
    That sweep'st their dewy diadems!

Why are not all things good and bright?
 Why are not all men kind and true?
O World so beauteous, wise, and right,
 Your Maker is our Maker too!

SANCTA MARIA.

V.

Mary! To thee the humble cry.
 What seek they? Gifts to pride unknown.
They seek thy help—to pass thee by:—
 They murmur, 'Show us but thy Son.'

The childlike heart shall enter in:
 The virgin soul its God shall see:
Mother, and maiden pure from sin,
 Be thou the guide: the Way is He.

The mystery high of God made Man
 Through thee to man is easier made:
Pronounce the consonant who can
 Without the softer vowel's aid!

FEST. NATIVITATIS B. V. M.

VI.

When thou wert born the murmuring world
 Rolled on, nor dreamed of things to be,
From joy to sorrow madly whirled,
 Despair disguised in revelry.

A princess thou of David's line;
　The mother of the Prince of Peace,
That hour no royal pomps were thine:
　The earth alone her boon increase

Before thee poured. September rolled
　Down all the vine-clad Syrian slopes
Her robes of purple and of gold;
　And birds sang loud from olive tops.

Perhaps old foes, they know not why,
　Relented. From a fount long sealed
Tears rose, perhaps, to Pity's eye:
　Love-harvests crowned the barren field.

The respirations of the year,
　At least, grow soft. O'er valleys wide
Pine-roughened crags again shone clear;
　And the great Temple, far descried,

To watchers, watching long in vain,
　To patriots grey, in bondage nursed,
Flashed back their hope—'The Second Fane
　In glory shall surpass the First!'

AB ANGELO SALUTATA.

VII.

That angel's voice is in her ear!
　Ah, not alone by Mary heard!
Like light it cleaves that region drear
　Where never sang the matin bird!

It thrills the expectant Hades! They,
  The pair that once through Eden ranged,
Amid their penal shadows grey
  Stand up and smile, this hour avenged!

They see their queenly daughter grasp
  The Fruit of Life, her bridal dower:
They see its boughs rush up, and clasp
  The sleeping earth with starry bower.

Once more they tread that Eden bound:
  Far up—all round—at last, at last
They see God's mountain city-crowned;
  In every fount they see it glassed.

Why saw they not, the hour they fell,
  Those hills, that City 'like a Bride'?
Then too it girt that garden dell,
  Predestined Heaven though undescried!

NIHIL RESPONDIT.

VIII.

She hid her face from Joseph's blame
  The Spirit's glory-shrouded Bride:
The sword comes next; but first the shame:
  Meekly she bore it; nought replied.

In mutual sympathies we live:
  The insulted heart forgives, but dies:
To her that wound was sanative
  For life to her was sacrifice.

At us no barbless shaft is thrown
    When charged with deeds by us unwrought;
For sins unchallenged, sins unknown,
    Worse sins have stained us, act, or thought.

Her humbleness no sin could find
    To weep for: yet, that hour, no less
Deeplier the habitual sense was shrined
    In her of her own nothingness.

That hour foundations deeper yet
    God sank in her; that so more high
Her greatness, spire and parapet,
    Might rise and nearer to the sky;

That, wholly over-built by grace,
    Nature might vanish, like some isle
In great towers lost—the buried base
    Of some surpassing fortress pile.

ST. JOSEPH'S DOUBT.

IX.

'The Angel of the Lord appeared unto him in a dream.'

'Twas not her tear his doubt subdued;
    No word of hers announced her Christ:
By him in dream that angel stood
    With warning hand. A dream sufficed.

Where faith is strong, though light be dim,
    How faint a beam reveals how much!
The Hand that made the worlds on him
    Descended with a feather's touch.

'Blessèd for ever who believed:'—
  Like Her, through faith his crown he won:
His *heart* the Babe divine conceived;
  His heart was sire of Mary's Son.

Hail, Image of the Father's Might!
  The Heavenly Father's human shade!
Hail, silent King whose yoke was light!
  Hail, Foster-sire whom Christ obeyed!

Hail, Warder of God's Church beneath,
  Thy vigil keeping at her door
Year after year at Nazareth!
  So guard, so guide it evermore!

FEST. VISITATIONIS.

X.

The hilly region crossed with haste,
  Its last dark ridge discerned no more,
Bright as the bow that spans a waste
  She stood beside her Cousin's door;

And spake:—that greeting came from God!
  Filled with the Spirit from on high
Sublime the aged Mother stood,
  And cried aloud in prophecy,

'Soon as thy voice had touched mine ears
  The child in childless age conceived,
Leaped up for joy! Throughout all years
  Blessed the Woman who believed.'

Type of Electing Love! 'tis thine
  To sound God's greeting from the skies!
Thou speak'st, and Faith, a babe divine,
  Leaps up thy Babe to recognise.

Within true hearts the second birth
  Exults, though blind as yet and dumb.
The child of Grace his hands puts forth,
  And prophesies of things to come.

AMOR INNOCENTIUM.

XI.

Ascending from the convent-grates,
  The children mount the woodland vale.
'Tis May-Day Eve; and Hesper waits
  To light them, while the western gale

Blows softly on their bannered line:
  And, lo! down all the mountain stairs
The shepherd children come to join
  The convent children at their prayers.

They meet before Our Lady's fane:
  On yonder central rock it stands,
Uplifting, ne'er invoked in vain,
  That Cross which blesses all the lands.

Before the porch the flowers are flung;
  The lamp hangs glittering 'neath the Rood;
The 'Maris Stella' hymn is sung;
  Their chant each morn to be renewed.

Ah! if a secular muse might dare,
 Far off, the children's song to catch;
To echo back, or burthen bear!—
 As fitly might she hope to match

The throstle's note as theirs, 'tis true:
 Yet, now and then, that borrowed tone,
Like sunbeams flashed on pine or yew
 Might shoot a sweetness through her own!

FEST. NATIVITATIS.

XII.

PRIMEVAL night had repossessed
 Her empire in the fields of space;
Calm lay the kine on earth's dark breast;
 The earth lay calm in heaven's embrace.

That hour, where shepherds kept their flocks,
 From God a glory sudden fell:
The splendour smote the trees and rocks,
 And lay, like dew, along the dell.

God's Angel close beside them stood:
 'Fear nought,' that Angel said, and then,
'Behold, I bring you tidings good:
 The Saviour Christ is born to men.'

And straightway round him myriads sang
 Again that anthem, and again,
Till all the hollow valley rang,
 'Glory to God, and peace to men.'

Thus in the violet-scented grove,
  The May breeze murmuring softly by them,
The children sang. Who Mary love
  The long year through have Christmas nigh them!

PROTEVANGELION.

XIII.

When from their lurking place the Voice
  Of God dragged forth that Fallen Pair
Still seemed the garden to rejoice,
  The sinless Eden still was fair.

They, they alone, whose light of grace
  But late made Paradise look dim
Stood now, a blot upon its face,
  Before their God, nor gazed on Him.

They glanced not up; or they had seen
  In that severe, death-dooming eye
Unutterable depths serene
  Of sadly-piercing sympathy.

Not them alone that Eye beheld,
  But, by their side, that other Twain
In whom the race whose doom was knelled
  Once more should rise; once more should reign.

It saw that Infant crowned with blood—
  And her from whose predestined breast
That Infant ruled the worlds. She stood
  Her foot upon the serpent's crest!

Voice of primeval prophecy!
  Of all the Gospels head and heart!
With Him, her Son and Saviour, she
  Possessed, that hour, in thee a part!

DEI GENITRIX.

XIV.

I SEE Him: on thy lap He lies
  'Mid that Judæan stable's gloom:
O sweet, O awful Sacrifice!
  He smiles in sleep, yet knows the doom.

Thou gav'st Him life! But was not this
  That Life which knows no parting breath?
Unmeasured Life? unwaning Bliss?
  Dread Priestess, lo! thou gav'st Him death!

Beneath the Tree thy Mother stood;
  Beneath the Cross thou too shalt stand:—
O Tree of Life! O bleeding Rood!
  Thy shadow stretches far its hand.

That God who made the sun and moon
  In swaddling bands lies dumb and bound—
Love's Captive! darker prison soon
  Awaits Thee in the garden ground.

He wakens. Paradise looks forth
  Beyond the portals of the grave.
Life, life thou gavest! life to Earth,
  Not Him! Thine Infant dies to save.

ADOLESCENTULÆ AMAVERUNT TE NIMIS.

XV.

'Behold! the wintry rains are past;
  The airs of midnight hurt no more:
The young maids love thee. Come at last!
  Thou lingerest at the garden-door.

'Blow over all the garden; blow,
  Thou wind that breathest of the south
Through all the alleys winding low
  With dewy wing and honeyed mouth!

'But wheresoe'er thou wanderest, shape
  Thy music ever to one Name:
Thou too, clear stream, to cave and cape
  Be sure thou whisper of the same.

'By every isle and bower of musk
  Thy crystal clasps as on it curls
We charge thee, breathe it to the dusk;
  We charge thee, grave it in thy pearls.'

The stream obeyed. That Name he bore
  Far out above the moon-lit tide:
The breeze obeyed. He breathed it o'er
  The unforgetting Pine; and died.

XVI.

The infant year with infant freak
　　Intent to dazzle and surprise,
Played with us long at hide and seek,
　　Turned on us now, now veiled her eyes.

Between the pines for ever green
　　And boughs by April half attired
She glanced; then sang, once more unseen,
　　'The unbeheld is more desired.'

With footsteps vague, and hard to trace,
　　She crept from whitening bower to bower;
Now bent from heaven her golden face
　　Now veiled her radiance in a shower.

Like genial hopes and thoughts devout
　　That touch some sceptic soul forlorn,
And herald clearer faith, and rout
　　The night, and antedate the morn,

Her gifts. But thou, all-beauteous May,
　　Art come at last. O! with thee bring
Hearts pure as thine with thee to play,
　　And own the consummated spring.

To hands by deeds unblest defiled
　　In vain the whiteness of thy thorn!
Proud souls, where lurks no more the child,
　　For them thy violet is unborn!

For breasts that know nor joy nor hope
　　Thy songstress sings an idle strain:
Thy golden-domed laburnums drop
　　O'er loveless hearts their bowers in vain.

FEST. EPIPHANIÆ.

XVII.

A VEIL is on the face of Truth :
   She prophesies behind a cloud ;
She ministers in robes of ruth
   Nocturnal rites and disallowed.

Eleusis hints, but dares not speak ;
   The Orphic minstrelsies are dumb ;
Lost are the Sibyl's books, and weak
   Earth's olden faith in Him to come.

But ah, but ah, that Orient Star !
   On straw-roofed shed and large-eyed kine
It flashes, guiding from afar
   The Magians' long-linked camel-line !

Gold, frankincense, and myrrh they bring—
   Love, Worship, Life severe and hard :
Their symbol gifts the Infant King
   Accepts ; and Truth is their reward.

Rejoice, O Sion, for thy night
   Is past : the Lord, thy Light, is born :
The Gentiles shall behold thy light ;
   The kings walk forward in thy morn.

FEST. EPIPHANIÆ.

XVIII.

They leave the land of gems and gold,
  The shining portals of the East;
For Him, 'the Woman's Seed' foretold,
  They leave the revel and the feast.

To earth their sceptres they have cast
  And crowns by Kings ancestral worn;
They track the lonely Syrian waste;
  They kneel before the Babe new-born.

O happy eyes that saw Him first!
  O happy lips that kissed His feet!
Earth slakes at last her ancient thirst;
  With Eden's joy her pulses beat.

True Kings are those who thus forsake
  Their kingdoms for the Eternal King—
Serpent! her foot is on thy neck!
  Herod! thou writh'st, but canst not sting!

He, He is King, and He alone,
  Who lifts that Infant hand to bless;
Who makes His Mother's knee His Throne,
  Yet rules the starry wilderness.

MATER DEI.

XIX.

How many a lonely hermit-maid
    Hath brightened like a dawn-touched isle
When, on her breast in vision laid,
    That Babe hath lit her with His smile!

How many an agèd Saint hath felt,
    So graced, a second spring renew
Her wintry breast; with Anna knelt
    And trembled like the matin dew!

How oft th' unbending monk, no thrall
    In youth of mortal smiles or tears,
Hath felt that Infant's touch through all
    The armour of his hundred years!

But Mary's was no transient bliss;
    Nor hers a vision's phantom gleam:
The hourly need, the voice, the kiss—
    That Child was hers! 'twas not a dream!

At morning hers, and when the sheen
    Of moonrise crept the cliffs along;
In silence hers, and hers between
    The pulses of the night-bird's song.

And as the Child, the love. Its growth
    Was, hour by hour, a growth in grace:
That Child was God; and love for both
    Advanced perforce with equal pace.

GAUDIUM ANGELORUM.

XX.

'He looked on her humility'—
    Ah humbler thrice that breast was made
When Jesus watched His mother's eye,
    When God each God-born wish obeyed!

In her with seraph seraph strove
    And each the other's purpose crost:
And now 'twas Reverence, now 'twas Love
    The peaceful strife that won or lost.

Now to that Infant she extends
    Those hands that mutely say 'mine own!'
Now shrinks abashed, or swerves and bends
    As bends a willow backward blown.

And ofttimes, like a roseleaf caught
    By eddying airs from fairy land,
The kiss a sleeping brow that sought
    Descends upon the unsceptred hand!

O tenderest awe whose sweet excess
    Had ended in a fond despair
Had not the all-pitying helplessness
    Constrained the boldness of her care!

O holiest strife! The angelic hosts
    That watched it hid their dazzled eyes,
And lingered from the heavenly coasts
    To bless that heavenlier Paradise!

LEGENDA.

XXI.

O WEARIED Souls, by earth beguiled,
  Round whom the world's enthralments close
Look back on her, that three-years' child,
  Who first the life conventual chose!

A nun-like veil was o'er her thrown,
  Her locks by fillet-bands made fast,
Swiftly she climbed the steps of stone;
  Into the Temple swiftly passed.

Not once she paused her breath to take;
  Not once cast back a homeward look:
As longs the hart his thirst to slake
  When noontide rages, in the brook,

So longed that child to live for God;
  So pined from earth's enthralments free,
To bathe her wholly in the flood
  Of God's abysmal purity!

Anna and Joachim from far
  Their eyes on that white vision raised;
And when, like caverned foam, or star
  Cloud-hid, she vanished, still they gazed.

FEST. PRESENTATIONIS.

XXII.

Twelve years had passed, and, still a child
    In brightness of the unblemished face,
Once more she scaled those steps, and smiled
    On Him who slept in her embrace.

As in she passed there fell a calm
    On all: each bosom slowly rose
Like the long branches of the palm
    When under them the south wind blows:

The scribe forgot his wordy lore;
    The chanted psalm was heard far off;
Hushed was the clash of golden ore;
    And hushed the Sadducean scoff.

Type of the Church, the gift was thine!
    'Twas thine to offer first, that hour,
Thy Son—the Sacrifice Divine,
    The Church's everlasting dower!

Great Priestess! round that aureoled brow
    Which cloud or shadow ne'er had crossed,
Began there not thenceforth to grow
    A milder dawn of Pentecost?

THE FIRST DOLOUR.

(Gladio Transfixa.)

XXIII.

To be the mother of her Lord—
  What means it? This; a bleeding heart!
The pang that woke at Simeon's word
  Worked inward, never to depart.

The dreadful might of Sin she knew
  As Innocence alone can know:
O'er her its deadliest gloom it threw
  As shades lie darkest on the snow.

Yet o'er her Sorrow's depth no storm
  Of earth's rebellious passion rolled:
So sleeps some lake no gusts deform
  High on the dark hills' craggy fold.

In that still glass the unmeasured cliff,
  With all its scars and clouds is shown:
And, mellowed in that mother's grief,
  At times, O Christ, we catch Thine own!

XXIV.

The golden rains are dashed against
  Those verdant walls of lime and beech
Wherewith our happy vale is fenced
  Against the north; yet cannot reach

The stems that lift you leafy crest
  High up above their dripping screen:
The chestnut fans are downward pressed
  On banks of bluebell hid in green.

White vapours float along the glen
  Or rise from every sunny brake;
A pause amid the gusts—again
  The warm shower sings across the lake.

Sing on, all-cordial showers, and bathe
  The deepest root of loftiest pine!
The cowslip dim, the 'primrose rathe'
  Refresh; and drench in nectarous wine

You fruit-tree copse, all blossomed o'er
  With forest foam and crimsoned snow—
Behold! above it bursts once more
  The world-embracing, heavenly bow!

LEGENDA.

XXV.

As, flying Herod, southward went
  That Child and Mother, unamazed,
Into Egyptian banishment,
  The weeders left their work, and gazed.

That bright One spake to them, and said,
  'When Herod's messengers demand,
Passed not that Infant, Herod's dread,—
  Passed not that Infant through your land?

'Then shall ye answer make, and say,
    Behold, since first the corn was green
No little Infant passed this way;
    No little Infant we have seen.'

Earth heard; nor missed the Maid's intent —
    As on the Flower of Eden passed
With Eden swiftness up she sent
    A sun-browned harvest ripening fast.

By simplest words and sinless wheat
    The messengers rode back beguiled;
And by that truthfullest deceit
    Which saved the little new-born Child!

THE SECOND DOLOUR.

(Cum Filio Profuga.)

XXVI.

THE fruitful River slides along;
    The Conqueror's City glitters nigh;
The Palm-groves ring with dance and song;
    Earth trembles, crimsoned from the sky.

Far down the sunset, lonely stands
    Some temple of a bygone age
Slow-settling into sea-like sands,
    Long served with prayer and pilgrimage.

Here ruled the Shepherd-Kings, and they
    That race from Sun and Moon which drew
The unending lines of Priestly sway:
    Here Alexander's standard flew.

Here last the great Cæsarian star
  Through Egypt's sunset flashed its beam
While pealed the Roman trump afar,
  And Earth's first Empire like a dream

Dissolved. But who are they—the Three
  That pierce thus late yon desert wide?
The Babe is on His Mother's knee;
  Low-bent an old Man walks beside.

What say'st thou, Egypt? 'Let them come!
  Of such as little note I keep
As of the least of flies that hum
  Above my deserts, or my deep!'

SAINT JOSEPH.

XXVII.

True Prince of David's line! thy chair
  Is set on every poor man's floor:
Labour through thee a crown doth wear
  More rich than kingly crowns of yore!

True Confessor! thine every deed,
  While error ruled the world, or night
Confessed aright the Christian creed,
  The Christian warfare waged aright.

Teach us, like thee, our heart to raise,
  In toil not ease contemplatist;
Like thee, o'er lowly tasks to gaze
  On her whose eyes are still on Christ.

O teach us, thou whose ebbing breath
    Was watched by Mary and her Son,
To welcome age, await in death
    True life's true garland, justly won.

'JOSEPH, HER HUSBAND.'

XXVIII.

Gladsome and pure was Eden's bower—
    Saint Joseph's house was holier far,
More rich in Love's auguster dower,
    More amply lit by Wisdom's star.

The Queen of Virgins where he sate
    Beside him stood and watched his hand:
His daughter-wife, his angel-mate
    Submissive to his least command.

Hail, Patriarch blest and sage! on earth
    Thine was the bridal of the skies!
Thy house was heaven: for by its hearth
    Thy God reposed in mortal guise.

Hail! life most sweet in life's decline!
    Hail death, than life more bright, more blest!
The hands of Mary clasping thine,
    Thy head upon the Saviour's breast!

SAINT JOSEPH'S PATRONAGE.

('Constituit eum dominum domus suæ.'
The Household Saints.)

XXIX.

The Apostle's life, the Martyr's death,
    The all-conquering Word, all-wondrous Sign,
Have greatness sense-discerned. By faith,
    And Faith's strong Love, we reach to thine.

Through lower heavens those others run,
    Fair planets kenned by feebler eyes:
Thy loftier light is later won,
    Serener gleam from lonelier skies.

Thou stand'st within: they move without:
    More near the God-Man was thy place:
It was: it is: we cannot doubt
    That as thy greatness was thy grace.

No priestly tiar, no prophet rod
    Were thine: with them thou art who zone
The altar of Incarnate God,
    Who throng the white steps of the Throne.

There Anna rests, and Joachim
    That Great One's Parents; at their side
Elizabeth, not far from Him
    Her Baptist Son for Right who died.

A hierarchy apart they sit,
    A Royal House benign yet dread,
In Godhead veiled, by Godhead lit—
    There highest shines thy silver head.

MATER CHRISTI.

XXX.

Daily beneath His mother's eyes
    Her Lamb matured His lowliness;
'Twas hers the lovely Sacrifice
    With fillet and with flower to dress.

Beside that mother's knee He knelt;
    With heavenly-human lips He prayed:
His Will within her will she felt;
    And yet His Will her will obeyed.

Gethsemané! when day is done
    Thy flowers with falling dews are wet:
Her tears fell never; for the sun
    Those tears that brightened never set.

The house was silent as that shrine
    The priest but entered once a year:
There shone His emblem. Light Divine!
    Thy presence and Thy power were here!

MATER CHRISTI.

XXXI.

He willed to lack; He willed to bear;
    He willed by suffering to be schooled;
He willed the chains of flesh to wear;
    Yet from her arms the worlds He ruled.

As tapers 'mid the noontide glow
   With merged yet separate radiance burn,
With human taste and touch even so
   The things He knew He willed to learn.

He sat beside the lowly door:
   His homeless eyes appeared to trace
In evening skies remembered lore
   And shadows of His Father's face.

One only knew Him. She alone
   Who nightly to His cradle crept
And, lying like the moonbeam prone,
   Worshipped her Maker as He slept.

MATER CREATORIS.

XXXII.

Bud forth a Saviour, Earth! fulfil
   Thy first of functions, ever new!
Balm-dropping heaven, for aye distil
   Thy grace like manna or like dew!

'To us, this day, a Child is born.'
   Heaven knows not mere historic facts—
Celestial mysteries night and morn
   Live on in ever-present Acts.

Calvary's dread Victim in the skies
   On God's great altar rests even now:
The Pentecostal glory lies
   For ever round the Church's brow.

From Son and Father, He, the Lord
　　Of Love and Life, proceeds alway:
Upon the first Creative Word
　　Creation, trembling, hangs for aye.

Nor less ineffably renewed
　　Than when on earth the tie began,
Is that mysterious Motherhood
　　Which re-creates the worlds and man.

MATER SALVATORIS.

XXXIII.

O Heart with His in just accord!
　　O Soul His echo, tone for tone!
O Spirit that heard and kept His word!
　　O Countenance moulded like His Own!

Behold, she seemed on Earth to dwell;
　　But hid in light she ever sat
Beneath the Throne ineffable
　　Chanting her clear Magnificat.

Fed from the boundless heart of God
　　The joy within her rose more high
And all her being overflowed,
　　Until that Hour decreed drew nigh.

That hour, there crept her spirit o'er
　　The shadow of that pain world-wide
Whereof her Son the substance bore—
　　Him offering, half in Him she died;

Standing, like that strange Moon whereon
    The mask of Earth lies dim and dead,
An orb of glory, shadow-strewn,
    Yet girdled with a luminous thread.

HER FOUNDATIONS ARE ON THE HOLY HILLS.

XXXIV.

Her Child, her God, in Nature's right
    She loved: we love Him but by Grace:
Behold! our Virtue's proudest height
    Is lower than her Virtue's base!

Alone by holy Nature taught
    All lesser mothers love their own:
Her love was Nature's love, heaven-caught,
    And lightning-lifted to the Throne.

Her God! alone through worship she
    Proportioned love for Him could prove!
Her God, and yet her Offspring! He
    Both loved her, and was bound to love!

MATER ADMIRABILIS.

XXXV.

O Mother-Maid! to none save thee
    Belongs in full a Parent's name;
So fruitful thy Virginity,
    Thy Motherhood so pure from blame!

All other parents, what are they?
   Thy types! In them thou stood'st rehearsed
As they in bird, and bud, and spray.
   Thine Antitype? The Eternal First!

Prime Parent He: and next Him thou!
   O'ershadowed by the Father's Might
Thy 'Fiat' was thy bridal vow:
   Thine offspring He, the 'Light from Light.'

Her Son Thou wert: her Son Thou art
   O Christ! Her substance fed Thy growth:
Alone, she shaped Thee in her heart—
   Thy Mother and Thy Father both.

MATER AMABILIS.

XXXVI.

MOTHER of Love! Thy love to Him
   Cherub and Seraph can but guess:
A mother sees its image dim
   In her own breathless tenderness.

That infant touch none else could feel
   Vibrates like light through all her sense:
Far off she hears his cry: her zeal
   With lions fights in his defence.

Unmarked his youth goes by: his hair
   Still smooths she down, still strokes apart;
The first white thread that meets her there
   Glides like a dagger through her heart.

Men praise him: on her matron cheek
  There dawns once more a maiden red:
Of war, of battle-fields they speak:
  She sees once more his father dead.

In sickness—half in sleep—she hears
  His foot, ere yet that foot is nigh:
Wakes with a smile; and scarcely fears
  If he but clasp her hand, to die.

THE THIRD DOLOUR.

(Filium quærens.)

XXXVII.

Three days she seeks her Child in vain:
  He who vouchsafed that holy woe
And makes the gates of glory pain
  He, He alone its depth can know.

She wears the garment He must wear;
  She tastes His chalice! From a Cross
Unseen she cries, 'Where art Thou, where?
  Why hast Thou me forsaken thus?'

With feebler hand she touches first
  That sharpest thorn in all His Crown,
Worse than the Nails, the Reed, the Thirst,
  Seeming Desertion's icy frown!

O Saviour! we, the weak, the blind
  We lose Thee, snared in Pleasure's bound:
Teach us once more Thy Face to find
  Where only Thou art truly found,

In Thy true Church, its Faith, its Love
   Its anthemed Rites or Penance mute
And that Interior Life whereof
   Eternal Life is flower and fruit.

MATER FILII.

XXXVIII.

Others, the hours of youth gone by,
   A mother's hearth and home forsake;
And, with the need, the filial tie
   Relaxes, though it does not break.

But Thou wert born to be a Son—
   God's Son in heaven, Thy will was this,
To pass the chain of Sonship on
   And bind in one whatever is.

Thou cam'st the *Son* of Man to be,
   That so Thy brethren too might bear
Adoptive Sonship, and with Thee
   Thy Sire's eternal kingdom share.

Transcendently the Son Thou art:
   In this mysterious bond entwine,
As in a single, two-celled heart,
   Thy natures, human and divine.

XXXIX.

When April's sudden sunset cold
   Through half-clothed boughs with watery sheen
Bursts on the high, new-cowslipped wold
   And bathes a world half gold half green

Then shakes the illuminated air
   With din of birds; the vales far down
Grow phosphorescent here and there;
   Forth flash the turrets of the town;

Along the sky thin vapours scud;
   Bright zephyrs curl the choral main;
The wild ebullience of the blood
   Rings joy-bells in the heart and brain:

Yet in that music discords mix;
   The unbalanced lights like meteors play;
And, tired of splendours that perplex,
   The dazzled spirit sighs for May.

XL.

Not yet, not yet! the Season sings
   Not of fruition yet but hope;
Still holds aloft, like balanced wings
   Her scales, and lets not either drop.

The white ash, last year's skeleton,
   Still glares uncheered by leaf or shoot
'Gainst azure heavens, and joy hath none
   In that pure primrose at her foot.

Yet Nature's virginal suspense
    Is not forgetfulness nor sloth:
Where'er we wander soul and sense
    Discern a blindly working growth.

Her throne once more the daisy takes
    That white star of our dusky earth;
And the sky-cloistered lark down-shakes
    Her passion of seraphic mirth.

'Twixt barren hills and clear cold skies
    She weaves, ascending high and higher,
Songs florid as those traceries
    Which won their name of old from fire.

Sing! thou that need'st no ardent clime
    To sun the sweetness from thy breast
And teach us those delights sublime
    Wherein ascetic spirits rest!

XLI.

The moon, ascending o'er a mass
    Of tangled yew and sable pine,
What sees she in yon watery glass?
    A tearful countenance divine.

Far down, the winding hills between,
    A sea of vapour bends for miles,
Unmoving. Here and there dim-seen
    The knolls above it rise like isles.

The tall rock glimmers spectre-white;
    The cedar in its sleep is stirred;
At times the bat divides the night;
    At times the far-off flood is heard.

Above, that shining blue!—below,
    That shining mist! Oh, not more pure
Midwinter's landscape, robed in snow
    And fringed with frosty garniture!

The fragrance of the advancing year
    Alone assures us it is May.
Make answer! in the heavenlier sphere
    Must all of earth have passed away?

NAZARETH.

XLII.

Before the Saviour's eyes unsealed
    The Beatific Vision stood—
If God from her that splendour veiled
    Awhile, in Him she gazed on God.

The Eternal Spirit o'er them hung:
    The Eternal Father moved beside:
With hands forth-held the Angelic throng
    Worshipped their Maker far descried.

Yet neither He who said of yore
    'Let there be light'—and all was day—
Nor she that, still a creature, wore,
    Creation's crown, and wears for aye,

To casual gazers wondrous seemed:
    The wanderer sat beside their door,
Partook their broken bread, and deemed
    The donors kindly; nothing more.

In Eden thus that primal Pair
    Ere sin had marred their first estate
Sate side by side in silent prayer,
    Their earliest sunset fronting, sate;

And now the lion now the pard
    Piercing the Cassia bower drew nigh;
Fixed on the twain a mute regard,
    Half pleased, half vacant; then passed by.

FŒDERIS ARCA.

XLIII.

From end to end, O God, Thy Will
    With swift yet ordered might doth reach:
Thy purposes their scope fulfil
    In sequence, resting each on each.

In Thee is nothing sudden; nought
    From harmony and law that swerves:
The orbits of Thine act and thought
    In soft gradation wind their curves.

O then with what a gradual care
    Must Thou have shaped that Ark and Shrine
Ordained the Eternal Word to bear,
    That Garden of Thy mystic Vine!

How white a gift within her breast
    Lay stored, for Him a couch to strew!
How vast a virtue lined His nest!
    How many a grace beside Him grew!

Of love on love what sweet excess!
  How deep a faith! a hope how high!—
Mary! on earth of thee we guess;
  But we shall see thee when we die.

SPIRITUS SPONSA.

XLIV.

As though, fast-borne the hills along,
  At dawn some shepherd girl or boy
Should wrestle with the lark in song
  And, shaft for shaft, retort his joy,

So walked, the hills of Truth above,
  The Bride Elect, the sinless Maid;
So, challenged by the all-heavenly Love
  The all-heavenly Lover's voice repaid.

From zenith heights incessant fell
  On her His Grace like sunny rain:
Unvanquished and invincible
  Her heart repaid that golden grain.

Perchance, in many an instant gleam
  She caught, unscorched and unabashed,
That vision of the Face supreme
  Which on her first-born spirit flashed!

Diseased are we: the infectious fire
  Corrupts our life-blood from our birth:
She, she was like the unfallen Sire,
  Compacted out of virgin earth.

In God she lived: His world she trod:
   Saw Him and His; saw nought beside—
He only *lives* who lives in God:
   That hour when Adam fell, he died.

ORANTE.

XLV.

She mused upon the Saints of old;
   Rock-like, on rock she stood, foot-bare:
On Him she mused, that Child foretold;
   To Him she held her hands in prayer,

Unwavering hands that, drawing fires
   Of grace from heaven, our earth endowed
With heavenly breath like mountain spires
   That suck the lightning from the cloud.

No moment passed without its crown;
   And each new grace was used so well
It dragged some tenfold talent down,
   Some miracle on miracle.

O golden House! O boundless store
   Of wealth by heavenly commerce won!
When God Himself could give no more,
   He gave thee all; He gave His Son!

RESPEXIT HUMILITATEM.

XLVI.

Not all thy Purity, although
   The whitest moon that ever lit
The peaks of Lebanonian snow
   Shone dusk and dim compared with it;

Not that great Love of thine whose beams
   Transcended in their virtuous heat
Those suns that melt the ice-bound streams
   And make earth's pulses newly beat;

It was not these that from the sky
   Drew down to thee the Eternal Word:
He looked on thy Humility;
   He knew thee, 'Handmaid of thy Lord.'

Let no one claim with thee a part,
   Let no one, Mary, name thy name,
While, aping God, upon his heart
   Pride sits, a Demon robed in flame.

Proud Vices, die! Where Sin has place
   Be Sin's avenger self-disgust:
Proud Virtues, doubly die, that Grace
   At last may burgeon from your dust!

MULIER FORTIS.

XLVII.

Supreme among the things create
  God's Image with the downward brow !
Greatness that know'st not thou art great !
  Thus great, Humility art thou.

All strength beside is weakness.   Might
  Belongs to God ; and they alone
Self-emptied souls and seeming-slight
  Are filled with God, and share His throne.

O Mary ! strong wert thou and meek ;
  Thy meekness gave thee strength divine :
Thyself in nothing didst thou seek ;
  Therefore thy Maker made Him thine.

Through Pride our parents disobeyed ;
  Rebellious Sense avenged the wrong :
The Soul, the body's captive made,
  No more was fruitful, or was strong.

With barrenness the earth was cursed ;
  Inviolate she brought forth no more
Her fruits, nor freely as at first :
  Thou cam'st, her Eden to restore !

Low breathes the wind upon the string ;
  The harp, responsive, sounds in turn :
Thus o'er thy *Soul* the Spirit's wing
  Creative passed ; and Christ was born.

MAY CAROLS.

PART II.
THE SPIRITUAL MOTHERHOOD.

'Behold thy mother.'—JOHN xix. 27.

AGIOS ATHANATOS.

I.

Cloud-piercing Mountains! Chance and Change
  More high than you their thrones advance!
Self-vanquished Nature's rockiest range
  Gives way before them like the trance

Of one that wakes. From morn to eve
  Through fissured clefts her mists make way;
At Night's cold touch they freeze, and cleave
  Her crags, and with a Titan's sway

Flake off and peel the rotting rocks,
  And heap the glacier tide below
With isles of sand and floating blocks
  Like leaves on streams when tempests blow.

Lo, thus the great decree all-just
  O Earth, thy mountains hear; and learn
Like man its awful import—'dust
  Thou art, and shalt to dust return.'

He only *is* Who ever was;
  The All-measuring Mind; the Will Supreme:
Rocks, mountains, worlds, like bubbles pass:
  God is; the things not God but seem.

PASTOR ETERNUS.

II.

I SCALED the hills. No murky blot
   No mist obscured the diamond air:
One time, O God, those hills were not!
   Thou spak'st: at Thy command they were!

O'er ebon meres the ledges hung;
   High up were summits white with snow:
Some peak athwart the mountains flung
   A crownéd Shadow creeping slow.

Still crept it onwards. Vague and vast
   From ridge to ridge the mountains o'er
That king-like Semblance slowly passed:
   A shepherd's crook for staff it bore.

O Thou that leadest like a sheep
   Thine Israel! all the earth is Thine!
Thy mystic Manhood still must sweep
   Thy worlds with healing shade divine.

The airy pageant died with day:
   The hills, the worlds themselves must die:
But Thou remainest such alway:
   Thy Love is from Eternity.

JESUM OSTENDE.

III.

Who doubts that thou art finite? Who
  Is ignorant that from Godhead's height
To what is loftiest here below
  The interval is infinite?

O Mary! with that smile thrice-blest
  Upon their petulance look down;
Their dull negation, blind protest:
  Thy smile will melt away their frown.

Show them thy Son! That hour their heart
  Will beat and burn with love like thine;
Grow large; and learn from thee that art
  Which communes best with things divine.

The man who grasps not what is best
  In *creaturely* existence, he
Is narrowest in the brain, and least
  Can grasp the thought of Deity.

TURRIS EBURNEA.

IV.

This scheme of worlds which vast we call
  Is only vast compared with man:
Compared with God, the One yet All,
  Its greatness dwindles to a span.

A Lily with its isles of buds
   Asleep on some unmeasured sea :—
O God, the starry multitudes
   What are they more than this to Thee?

Yet, girt by Nature's petty pale
   Each tenant holds the place assigned
To each in Being's awful scale :
   The last of creatures leaves behind

The abyss of Nothingness : the first
   Into the abyss of Godhead peers
Waiting that Vision which shall burst
   In glory on the eternal years.

Tower of our Hope! through thee we climb
   Finite creation's topmost stair ;
Through thee from Sion's height sublime
   Towards God we gaze through clearer air.

Infinite distance still divides
   Created from Creative Power ;
But all which intercepts and hides
   Lies dwarfed by that surpassing Tower!

CONSERVABAT IN CORDE.

V.

As every change of April sky
   Is imaged in the unchangeful brook
Her meditative memory
   Mirrored His every deed and look.

As suns through summer ether rolled
  Mature each growth the spring has wrought,
Her love's calm solstice turned to gold
  Her harvests of quiescent thought.

Her soul was as a vase, and shone
  Illumed but with the interior ray;
Her Maker's finger wrote thereon
  A mystic Bible new each day.

Deep Heart! In all His sevenfold might
  The Paraclete with thee abode,
And, sacramented there in light,
  Bare witness of the things of God.

THE KINDLY TRANSIENCE.

VI.

'Like flowers,' they tell us, 'Life must fade!'
  Ah flower-faced Friend! if flowers must die
Immortal sweets of these are made:
  Thus Time bequeaths Eternity.

'Life is a fleeting shade!' What then?
  The Substance doth the Shadow cast:
Essential Life, it recks not when,
  Shall crown this seeming Life at last!

Thus, while May breezes whirling caught
  Dead leaves poor spoils of winter gone
Half-truths, deciduous spoils of Thought,
  Their clothing from on high put on:

And better far it seemed to plight
    To earth a transient troth and trust
Than with corruption wed, and blight
    The Spirit's hope with deathless dust.

VII.

Stronger and steadier every hour
    The pulses of the season's glee
As higher climbs that vernal Power
    Which rules the azure revelry.

Trees that from winter's grey eclipse
    Of late but pushed their topmost plume
Or felt with green-touched finger-tips
    For spring, their perfect robes assume.

Like one that reads not one that spells
    The unvarying rivulet onward runs;
And bird to bird from leafier cells
    Sends forth more leisurely response.

Through gorse-gilt coverts bounds the deer;
    The gorse, whose latest splendours won
Make all the fulgent wolds appear
    Bright as the pastures of the sun.

A balmier zephyr curls the wave;
    More purple flames o'er ocean dance;
And the white breaker by the cave
    Falls with more cadenced resonance;

While, vague no more, the mountains stand
    With quivering line or hazy hue,
But drawn with finer firmer hand,
    And settling into deeper blue.

MARIÆ CLIENS.

VIII.

A LITTLE longer on the earth
   That aged creature's eyes repose
Though half their light and all their mirth
   Are gone; and then for ever close.

She thinks that something done long since
   Ill pleases God: or why should He
So long delay to take her hence
   Who waits His will so lovingly?

Whene'er she hears the church-bells toll
   She lifts her head, though not her eyes
With wrinkled hands, but youthful soul
   Counting her lip-worn rosaries.

And many times the weight of years
   Falls from her in her waking dreams:
A child her mother's voice she hears:
   To tend her father's steps she seems.

Once more she hears the whispering rains
   On flowers and paths her girlhood trod;
Yet of things present nought remains
   Save one abiding sense of God.

Mary! make smooth her downward way!
   Not dearer to the young thou art
Than her. Make glad her latest May;
   And hold her, dying, on thy heart!

IN MORTE TUTAMEN.

IX.

It was the dread last Eucharist:
　The hopes and fears of earth were gone;
The latest, lingering friend dismissed;
　The bed was ashes strewed o'er stone.

It was the dear last Eucharist:
　The old man lay in silent prayer:
His heart was now a shrine; and Christ
　Was with His Mother whispering there.

He heard them; heard within that veil
　Voices that Angels may not hear,
Not he that said to Mary, 'hail,'
　Not he that watched the Sepulchre;

Voices that met with touch like light;
　Murmurs that mixed, as when their breath
Two pine trees, side by side, unite:
　Of Love one whispered; one of Death.

SPECULUM JUSTITIÆ.

X.

Not in Himself the Eternal Word
　Lay hid upon Creation's day:
His Loveliness abroad He poured
　On all the worlds, and pours for aye.

Not in Himself the Incarnate Son
   In whom Man's race is born again
His glory hides. The victory won
   He rose to send His 'Gifts on Men.'

In sacraments, His dread behests,
   In Providence, in granted prayer,
Before the time He manifests
   His Presence, far as man may bear.

He shines not from a vault of gloom;
   The horizon round His splendour paints:
The sphere of Souls His beams illume;
   His light is glorious in His Saints.

He shines upon His Church that Moon
   Who, in the watches of the night,
Transmits to Earth the entrusted boon,
   A sister orb of sacred light.

And thou, pure mirror of His grace!
   As sun reflected in a sea,
So, Mary, feeblest eyes the face
   Of Him thou lov'st discern in thee.

AUXILIUM CHRISTIANORUM.

XI.

Not for herself doth Mary hold
   That Mother-Crown, that Queenly Throne;
The loftiest in the Saviour's Fold
   The least possesses of her own.

Pure thoughts that make to God their quest
  With her find footing o'er the clouds,
Like those sea-crossing birds that rest
  A moment on the sighing shrouds.

In her our hearts, no longer nursed
  On dust, for spiritual beauty yearn;
From her our instincts, as at first,
  An upward gravitation learn.

Through her draw nigh the things remote:
  For in true love's supernal sphere
No more round self the affections float,
  More near to God, to man more near.

In her, the weary warfare past,
  The port attained, the exile o'er,
We see the Church's bark at last
  Close-anchored on the eternal shore!

XII.

O COWSLIPS sweetening lawn and vale,
  O Harebells drenched in noontide dew,
O moon-white Primrose, Wind-flower frail!
  The song should be of her, not you!

The May breeze answered, whispering low,
  'Not *thine*: they sing her praises best!
The flowers her grace in theirs can show:
  Her claims they prove not, yet attest.

'Beneath all fair things round thee strewn
  Her beauty lurks, by sense unseen:
Who lifts their veil uprears a throne
  In holy hearts to Beauty's Queen.'

AB ETERNO ORDINATA.

XIII.

Eternal Beauty, ere the spheres
  Had rolled from out the gulfs of night,
Sparkled, through all the unnumbered years
  Before the Eternal Father's sight:

Truth's solemn reflex—not a Dream—
  Created Wisdom's smile unpriced —
Before His eyes it hung, a gleam
  Flashed from the eternal Thought of Christ.

It hung, the unbodied antitype
  Of all Creation shapes and sings;
That finite world which Time makes ripe,
  Which Uncreated Light enrings.

Star-like within the depths serene
  Of that still vision, Mary, thou
With Him, thy Son, of God wert seen
  Millenniums ere the lucid brow

Of Eve o'er Eden founts had bent,
  Millenniums ere that *second* Pair
With shame the hopes of man had blent,
  Had stained the brightness once so fair.

Elect of Creatures! Man in thee
  Beholds that primal Beauty yet;
Sees all that Man was formed to be,
  Sees all that Man can ne'er forget!

XIV.

Three worlds there are—the first of Sense—
    That sensuous earth which round us lies;
The next, of Faith's Intelligence;
    The third, of Glory, in the skies.

The first is palpable, but base;
    The second heavenly, but obscure;
The third is star-like in the face,
    But ah! remote that world as pure.

Yet, glancing through our misty clime,
    Some sparkles from that loftier sphere
Make way to earth; then most what time
    The annual spring-flowers re-appear.

Amid the coarser needs of earth
    All shapes of brightness, what are they
But wanderers exiled from their birth
    Or pledges of a happier day?

Yea, what is Beauty, judged aright,
    But some surpassing, transient gleam;
Some smile from heaven, in waves of light
    Rippling o'er life's distempered dream?

Or broken memories of that bliss
    Which rushed through first-born Nature's blood
When He who ever was, and is
    Looked down, and saw that all was good?

XV.

Alas! not only loveliest eyes
    And brows with lordliest lustre bright
But Nature's self, her woods and skies
    The credulous heart can cheat or blight.

And why? Because the sin of man
    'Twixt Fair and Good has made divorce
And stained, since Evil first began,
    That stream so heavenly at its source.

O perishable vales and groves!
    Your master was not made for you:
Ye are but creatures! human loves
    Are to the great Creator due.

And yet, through Nature's symbols dim
    There are with keener sight that pierce
The outward husk and reach to Him
    Whose garment is the universe.

For this to earth the Saviour came
    In flesh; in part for this He died;
That man might have in soul or frame
    No faculty unsanctified.

That Fancy's self, so prompt to lead
    Through paths disastrous or defiled,
Upon the Tree of Life might feed;
    And Sense with Soul be reconciled.

IDOLATRIA.

XVI.

The fancy of an age gone by
   When Fancy's self to earth declined
Still thirsting for Divinity
   Yet still, through sense, to Godhead blind

Poor mimic of that Truth of old
   The Patriarchs' Faith—a Faith revealed—
Compressed its God in mortal mould
   Poor prisoner of Creation's field.

Nature and Nature's Lord were one!
   Then countless gods from cloud and stream
Glanced forth; from sea, and moon, and sun:
   So ran the Pantheistic dream.

And thus the All-Holy, thus the All-True,
   The One Supreme, the Good, the Just,
Like mist was scattered, lost like dew,
   And vanished in the wayside dust.

Mary! through thee the idols fell:
   When He the Nations longed for* came—
True God yet Man, with man to dwell,
   The phantoms hid their heads for shame.

His place, or thine, removed, ere long
   The Bards would push the Seers aside;
And, lifted by the might of song,
   Olympus stand re-edified!

      * 'The Desire of the Nations.'

'IN HIM WE HAVE OUR BEING.'

XVII.

The God who lives in those bright flowers
    That wave and flash from yonder rock
O children singing 'mid your bowers
    In you lives also, pleased to mock

His own unmoved Immensity
    With you—in you—to sport and play:
As ripples on a summer sea
    Are ye: unchanged that sea for aye!

Thus much of Truth they knew that feigned
    Of old, their God with Nature one:
Another, loftier truth remained
    For us, which now they read who run.

Half-truths are Falsehood's baits: too near
    They roam to Error's maze of doubt,
And, like some scared, outlying deer,
    O'er-leap the limit, in and out.

Such quarry, hunter youths, beware!
    That bourne is demon-haunted ground;
And, bone from bone, the demons tear
    The man who steps beyond its bound.

TOTA PULCHRA.

XVIII.

A BROKEN gleam on wave and flower,
   A music that in utterance dies,
A redd'ning leaf, a falling shower,
   Behold that Beauty which we prize!

And ah! how oft Corruption works
   Through that brief Beauty's force or wile!
How oft a gloom eternal lurks
   Beneath an evanescent smile!

But thou, serene and smiling light
   Of every grace to man benign,
In thee all harmonies unite;
   All minstrelsies of Truth are thine.

Of old whate'er to mind or heart
   Was dear 'had leave' with thee to rest:
The 'little birds' of every Art
   Hung on thy Fane their procreant nest.

'AD NIVES.'

XIX.

BEFORE the morn began to break
   The Bright One bent above that pair
Whose childless vows aspired to take
   The Mother of their Lord for heir.

'Twas August: even in midnight shade
    The roofs were hot, and hot the street:
' Build me a fane,' that Vision said,
    ' Where first your eyes the snow shall meet.' *

With snow the Esquiline was strewn
    At morn!—Fair Legend! who but thinks
Of thee, when first the breezes blown
    From summer Alp to Alp he drinks?

He stands: he hears the torrents dash:
    The sultry valley steams; and lo!
Through chasms of endless azure flash
    The peaks of everlasting snow!

He stands; he listens; on his ear
    Swells softly forth some virgin hymn,
The white procession winding near
    With glimmering lights in sunshine dim.

Mother of Purity and Peace!
    They sing the Saviour's name and thine—
Clothe them for ever with the fleece
    Unspotted of thy Lamb divine!

FEST. PURITATIS.

XX.

FAR down the bird may sing of love;
    The honey-bearing blossom blow:
But hail ye hills that rise above
    The limit of perpetual snow!

* Santa Maria Maggiore, on the Esquiline, at Rome.

O Alpine City, with thy walls
  Of rock eterne and spires of ice
Where torrent still to torrent calls
  And precipice to precipice;

How like that holier City thou
  The heavenly Salem's earthly porch,
Which rears among the stars her brow
  And plants firm feet on earth—the Church!

'Decaying, ne'er to be decayed,'
  Her woods like thine renew their youth:
Her streams, in rocky arms embayed,
  Are clear as virtue, strong as truth.

At times the lake may burst its dam;
  Black pine and rock the valley strew;
But o'er the ruin soon the lamb
  Its flowery pasture crops anew.

Like thee in regions near the sky
  She piles her cloistered snows, and thence
Diffuses gales of purity
  O'er fields of consecrated sense.

On those still heights a lovelight glows
  The plains from them above receive;
Not all the Lily! There *thy* Rose,
  O Mary, triumphs, morn and eve!

Through thee Art preached, 'mid change and strife,
  The eternal Peace, the immortal Love,
And o'er the weeping vale of life
  Her heavenly rainbow Painting wove.

Those pictures, fair as moon or star,
  The ages dear to Faith brought forth
Formed but the illumined calendar
  Of her that Church which knows thy worth.

Not less doth Nature teach through thee
  That mystery hid in hues and lines:
Who loves thee not hath lost the key
  To all her sanctuaries and shrines.

XXI.

The night through yonder cloudy cleft
  With many a lingering last regard,
Withdraws—but slowly—and hath left
  Her mantle on the darksome sward.

The lawns with silver dews are strewn!
  The winds lie hushed in cave and tree;
Nor stirs a flower, save one alone
  That bends beneath the earliest bee.

Peace over all the garden broods;
  Pathetic sweets the thickets throng;
Like breath the vapour o'er the woods
  Ascends, dim woods without a song;

Or hangs, a shining, fleece-like mass
  O'er half yon lake that winds afar
Among the forests, still as glass,
  The mirror of that Morning Star

Which, halfway wandering from the sky,
  Amid the glimmering dawn delays,
And, large and less alternately,
  Bends down a lustrous, tearful gaze.

Mother and home of Spirits blest!
   Bright gate of Heaven and golden bower!
Thy best of blessings, love and rest,
   On earth, ere yet thou leav'st her, shower!

STELLA MATUTINA.

XXII.*

Shine out, O Star, and sing the praise
   Of that unrisen Sun whose glow
Thus feeds thee with thine earlier rays:
   The secret of thy song we know.

Thou sing'st that Sun of Righteousness,
   Sole light of this benighted globe
Whose beams, from Him reflected, dress
   His Mother in her shining robe!

Pale Lily, pearled around with dew,
   Lift high that heaven-illumined vase
And sing the glories ever new
   Of her, God's chalice, 'full of grace.'

Cerulean Ocean fringed with white
   That wear'st her colours evermore
In all thy pureness, all thy might,
   Resound her name from shore to shore,

Her name, and His, that, like thy rim
   Of light the dusky lands around,
Still girds Creation's shadow dim
   With Incarnation's shining bound.

Transfigured Earth, disguised too long,
    It falls—that Pagan mask of Sense!
Burst forth, dumb worlds, at last in song
    Of spiritual Intelligence!

THE FLESH AND THE SPIRIT.

XXIII.

Man's soul a palace is: therein
    A kingly senate sits in state:
But under-winding caves of Sin
    A pestilence all round create.

Man's head uptowers in arctic air:
    O'er temperate zones his heart hath sway:
But tropic sands there are; and there
    The lions of our nature prey.

Dread Maker of our twofold being
    In night and day alternate robed,
Shine on us, that the monsters, fleeing,
    May leave Thine Image throned and globed!

Shine on us;—and thou shinest! sun-bright
    Flash back the ransomed fields and meads
Trod by that Form compact of light
    That only mid the lilies feeds.

O earth, partaker of the curse,
    Thy glory fled when Adam fell:
Yet, not her mother but her nurse,
    Of Mary earth was capable!

MADE SUBJECT TO VANITY.

XXIV.

Poor earthly House of flesh and blood!
   Imprisoned Spirit's mortal mould
What rapture-thrills in fount and flood
   Are thine, and on the windy wold!

And yet what art thou? Bond and chain!
   To cheat the whole, thou giv'st the part:
The mother clasps her babe—'tis vain;
   She cannot hide him in her heart!

The *whole* great Soul would hear, would see:
   The sense is bound to eye, to ear:
Still 'Touch me not,' remains for thee:
   'Not yet ascended,' still we hear!

O pure in life, O sweet in death
   O sweet and sinless flesh of flowers
I would that life with such light breath
   Such sweetness born of death, were ours!

XXV.

MATER DIVINÆ GRATIÆ.

The gifts a mother showers each day
   Upon her softly-clamorous brood,
The gifts they value but for play,
   The graver gifts of clothes and food,

Whence come they but from him who sows
  With harder hand, and reaps, the soil;
The merit of his labouring brows,
  The guerdon of his manly toil?

From Him the Grace: through her it stands
  Adjusted, meted, and applied;
And ever, passing through her hands,
  Enriched it seems, and beautified.

Love's mirror doubles Love's caress:
  Love's echo to Love's voice is true:
Their Sire the children love not less
  Because they clasp a Mother too.

MATER DIVINÆ GRATIÆ.

XXVI.

'They have no wine.' The tender guest
  Was grieved their feast should lack for aught:
He seemed to slight her mute request:
  Not less the grace she wished He wrought.

O great in Love! O full of Grace
  That winds in thee a river broad
From Christ, with heaven-reflecting face,
  Gladdening the City of thy God!

Be this thy gift: that man henceforth
  No more should creep through life content,
Draining the springs impure of earth
  With life's material element.

Let sacraments to sense succeed :
  Let nought be winning, nought be good
Which fails of Him to speak, and bleed
  Once more with His all-cleansing blood !

'They have no wine.' At heaven's high Feast
  That soft petition still hath place,
And bathes—so wills that Kingly Priest
  Whose ' Hour *is* come '—the worlds with Grace.

DETACHMENT.

XXVII.

From sin but not alone from sin
  That Bright One of the worlds was free ;
Never there stirred her breast within,
  That downward Creature-Sympathy

Which clouds the strong eyes that discern
  Through all things, One, the All-True, All-just,
And bids the infirmer instinct yearn
  To beauteous nothings writ in dust.

Clear shines o'er glooming waves afar
  Yon cottage fire, as daylight dies,
How pure—till comes the evening star
  To shame it from untainted skies !

O Mary, in thy Daughters still
  Thine image pure, if pale, we find ;
The crystal of the flawless will ;
  The soul irradiating the mind ;

The heart where live, in memory sheathed,
    But ghosts of mortal joy or grief
Like wood-scents through a Bible breathed
    By some thin-pressed long-cherished leaf;

The tender strength, the bliss heaven-taught,
    Unguessed by Time's distempered thrall;
The lucid depth of loving thought,
    The peace divine encircling all.

In Him, the Unseen, their wealth they hoard:
    They sit, in self-oblivion sweet
The Virgin-Spouses of their Lord,
    Beside the Virgin-Mother's feet.

THE BEGINNING OF MIRACLES.

XXVIII.

The water changed to wine she saw:
    She saw nought else of shapes around:
With such a trance of loving awe
    That first of signs her spirit bound.

She saw in perspective benign
    Whate'er that first of signs rehearsed,
That later chalice, and the wine
    More changed, that slaked a holier thirst.

She saw calm homes of love and rest
    The earthly life to heaven allied
The deaths sabbatical and blest
    Of Saints that died as Joseph died.

She saw a world serene, august,
    A world new-made, whose every part
Was fashioned, not of sinful dust,
    But in, and from the Saviour's Heart.

She saw the stream of human kind
    So long defiled with weeds and mud
In fontal pureness onward wind
    To meet the eternal ocean flood

Within whose breast a love-star shook
    More fair than he that from the skies,
As home their silent way they took,
    Illlumed her never tearless eyes.

FILIA MARIAE.

XXIX.

One thought alone 'mid all this sea
    Of vernal bliss disturbs my breast:
What have I suffered, Lord, for Thee,
    Or how my love aright confessed?

Command me tasks that Love may show
    He needs no violet-scented bowers;
Some pain to bear, some joy forego,
    Some task, not chos'n, of arduous hours.

I mused upon Thy work and Thee:
    Hardness I sought, and shunned delights:
Where blows the flower and sucks the bee
    I found Thee not; I clomb the heights.

Them, too, I feared ; to city-ways
  I fled ; hot court, and fevered stair :
There too were beauty, love, and praise :
  The Saviour's bleeding steps were there.

EXPECTATIO.

XXX.

A SWEET exhaustion seems to hold
  In spells of calm the shrouded eve :
The gorse itself a beamless gold
  Puts forth : yet nothing seems to grieve.

The dewy chaplets hang on air ;
  The willowy fields are silver-grey ;
Sad odours wander here and there ;
  And yet we feel that it is May.

Relaxed and with a broken flow
  From dripping bowers low carols swell
In mellower, glassier tones, as though
  They mounted through a bubbling well.

The crimson orchis scarce sustains
  Upon its drenched and drooping spire
The burden of the warm soft rains ;
  The purple hills grow nigh and nigher.

Nature, suspending lovely toils,
  On expectations lovelier broods,
Listening, with lifted hand, while coils
  The flooded rivulet through the woods.

She sees, drawn out in vision clear,
  A world with summer radiance drest
And all the glories of that year
  Still sleeping in her sacred breast.

XXXI.

Whitens the green field, daisy-strewn;
  A richer fragrance loads the breeze;
Full-flowering meadows sweep, tall-grown,
  The bending boughs of greener trees.

Whitens the thorn, like yonder snow
  That crowns, not clothes, the hills aloof:
Empurpled skies more darkly glow
  Through chasms of denser forest roof.

The silver treble of the bird
  O'erruns her music's graver base
That golden murmur always heard
  That dins the universal space,

Commingled sound of insect swarm
  And vagrant bee, and wandering stream,
And workings of the woodlands warm
  By summer yearnings touched in dream.

O Nature, make thy children thine!
  Erase the stain; burn out the blot;
Like her of Mothers most benign,
  The sole that, loving, flatters not.

'JESUS AND HIS MOTHER WERE THERE.'

XXXII.

Love, youthful love, that mean'st so well,
    And spread'st thy wings to soar so high,
Yet, backward blown by gusts from hell
    On desert sands so oft dost die!

For thee what help? From pride? from scorn?
    Ah! love alone is love's defence,
True love, of love celestial born,
    And nursed in caves of Reverence.

Childhood thrice-blest! thine every thought
    Reveres superior mind or power
That, sown in darkness, may be wrought
    From Reverence love's consummate flower!

A sinless man, a sinless mate
    Walked, linked in God, o'er Eden's sward:
But He who links holds separate:—
    Between them paced Whom both adored!

O Face so like thy Son's look forth
    Through clouds that blot this mortal scene
And, teaching woman's spiritual worth,
    The heart of man with fire make clean:

That so once more with spotless feet
    Upon a world-wide Eden's sod
Humanity may stand complete
    One image, dual-cast from God;

And, dual-crowned—like that fair hill
    Parnassian, which from summits twain
Flashed back the morning bright and still
    Echoing the Muses' vestal strain—

May sing the Heavenly Lover's praise
    With voices twain, yet lost in one,
And learn that only when we raise
    Our hearts, they beat in unison.

LUMEN NUPTIARUM.

XXXIII.

Say, who is she that walks on air
    Nor stains her foot with sinful earth?
The all-tender Vestal, chaste and fair,
    In death more blameless than at birth.

Say, who is she serenely blest
    That walks the dustier ways of life
With foot immaculate as her breast?
    That Woman maid, the Christian Wife!

Her love, a full-blown rose, each hour
    Its snowy bud regerminates;
The star of Eden lights her bower;
    Her children's laughter cheers its gates.

Yet half she is, that wife—still bride—
    Owes to that vestal never wed,
As Homes through Him are sanctified
    Who had not where to lay His head.

XXXIV.

The golden day is dead at last,
    And hiding all their blossoms white
In one deep shade the bowers are massed,
    So feebly o'er them plays the light

Of those uncertain, moonless skies
    Bewildered with a silver haze,
Through which the unnumbered starry eyes
    Bend tearful down a trembling gaze.

Against the horizon's pallid line
    Where western heaven with ocean blends,
Far seen yon solitary Pine
    Its cloud-like canopy suspends.

Ah! hark, that Convent's chime! It swells
    From dusky turrets far away:
To shepherds half asleep it tells
    That Mary's daughters watch and pray.

XXXV.

If God for each fair action wrought
    On earth, with *wholly* pure intent,
Should call an Angel out of nought
    Thenceforth in heaven its monument,

To prove the all-fruitful strength and worth
    Of pureness perfect; and to show
That life in heaven may owe its birth
    To humblest Virtue tried below;

How often angel choirs would fleet
   From heaven the shadowy gulf across,
Some death-delivered Soul to greet
   Assoiled, ere death, from mortal dross;

Some Vestal from the cloister shade
   Still pale, some village maid as pure,
That smiled to see her beauty fade,
   Worked on for God in age obscure—

'Hail, Mother of our Joy!' how oft
   In hearts that knew not earthly ties
That angel Salutation soft
   Would wake the beautiful surprise,

As forward through the realms of light
   That Soul, on angel-litter borne,
Made way, an eddy silver-bright
   Through gold seas of the eternal morn!

'WHEN THOU HAST SET MY HEART AT LIBERTY.'

XXXVI.

How narrow earthly loves, even those
   Clouded the least by earthly stain!
What bars of Self around them close!
   Not Death itself can burst that chain.

We love amiss; we sorrow worse;
   Wan vintage of a barren sun
We drain around an ill-waked corse
   In death-vaults of delight foregone.

O thou whose love to Him was knit
    So near thee, yet so high above;
In whom to love was to submit,
    In whom Submission meant but Love;

Whose heart great Love dilated so
    That by His Cross, a Mother twice,
All men thy sons became; whose Woe
    But crowned true Love's Self-Sacrifice;

Make thou the bosom, pure before,
    Through grief more solid-pure to grow;
The lily vase that shook of yore
    Make thou the lily filled with snow!

The thought of thee among the Blest
    O'er earth a bliss snow-pure doth breathe:
Thy rest in heaven diffuses rest
    O'er those who love and mourn beneath.

GRATIÆ PLENA.

XXXVII.

If he of Angels first and best
    Chief Ardour of the Seraph fires
More graces clasps than all the rest,
    Perchance than all their ninefold choirs,

(That so proportioned worth and place
    May wed, nor even war with odd)
What plenitude of conquering grace
    Must fill the Mother of her God!

Their greatness stands in limits curbed
    Of sequent rank and grade; but she
Is one and whole, a world full-orbed,
    An Order sole, and Hierarchy:

Of things create both last and first;
    Added, that so from Adam's crime
Her Son might save the race accursed;
    Decreed before the birth of time.

Hail, Full of Grace! To eyes of men
    Light shows not mid excess of light:
Thy glory mocks the angelic ken,
    The peerless whiteness of thy white!

And yet 'twixt her and us but small
    The distance:—finite it must be:
'Twixt her and God the interval
    Is evermore infinity.

VAS INSIGNE DEVOTIONIS.

XXXVIII.

O STRONG in prayer! our spirits bind
    To God: our bodies keep from sin:
Live in our hearts that Christ may find
    An incorrupt abode therein:

That He, the Eternal Spirit, He
    Who overshadowed with His Grace
The depths of thy Humility
    In us may have a resting-place.

Who love thee prosper! As a breeze
  Thou waft'st them o'er the ways divine:
Strange heights they reach with magic ease
  Through music-moulded discipline.

'If I but touch His vesture's hem
  I shall be healed, and strong, and free'—
Thou wert His Vesture, Mary! them
  His virtue heals that reach to thee.

THE LETTER AND THE SPIRIT.

XXXIX.

How oft that Sadducean fool
  That imped with feathers from the jay
As hard a heart, a brain as dull
  As e'er were bubble-blown from clay,

How oft his half-shut eye had roved
  From sacred page to page, and read
Those words that, unaffirming, proved
  The Resurrection from the Dead! *

Words plainer were there: 'I shall go
  To him; he cannot come to me'—
'Though worms consume this Body, lo!
  I in my flesh my God shall see.'

Such words the Saviour challenged not:
  He willed to prove that at the core
Of well-known words to reverent Thought
  There lurked a mine of unknown lore.

  * 'The God of Abraham, Isaac, and Jacob.'

'What texts avouch her greatness?' Two,
   For those the Letter's rind who pierce;
The Ancient Record and the New:
   In Christ they meet; and Christ is hers.

THE 'SINGLE EYE.'

XL.

THE spirit intricately wise
   That bends above his ciphered scroll
Only to probe and analyse,
   The self-involved and sunless soul

Has not the Truth he holds, though plain;
   For Truth divine is gift, not debt:
Her living waters wouldst thou drain?
   Let down the pitcher, not the net!

But they, the spirits frank and meek,
   Nor housed in self, nor science-blind,
Who welcome Truths they did not seek;—
   Truth comes to them in every wind.

Beside his tent's wide open door
   With open heart, and open eye
The Patriarch sat, when they who wore
   That triad type of God drew nigh.

The world of Faith around us lies
   Like nature's world of life and growth:
Seeing to see it needeth eyes
   And heart, profound and simple both.

MYSTICA.

XLI.

As pebbles flung for sport, that leap
  Along the superficial tide
But enter not those chambers deep
  Wherein the jewel'd beds abide,

Such those light minds that, grazing, spurn
  The surface text of Sacred Lore,
Yet ne'er its deeper sense discern
  Its halls of mystery ne'er explore.

Ah! not for such the unvalued gems!
  The priceless pearls of Truth they miss:
Not theirs the starry diadems
  That light God's temple in the abyss!

Ah! not for such to gaze on her
  That moves through all that empire pale;
At every shrine doth minister,
  Yet never lifts her sacred veil!

'The letter kills.' Make pure thy Will;
  So shalt thou pierce the Text's disguise:
Till then, revere the veil that still
  Hides Truth from truth-affronting eyes.

BEATI QUI AUDIUNT VERBUM DEI.

XLII.

When from the crowd that voice was raised
   That blessed the Mother of the Lord
Not her the Son who loved her praised
   But all who heard, and kept His word.

O answer meet! to her how dear
   To her too great her crown to boast!
The meek were glad that praise to hear:
   The meekest, loftiest, joyed the most.

Above her soul's pure mirror crept
   No mist: no doubt within her stirred:
She asked not 'who His words hath kept
   Like her, the mother of the Word?'

Her tender heart rejoiced to think
   That all who say, 'Thy Will be mine,'
Without, or with the external link,
   In heart bring forth the Babe divine.

Chief of the Prophets John might be,
   Yet, but for that his happier place
In Jesus' kingdom, less than he
   The least one in the realm of Grace.

The mother of Incarnate God
   Some Prophet's mother *seemed*, alone:
His hour not yet was come: abroad
   To noise her fame had noised his own.

AUTHENTIC THEISM.

XLIII.

A TRIVIAL age with petty sneer
    Rebukes a creed for it too large
And little deems how subtly near
    To falsehood's blindest is its charge.

The authentic Thought of God at last
    To it grows pale through Error's mist:
Upon that mist Man's image cast
    Becomes the new God-Mechanist.

The vast *Idea* shrivels up:
    Truth narrows with the narrowing soul:
Men sip it from the acorn's cup:
    Their fathers drained the golden bowl.

Shrink, spelled and dwarfed, *their* earth, *their* skies;
    Shrinks in *their* hand the measuring-rod;
With dim yet microscopic eyes
    They chase a daily-dwindling God.

His temple, thus to crypt reduced
    For ancient Faith has space no more
Or her, its Queen. To hearts abused
    By sense, prime truths are true no more.

'TESTE DAVID CUM SIBYLLA.'
(Plato.)

XLIV.

O Thou of amplest brow, and eye
    Resplendent most with piercing beam,
Prime Teacher of antiquity
    That through thy shadowy Academe

Didst walk, the boast of Grecian years,
    Of man conversing and the Soul
Until the music of the spheres
    Around thy listeners seemed to roll;

Thy theme was still the unsensuous Mind
    That moulds and makes our worlds of sense,
The Truth in fleeting forms enshrined
    Its own all-conquering evidence:

Olympian fancies, winged with speech
    Descending lit that arduous theme
Like Pindan swans, each following each,
    Adown some forest-darkened stream.

Ilyssus 'mid the reeds withheld
    His wave to list a statelier ode
Than ever in that holy eld
    From Sophoclean chorus flowed:

Man, man thou sang'st in strain heaven-taught,
    Thy State's Exemplar, Type, and Plan,
Man, born of God's eternal Thought—
    Ah, hadst thou heard of God made man!

'TESTE DAVID CUM SIBYLLA.'
(Plato.)

XLV.

He looked on the transcendent light,
   And, by the greatness of the fall
Measuring the unfallen Spirit's height
   That Spirit deemed the body's thrall.

He knew the light, but not the love,
   The sin, but not that Cross of shame
Which raised us sinless spheres above!
   Perhaps in death that knowledge came

In death that vision o'er him stood
   Which all atoned, and all sufficed,
That Vision of Incarnate God,
   The Mother-maid, the Infant Christ!

Perhaps, where'er the heart is pure
   In Gentile or in Christian lands,
Despite dim clouds of faith obscure
   By dying beds that Vision stands

To ripen in a moment's space
   Truth's harvest, slumbering long in seed,
And fit—to meet the Judge's face—
   With love in fear the Spirit freed!

'TESTE DAVID CUM SIBYLLA.'

(Idea Platonica.)

XLVI.

'The everlasting hills present
   God's Steadfastness to mortal ken:
His Ways the trackless firmament:
   The deep His Counsels hid from men.'

What follows? *All* that meets our eyes
   Now dimmed by life's distempered dream
Is revelation in disguise;
   It shrouds, yet shows, the One supreme!

Throughout all worlds there liveth nought
   But lived, unmade, unchangeable
For aye in God's creative Thought
   Which cast Creation's glistening shell.

Him first, Him most, His works express:
   But Nature's myriad-minded plan
Hath lesser meanings; and the less
   Charm most the petty mind of man.

Poor captive of a sensuous heart,
   That mind no longer by the whole
Interprets Nature's meaner part—
   We live in surburbs of the soul!

O Death! fling back the gates of sense
   That man, redeemed from thraldom base,
With glorified intelligence
   At last may see his Maker's Face!

Then type to antitype shall yield:
　Then Truth no more shall show reversed:
The golden side of nature's shield
　Shall smite our vision as at first

When God His creatures bade to pass
　Beneath their master's eye, and he,
Fresh from the Godhead, as through glass
　Discerned in each its mystery;

Descried its supernatural law,
　Inferred its place in nature's frame,
And, in the tongue of Gods, with awe
　Assigned to each its destined Name.

DEUS ABSCONDITUS.

XLVII.

He was no conqueror borne abroad
　On all the fiery winds of fame
That over-sweeps a world o'er-awed
　In ruin-heaps to write—a Name.

No Act triumphant crushed the foe:
　No word of power redeemed the thrall:
By Suffering He prevailed that so
　His Father might be all in all.

His Godhead veiled from mortal eyes
　Showed forth that Father's Godhead still
As calm seas mirror starry skies
　Because themselves invisible.

Thus Mary in the Son was hid:
   That Son alone that Mother's boast;
She nothing said, she nothing did:
   Her light in His was merged and lost.

THE VEIL.

XLVIII.

For thirty years with her He lurked
   As secret as the unrisen sun:
In three short years His Work He worked:
   That work we know. The victory won,

Once more the veil descends, and shrouds
   That trance of Love, the Forty Days:
Like mountains lost in luminous clouds
   Their marvels cheat our yearning gaze.

The Saints who rose when Jesus died,
   Lazarus, twice cast from nature's womb,
Hidden their after days abide
   As Enoch's life or Moses' tomb.

The Work, the Work, no more, is told:
   The lore man needs not shuns his sight:
Thy Work was this, to clothe in mould
   Of Adam's race the Infinite.

Thy Motherhood thine endless Act
   In this all lesser praise is drowned:
To this to add were to detract:
   Sole-throned it bideth and self-crowned.

'THE SECRET OF GOD IS WITH THEM THAT FEAR HIM.'

XLIX.

Flower of the darkness that unseen
    With fragrance fill'st the vernal grove
Where hid'st thou? 'Mid the grasses green,
    Or boughs that bar the blue above?

Thou bird that, darkling, sing'st a song
    That shook the bowers of Paradise
Thou too art hid thy leaves among;
    Thou sing'st unseen of mortal eyes.

Of her thou sing'st whose every breath
    Sweetens a world too base to heed;
Of Him, Death's Conqueror, who from Death
    Alone would take the crown decreed.

Thou sing'st that secret gifts are best;
    That only like to God are they
Who keep God's Secret in their breast
    And hide, as stars are hid by day.

JANUA CŒLI.

L.

They seek not; or amiss they seek;
    The coward soul, the captious brain:
To Love alone those instincts speak
    Whose challenge never yet was vain.

True Gate of Heaven! As light through glass,
  That God who might—not born of thee—
Have come, was pleased to earth to pass
  Through thine unstained Virginity:

Lo! thus aright to *know* thy Son
  Through knowledge comes of thee in part,
Interior Vision, Spirit-won,
  High wisdom of the virgin heart.

Summed up in thee our hearts behold
  The glory of *created* things:
From His, thy Son's, corporeal mould
  Looks forth the eternal King of kings!

LI.

If sense of Man's unworthiness
  With Nature's blameless looks at strife,
Should wake with wakening May, and press
  New-born contentment out of life;

If thoughts of breed unblest and blind
  Should stamp upon the springing flower,
Or blacker memories haunt the mind
  As ravens haunt the ruined tower;

O then how sweet in heart to breathe
  Those pure Judean gales once more;
From Bethlehem's crib to Nazareth
  In heart to tread that Syrian shore!

To watch that star-like Infant bring
    To one of soul as clear and white
May-lilies, fresh from Siloa's spring
    Or Passion-flower with May-dews bright;

To follow, earlier yet, the feet
    Of her the 'hilly land' who trod
With true love's haste, intent to greet
    That aged saint beloved of God:

Before her like a stream let loose
    The long vale's flowerage, winding, ran:
Nature resumed her Eden use;
    And Earth was reconciled with Man!

CAUSA NOSTRÆ LÆTITIÆ.

LII.

WHATE'ER is floral on the earth
    To thee, O Flower, of right belongs,
Whate'er is musical in mirth,
    Whate'er is jubilant in songs.

Childhood and springtide never cease
    For him thy freshness keeps from stain:
Dew-drenched for him, like Gideon's fleece,
    The dusty paths of life remain.

For all high thoughts thou bring'st to mind,
    We love thee:—love thee better yet
For all that taint on human kind
    Thy brightness helps us to forget!

Hope, Hope is Strength! That smile of thine
　　To us is Glory's earliest ray!
Through Faith's dim air, O star benign,
　　Look down, and light our onward way!

STELLA MARIS.

LIII.

I LEFT at morn that blissful shore
　　O'er which the fruit-bloom fluttered free;
And sailed the wildering waters o'er,
　　Till sunset streaked with blood the sea.

My sleep the hoarse sea-thunders broke—
　　Death-visaged cliffs, with feet foam-hid
Leaned forth their brows through vapour-smoke
　　Like tower, and tomb, and pyramid.

In death-black shadow, ghostly white,
　　The breaker raced o'er foaming shoals:
From caverns cold as death all night
　　Came wailings as of suffering Souls.

At morn, through clearing mist the star
　　Of ocean o'er the billow rose:
Down dropped the elemental war;
　　Tormented chaos found repose.

Star of the ocean! dear art thou,
　　Ah! not to sea-worn men alone:
The suffering Church, when shines thy brow
　　Upon her penance, stays her moan:

The Holy Souls draw in their breath :
   The sea of anguish rests in peace :
And from beyond the gates of death
   Up swell the anthems of release.

AARONIS VIRGA.

LIV.

Blossom for ever, blossoming Rod !
   Thou didst not blossom once to die :
That Life which, issuing forth from God
   Thy life enkindled runs not dry.

Without a root in sin-stained earth
   'Twas thine to bud Salvation's flower :
No single soul the Church brings forth
   But blooms from thee and is thy dower !

Rejoice, O Eve ! thy promise waned ;
   Transgression nipt thy flower with frost :
But, lo ! a Mother man hath gained
   Holier than she in Eden lost.

UNICA.

LV.

While all the breathless woods aloof
   Lie hushed in noontide's deep repose,
That dove, sun-warmed on yonder roof,
   Ah what a grave content she knows !

One note for her!   Deep streams run smooth:
    The ecstatic song of transience tells;
What depth on depth of loving truth
    In that divine content there dwells!

All day with down-dropt lids I sat
    In trance; the present scene forgone:
When Hesper rose, on Ararat,
    Methought, not English hills, he shone.

Back to the ark the waters o'er
    That primal dove pursued her flight:
A branch of that blest tree she bore
    Which feeds God's Church with holy light.

I heard her rustling through the air
    With sliding plume—no sound beside
Save the sea-sobbings everywhere,
    And sighs of that subsiding tide.

REGINA PROPHETARUM.

LVI.

She took the timbrel, as the tide
    Rushed, refluent, down the Red Sea shore:
'The Lord hath triumphèd,' she cried:
    Her song rang out above the roar

Of lustral waves that wall to wall
    Fell back upon that host abhorred:
Above the gloomy watery pall
    As eagles soar her anthem soared.

Miriam, rejoice! a mightier far
　　Than thou one day shall sing with thee!
Who rises, brightening like a star
　　Above yon bright baptismal sea?

That harp which David touched who rears
　　Heaven-high above those waters wide?
The Prophet-Queen! Throughout all years
　　She sings the Triumph of the Bride!

LVII.

Still on the gracious work proceeds,
　　The good, great tidings preached anew
Yearly to green enfranchised meads
　　And fire-topped woodlands flushed with dew.

Yon cavern's mouth we scarce can see;
　　Yon rock in gathering bloom lies meshed;
And all the wood-anatomy
　　In thickening leaves is over-fleshed.

That hermit oak, which frowned so long
　　Upon the spring with barren spleen,
Yields to the sinless Siren's song,
　　And bends above her goblet green.

Young maples, late with gold embossed
　　Lucidities of sun-pierced limes
No more surprise us merged and lost
　　Like prelude notes in deepening chimes.

Disordered beauties and detached
   Demand no more a separate place:
The abrupt, the startling, the unmatched,
   Submit to graduated grace;

While upward from the ocean's marge
   The year ascends with statelier tread
To where the sun his golden targe
   Finds, setting, on yon mountain's head.

TURRIS DAVIDICA.

LVIII.

The towerèd City loves thee well,
   Strong Tower of David's House! In thee
She hails the unvanquished citadel
   That frowns o'er Error's subject sea.

With magic might that Tower repels
   A host that breaks where foe is none,
No foe but statued Saints in cells
   High-ranged and smiling in the sun.

There stands Augustin; Leo there;
   And Bernard with a maiden face
Like John's; and, strong at once and fair,
   That Spirit-Pythian, Athanase.

Upon thy star-surrounded height
  God's Angel keepeth watch and ward;
And sunrise flashes thence ere night
  Hath left dark street and dewy sward.

'TU SOLA INTEREMISTI OMNES HÆRESES.'

LIX.

What tenderest hand uprears on high
  The standard of Incarnate God?
Successive portents that deny
  Her Son, who tramples? She who trod

Long since on Satan! Who were those
  That, age by age, their Lord denied?
Their seats they set with Mary's foes:
  They mocked the Mother as the Bride.

Of such was Arius; and of such
  * He whom the Ephesian Sentence felled:
† Her Title triumphed. At the touch
  Of Truth the insurgent rout was quelled:

Back, back the hosts of Hell were driven
  As forth that sevenfold thunder rolled:
And in the Church's mystic Heaven
  There was great silence as of old.

  * Nestorius.   † Deipara.

UT ACIES ORDINATA.

LX.

The watchman watched along the walls:
    And lo! an hour or more ere light
Loud rang his trumpet. From their halls
    The revellers rushed into the night.

There hung a terror on the air;
    There moved a terror under ground;
The hostile hosts, heard everywhere,
    Within, without, were nowhere found.

'The Christians to the lions! Ho!'
    Alas! self-tortured crowds, let be!
Let go your wrath; your fears let go:
    Ye gnaw the net, but cannot flee.

Ye drank from out Orestes' cup;
    Orestes' Furies drave you wild.
Who conquers from on high? Look up!
    A Woman, holding forth a Child!

LXI.

As children when, with heavy tread,
    Men sad of face, unseen before,
Have borne away their mother dead,
    So stand the nations thine no more.

From room to room those children roam,
    Heart-stricken by the unwonted black:
Their house no longer seems their home:
    They search; yet know not what they lack:

Years pass: Self-Will and Passion strike
    Their roots more deeply day by day;
Old kinsmen sigh; and 'how unlike'
    Is all the tender neighbours say:

And yet at moments, like a dream
    A mother's image o'er them flits:
Like hers their eyes a moment beam;
    The voice grows soft: the brow unknits:

Such, Mary, are the realms once thine
    That know no more thy golden reign:
Hold forth from heaven thy Babe divine!
    O make thine orphans thine again!

SEDES SAPIENTIÆ.

LXII.

O THAT the wordy war might cease!
    Self-sentenced Babel's strife of tongues:
Loud rings the arena. Athletes, peace!
    Nor drown the wild-dove's Song of Songs.

Alas, the wanderers feel their loss:
    With tears they seek—ah, seldom found—
That peace whose Volume is the Cross;
    That peace which leaves not holy ground.

Mary, the peaceful soul loves thee!
   A happy child not taught of Scribes
He stands beside the Church's knee;
   From her the lore of Christ imbibes.

Hourly he drinks it from her face:
   For there his eyes, he knows not how,
The face of Him she loves can trace,
   And crowned with thorns the sovereign brow.

'Behold! all colours blend in white!
   Behold! all Truths have root in Love!'
So sings, half lost in light of light,
   Her Song of Songs the mystic Dove.

TRUTH.

LXIII.

Profane are they, and without ruth,
   Unclean, unholy, and unjust,
Who, loving knowledge, love not Truth:
   Such love is intellectual lust.

He loves not Truth who over-runs
   Like hunting-ground her harvest store
Trampling the birthright of his sons;
   Truth's gambler, staking 'all' on 'more.'

Who Truth from Error scorns to sift;
   Contemns that Truth enthroned in state,
God's Vestal keeping her sweet gift
   In fruitfulness inviolate;

Who thirsts for truths of lesser place,
  Discovered Fact, or Natural Law,
Yet spurns the supernatural base
  Of Truth's whole kingdom without flaw:

For on the adamantine Rock
  Of Truth, Revealed, and Spirit-proved
Stands Faith, and meets the warring shock
  Of world on world with face unmoved,

Thrice blest because not 'Flesh and Blood'
  That knowledge certain and serene
To Peter taught of old, but God
  Sole Teacher of the things unseen.

IMPLICIT FAITH.

'MULTUM NON MULTA.'

LXIV.

Of all great Nature's tones that sweep
  Earth's resonant bosom, far or near,
Low-breathed or loudest shrill or deep
  How few are grasped by mortal ear!

Ten octaves close our scale of sound:
  Its myriad grades, distinct or twined,
Transcend our hearing's petty bound
  To us as colours to the blind.

In Sound's unmeasured empire thus
  The heights, the depths alike we miss:
Ah, but in measured sound to us
  A compensating spell there is!

In holy music's golden speech
    Remotest notes to notes respond:
Each octave is a world; yet each
    Vibrates to worlds its own beyond.

Our narrow pale the vast resumes;
    Our sea-shell whispers of the sea:
Echoes are ours of angel plumes
    That winnow far infinity.

Clasp thou of Truth the central core!
    Hold fast that Centre's central sense!
An atom there shall fill thee more
    Than realms on Truth's circumference.

That cradled Saviour, mute and small,
    Was God—is God while worlds endure!
Who holds Truth truly holds it all
    In essence, or in miniature.

Know what thou know'st! He knoweth much
    Who knows not many things: and he
Knows most whose knowledge hath a touch
    Of God's divine simplicity.

MATER VIVENTIUM.

LXV.

In vain thine altars do they heap
    With blooms of violated May
Who fail the words of Christ to keep;
    Thy Son who love not nor obey.

Their songs are as a serpent's hiss;
    Their praise a poniard's poisoned edge;
Their offering taints, like Judas' kiss,
    The shrine; their vows are sacrilege.

Sadly from such thy countenance turns:
    Thou canst not stretch thy Babe to such
Albeit for all thy pity yearns
    As greet Him with a leper's touch.

Who loveth thee must love thy Son:
    Weak Love grows strong thy smile beneath;
But nothing comes from nothing; none
    Can reap Love's harvest out of Death.

GEUS NON SANCTA.

LXVI.

I TOILED along the public path:
    Loud rang the booths with knave and clown;
Now laughter peals, now cries of wrath
    Assailed the suburb from the town.

Pleasure, the kennel Circe, brimmed
    Her cup for him that passed. Hard by
Sabbathless labour, dust-begrimmed
    Alternated the curse and sigh.

'Alas,' I said, 'no God is here!
    The World, the Flesh, rule here confest:'
I heard a voice; an Angel near
    On sailed; an altar touched his breast.

He placed it by me, and I knelt;
   Clamour and shout and dust were gone:
I prayed, and in my prayer I felt
   The peace of God, and heard, 'walk on;

'Walk on: the Lands this hour that sleep
   A sleep of storm, shall wake to pray
And, praying, rest; her Feasts shall keep;
   Their long, sad years thenceforth a May!'

MATER VENERABILIS.

LXVII.

Come from the midnight mountain tops,
   The mountains where the panthers play:
Descend! the cowl of darkness drops;
   Come fair and fairer than the day!

Our hearts are wounded with thine eyes:
   They stamp thereon in words of light
The mystery of the starry skies;
   The 'Name o'er every name' they write.

Come from thy Lebanonian peaks
   Whose sacerdotal cedars nod
Above the world when morning breaks;
   The Mountain of the House of God.

Weakness and Dream have passed like night;
   Religion claims her ancient bound
On-borne in venerable might
   By lions haled and turret-crowned.

LXVIII.

The sunless day is sweeter yet
   Than when the golden sun-showers danced
On bower new-glazed or rivulet;
   And Spring her banners first advanced.

By wind unshaken hang in dream
   The wind-flowers o'er their dark green lair;
And those ensanguined cups that seem
   Not bodied forms but woven of air.

Nor bird is heard nor insect flits:
   A tear-drop glittering on her cheek
Composed but shadowed, Nature sits
   Yon primrose not more staid and meek.

The light of pensive hope unquenched
   On those pathetic brows and eyes,
She sits, by silver dew-showers drenched
   Through which the chill spring odours rise.

Was e'er on human countenance shed
   So sweet a sadness? Once: no more;
Then when his charge the Patriarch led
   Dream-warned to Egypt's distant shore:

Down on her Infant Mary gazed;
   Her face the angels marked with awe;
Yet 'neath its dimness, undisplaced,
   Looked forth that smile the Magians saw.

THE FOURTH DOLOUR.

(The Meeting on Calvary.)

LXIX.

She stands before Him on the Road :
    He bears the Cross ; He climbs the Steep :
Three times He sinks beneath His load :
    He sinks to earth : she does not weep.

She may not touch that Cross whose weight
    Against His will a stranger bears :
In heart to bear it, and to wait,
    His upward footsteps, this is hers.

She may not prop that thorn-crowned Head :
    The waves of men between them break :
Another's hand the veil must spread
    Against that forehead and that cheek.

Her eyes on His are fastened. Lo !
    There stand they, met on Calvary's height,
Twin mirrors of a single woe
    Made by reflection infinite.

The sons of Sion round them rave :
    The Roman trumpet storms the wind :
They goad him on with spear and stave :
    He passes by : she drops behind.

REFUGIUM PECCATORUM.

LXX.

SAY, who are those that beat with brands
    Like bandits on our palace-gate?
That storm our keep like rebel-bands?
    That come like Judgment or like Fate?

Say, who are those that spurn by night
    Our sumptuous floors with brazen shoon
And banquet halls whose latest light
    Is lightning, or a dying moon?

Say, who are those that by our bed
    Like giants tower in iron mail;
That press against the prostrate head
    Their foot, and wind through heaven the flail?

The Sins are these! Sin-pasturing Past!
    How in thy darkness they have grown
That seemed to die! How we at last
    To pigmy size have shrunk, self-known!

Help, sinless Mother! Bid Him spare!
    He loves us more—that Judge benign—
Than thou. 'Tis He that wills thy prayer:
    From Him it comes, that love of thine!

THE FIFTH DOLOUR.

(Beside the Cross.)

LXXI.

She stood in silence. Slowly passed
  The hours whose moments dropped in blood:
Its frown the Darkness further cast:
  She moved not: silently she stood.

No human sympathy she sought:
  Her help was God, and God alone;
Not even the instinctive respite caught
  From passionate gesture, sigh or moan.

Her silence listened. On the air
  Like death-bells tolled that prime Decree
Which bade the Eternal Victim bear
  Man's Sin primeval. Let it be!

The Women round her heard all day
  The clash of arms, the scoffing tongue:
She heard the breaking of that spray
  Whereon the fruit of Knowledge hung.

Behold the Babe of Bethlehem! Ay!
  The Infant slumbered on thy breast;
And thou that heard'st His earliest cry
  Must hear His 'Consummatum est.'

STABAT MATER.

LXXII.

She stood: she sank not. Slowly fell
  Adown the Cross the atoning blood:
In agony ineffable
  She offered still His own to God.

No pang of His her bosom spared;
  She felt in Him its several power:
But she in heart His Priesthood shared:
  She offered Sacrifice that hour.

'Behold thy Son!' Ah, last bequest!
  It breathed His last farewell! The sword
Predicted pierced that hour her breast:
  She stood: she answered not a word.

His own in John He gave. She wore
  Thenceforth the Mother-crown of Earth.
O Eve! thy sentence too she bore;
  That hour in sorrow she brought forth.

REGINA MARTYRUM.

LXXIII.

That tie, the closest ever twined,
  That linked a Creature with her God
All ties of man in one combined
  When by His Cross that Creature stood.

In both, one Will all wishes quelled:
    On one great Sire were fixed their eyes:
From sister hearts the death-stream welled:—
    Twins of a single Sacrifice.

In death her Spouse, her Son in life,
    Her wedding-garment was His blood:
It clasped her close enough a wife
    To wear the crown of Widowhood.

O Love! alone thy topmost height
    They tread who stand—thy clouds above—
Where *all* the rock-hewn paths unite
    That branch from God, and lead to love!

THE SIXTH DOLOUR.

(Taken down from the Cross.)

LXXIV.

The Saviour from the Cross they took:
    Across His Mother's knee He lies:
She wept not but a little shook
    As with dead hand she closed dead eyes.

The surface wave of grief we know:
    By us its depths are unexplored:
She treads the still abyss below
    Following the footsteps of her Lord.

Above her head the great floods roll:
    Before her still He moves—her Hope:
And calm in heart of storm her Soul,
    Calm as the whirlpool's central drop.

The Saviour from the Cross they took:
  Across His Mother's knee He lay:
O passers by! be still and look!
  That Twain compose one Cross for aye.

THE SEVENTH DOLOUR.

(Before the Tomb.)

LXXV.

Before the Tomb the Mother sate
  Amid the new-delved garden ground:
Her eyes upon its stony gate
  Were fixed, while darkness closed around.

A wind above the olives crept:
  It seemed the world's collected sigh:
That Mother's eyes their vigil kept:
  She felt but this; her Lord was nigh.

Behind her leaning each on each
  The Holy Women waited near:
Nor any spake of comfort: speech
  Was slain by sorrow and by fear.

From realm to realm of night He passed,
  That Soul which smote the dark to-day:
That Mother's eyes were settled fast
  Upon the Tomb where Jesus lay.

MATER DOLOROSA.

LXXVI.

From her He passed; yet still with her
  The endless thought of Him found rest,
A sad but sacred branch of myrrh
  For ever folded in her breast.

A Boreal winter void of light—
  Such seemed her widowed days forlorn:
She slept; but in her breast all night
  Her heart lay waking till the morn.

Sad flowers on Calvary that grew;
  Sad fruits that ripened from the Cross;
These were the only joys she knew:
  Yet all but these she counted loss.

Love strong as Death! She lived through thee
  That mystic life whose every breath
From Life's low harpstring amorously
  Draws out the sweetened name of Death.

Love stronger far than Death or Life!
  Thy martyrdom was o'er at last:
Her eyelids dropped; and without strife
  To Him she loved her spirit passed.

MAY CAROLS.

PART III.

MARIE IN CŒLIS.

'And a great sign appeared in heaven: a woman clothed with the sun, and the moon under her feet, and on her head a crown of twelve stars.

. . . .

'And she brought forth a man-child, who was to rule all nations with an iron rod: and her son was taken up to God, and to His throne.'—APOCALYPSE xii. 1, 5.

THE 'UNKNOWN GOD.'

I.

Behind this vast and wondrous frame
    Of worlds whereof we nothing know
Except their aspect and their name,
    Beneath this blind, bewildering show

Of shapes that on the darkness trace
    Transitions fair and fugitive
Lies hid that Power upon whose Face
    No child of man shall gaze and live.

Like one on purple heights that stands
    While mountain echoes round him roll
Screening his forehead with his hands
    And following far through gulfs of soul

Some thought that still before him flies —
    Thus, Power eternal and unknown,
We muse on Thine immensities
    Yet find Thee in Thy Son alone.

Emanuel, God with us, in Him
    We see the Unmeasured, and the Vast
Like mountain outlines, large and dim,
    On lifted mists at sunrise cast.

'The Word made Flesh!' O Power Divine
    Through Him alone we guess at Thee,
And deepliest feel that He is Thine
    When throned upon His Mother's knee.

ASCENSIO DOMINI.

II.

Rejoice, O Earth, thy crown is won!
    Rejoice, rejoice, ye heavenly host!
And thou, the Mother of the Son,
    Rejoice the first; rejoice the most!

Who captive led captivity,
    From Hades' void circumference
Who raised the Patriarch Band on high,
    There rules, and sends us graces thence.

Rejoice, glad Earth, o'er winter's grave
    With altars wreathed and clarions blown;
And thou, the Race Redeemed, out-brave
    The rites of Nature with thine own!

Rejoice, O Mary! thou that long
    Didst lean thy breast upon the Sword—
Sad nightingale, the Spirit's song
    That sang'st all night! He reigns, restored!

Rejoice! He goes, the Paraclete
    To send! Rejoice! He reigns on high!
That Sword lies broken at thy feet!
    His triumph is thy victory.

ASCENSIO DOMINI.

III.

I take this reed—I know the hand
    That wields it must ere long be dust—
And write upon the fleeting sand
    Each tide o'er-sweeps, the words 'I trust.'

And if that sand one day was stone
    And stood in courses near the sky
For towers by earthquake overthrown
    Or mouldering piecemeal, what care I?

Things earthly perish: life to death
    And death to life in turn succeeds:
The Spirit never perisheth:
    The chrysalis its Psyche breeds.

True life alone is that which soars
    To Him who triumphed o'er the grave:
With Him on life's eternal shores
    I trust one day a part to have.

Ah, hark! above the springing corn
    That chime! in every breeze it swells!
Ye bells that wake the Ascension morn,
    Ye give us back our Paschal bells!

IV.

A sudden sun-burst in the woods
  But late sad Winter's palace dim!
O'er quickening boughs and bursting buds
  Pacific glories shoot and swim.

As when some heart, grief-darkened long
  Conclusive joy by force invades,
So swift the new-born splendours throng;
  Such lustre swallows up the shades.

The sun we see not; but his fires
  From stem to stem obliquely smite
Till all the forest aisle respires
  The golden-tongued and myriad light:

The caverns blacken as their brows
  With floral fire are fringed: but all
Yon sombre vault of meeting boughs
  Turns to a golden fleece its pall

As o'er it breeze-like music rolls:
  O Spring, thy limit-line is crossed!
O Earth, some orb of singing Souls
  Brings down to thee *thy* Pentecost!

DOMINICA PENTECOSTES.

V.

CLEAR as those silver trumps of old
   That woke Judea's jubilee;
Strong as the breeze of morning, rolled
   O'er answering woodlands from the sea

That Evangelic anthem vast
   Which winds, like sunrise, round the globe,
Following that sunrise, far and fast
   And trampling on his fiery robe.

Once more the Pentecostal torch
   Lights on the courses of the year:
The 'Upper Chamber' of the Church
   Is thrilled once more with joy and fear.

Who rears her brow from out the dust?
   Who fixes on a world restored
A gaze like Eve's, but more august?
   Who lifts it heaven-ward on her Lord?

It is the Birthday of the Bride!
   The new begins; the ancient ends:
From all the gates of Heaven flung wide
   The promised Paraclete descends.

He who o'ershadowed Mary once
   O'ershades Humanity to-day;
And bids her fruitful prove in sons
   Co-heritors with Christ for aye.

DOMINICA PENTECOSTES.

VI.

The Form decreed of tree and flower
  The Shape susceptible of life
Without the infused, vivific Power
  Were but a slumber or a strife.

He whom the plastic Hand of God
  Himself created out of earth
Remained a statue and a clod
  Till Spirit infused to life gave birth.

So till that hour the Church. In Christ
  Her awful structure, nerve and bone,
Though founded, shaped, and organized
  Existed but in skeleton

Till down on that predestined frame,
  Complete through all its sacred mould
That Pentecostal Spirit came,
  The self-same Spirit Who of old

Creative o'er the waters moved :
  Thenceforth the Church, made One and Whole,
Arose in Him, and lived, and loved ;
  His Temple she, and He her Soul.

VII.

Here, in this paradise of light,
   Superfluous were both tree and grass:
Enough to watch the sunbeams smite
   Yon white flower sole in the morass!

From his cold nest the skylark springs
   Soars, pauses, sings; shoots up anew;
Attains his topmost height, then sings
   Quiescent in his vault of blue.

With eyes half-closed I watch that lake
   Flashed from whose plane the sun-sparks fly
Like Souls new-born that shoot and break
   From thy deep sea, Eternity!

Ripplings of sunlight from the wave
   Ascend the white rock high and higher;
Soft gurglings fill the satiate cave;
   Soft airs amid the reeds expire.

All round the lone and luminous meer
   The dark world stretches far and free
That skylark's song alone I hear;
   That flashing wave alone I see.

O myriad Earth! Where'er a Word
   Of thine makes way into the soul
An echo million-fold is stirred:
   Of thee the part is as the whole!

REGINA CŒLI.

VIII.

In some celestial realm we know
    The God-man keeps His court sublime
As Adam ruled the sphere below
    In that first Eden's sinless prime.

He too, that second Adam, hears
    Those rivers four engird His bound;
Serene advance of sleepless years
    With God's accomplished Counsels crowned,

Around Him, close as Eden leaves,
    The Souls consummate hang in trance:
Like wind the Spirit among them weaves
    Eternal song, or through the expanse

On-wafts, like snowy clouds high-piled
    Those pilgrims of God's trackless Will,
The white hosts of the Undefiled
    Whom love divine alone could fill.

The lustral mist for aye ascends:
    All creatures mix secure from strife:
At last the Tree of Knowledge blends
    Its branches with the Tree of Life.

An Eve partakes that Eden. She
    Who decked His cradle shares His throne:—
The Solitudes of Deity
    These, these are His, and His alone.

FEST. SS. TRINITATIS.

IX.

Fall back, all worlds, into the abyss
   That man may contemplate once more
That which He ever was Who is;
   The Eternal Essence we adore.

Angelic hierarchies! recede
   Beyond extinct Creation's shade—
What were ye at the first? Decreed:
   Decreed, not fashioned! thought, not made!

Like wind the untold Millenniums passed:
   Sole-throned He sat; yet not alone:
Godhead in Godhead still was glassed;
   The Spirit was breathed from Sire and Son.

Prime Virgin, separate and sealed;
   Nor less of social Love the root!
Dimly in lowliest shapes revealed;
   Entire in every Attribute:

Thou liv'st in all things and around;
   To Thee external is there nought;
Thou of the boundless art the bound;
   And still Creation is Thy Thought.

In vain, O God, our wings we spread;
   So distant art Thou—yet so nigh.
Remains but this when all is said
   For Thee to live; in Thee to die.

FESTUM SS. TRINITATIS.

X.

Like some broad flood whose conquering course
    Shakes the dim forests night and day
On sweeps the prime Creative Force,
    And re-creates the worlds alway.

The eternal Mind, the sole-born Thought
    Shape-entering matter's stamp and mould,
Through all the spaces wonder-fraught
    Speaks Law and Order as of old.

That Love which, ere it overflowed
    And beat on lone Creation's shore
Issuing from Both with Both abode
    Proceeds, abides, for evermore.

Yet man who—not in brow or breast
    But soul, and reason, and free-will—
Imaged his Maker and expressed
    Ignored that Triune Mystery still!

Here failed his science, failed as sight
    Earth's motion fails to mark! Ah me!
Our eye can track the swallow's flight;
    The circling sphere it cannot see!

And yet as Sense, abashed, down kneels
    And wins from Science lore sublime
To kneeling science Faith reveals
    Mysteries transcending space and time.

The Infinite remains unknown
    Too vast for man to *understand:*
In Him, the 'Woman's Seed,' alone
    We trace God's footprint in the sand.

THRONUS TRINITATIS.

XI.

Each several Saint the Church reveres,
    What is he but an altar whence
Some separate Virtue ministers
    To God a separate frankincense?

Each beyond each, not made of hands
    They rise, a ladder angel-trod:
Star-bright the last and loftiest stands:
    That altar is the Throne of God.

Lost in the uncreated light
    A Form all Human rests thereon:
His shade from that surpassing height
    Beyond Creation's verge is thrown.

Him 'Lord of lords, and King of kings,'
    The chorus of all worlds proclaim:
'He took from her,' one angel sings
    At intervals, 'His human frame.'

REGINA SANCTORUM OMNIUM.

XII.

He seemed to linger with them yet:
    But late ascended to the skies
They saw—ah, how could they forget?—
    The form they loved, the hands, the eyes.

From anchored boat, in lane or field
  He taught; He blessed, and brake the bread;
The hungry filled; the afflicted healed;
  And wept, ere yet He raised, the dead.

But when, like some supreme of hills
  Whose feet shut out its summit's snow
That, hid no longer, heavenward swells
  As further from its base we go,

Abroad His perfect Godhead shone
  Each hour more plainly kenned on high
And clothed His Manhood with the sun
  And, lifting, cleansed the adoring eye;

Then fixed His Church a deepening gaze
  Upon His Saints. With Him they sate
And, burning in that Godhead's blaze,
  They seemed that Manhood to dilate.

His were they: of His likeness each
  Had grace some fragment to present
And nearer brought to mortal reach
  Some imitable lineament.

ADVOCATA.

XIII.

I saw, in visions of the night
  Creation like a sea outspread
With surf of stars and storm of light
  And movements manifold and dread.

Then lo, within a Human Hand
    A Sceptre moved that storm above:
Thereon, as on the golden wand
    Of kings new-crowned, there sat a Dove.

Beneath her gracious weight inclined
    That Sceptre drooped. The waves had rest:
And Sceptre, Hand, and Dove were shrined
    Within a glassy ocean's breast.

His Will it was that placed her there!
    He at whose word the tempests cease
Upon that Sceptre planted fair
    That peace-bestowing type of Peace!

EXALTAVIT HUMILES.

XIV.

The Chief of Creatures lived unknown
    Sharing her Maker's sacred cloud
Like some fair headland flower-bestrewn
    That sleeps within its sea-born shroud.

The Brethren sought precedence: Christ
    To them gave titles. He, their God,
For Him 'the Son of Man' sufficed:
    The hidden way with Him she trod.

She died: the idols sank, and they
    Those four great Heresies, whose pride
Successive blurred the fount of day
    Her Son's Divinity denied:

As God, as Man, secure He reigned :
    Then came her hour : then shone her crown
And theirs, that Saintly Court unstained
    While guests of earth, by earth's renown.

Humility was crowned though late :
    That boastful, pagan greatness fell :
And on their thrones the Meek ones sate
    'Judging the tribes of Israel.'

XV.

WHERE is the crocus now that first
    When earth was dark and heaven was grey
A prothalamion flash, up burst ?
    Ah, then we thought not of the May !

The clear stream stagnates in its course ;
    Narcissus droops in pallid gloom ;
Far off the hills of golden gorse ;
    A dusk Saturnian face assume.

The seeded dandelion dim
    Casts loose its air-globe on the breeze ;
Along the grass the swallows skim ;
    The cattle couch among the trees.

Yet ever lordlier loveliness
    Succeeds the charm that cheats our hold :
The thorn assumes her snowy dress ;
    Laburnum bowers their robes of gold.

Down waves successive of the year
    The season slides ; but sinks to rise
With ampler view, as on we steer,
    Of lovelier lights and loftier skies.

XVI.

A low ground-mist, the hills between
    Measuring their intervals, distends
Ridge beyond ridge, the sylvan scene ;
    Far off the reddening river bends

From bridge to town. On hueless air
    The moon suspends her pearly shell
Above the eastern ledges bare ;
    But sunset throngs yon western dell

That pants through amethystine mist
    And gleams as though the Sons of God
Through golden ether stooped, and kissed
    Some Syrian vale the Saviour trod !

The beatific Splendours wane :
    The hills, of all that sweetness gone,
A roseate memory still retain :
    Thou compline chime, peal on, peal on !

Of Him thou sing'st whose Blood erased
    Earth's ancient stain by power divine ;
Of them, that second Pair, who paced
    That second Eden, Palestine.

IN CIVITATE SANCTIFICATA REQUIEVI.

XVII.

In silence, like a ridge of snows
  Slow reared in lands for ever calm,
On Sion's brow the Temple rose;
  In stillness grew as grows the palm.

Far off, on ridges vapour-draped,
  Was hewn and carved each destined stone:
Far off the axe the cedars shaped
  Upon their native Lebanon.

So rose that Temple holier far
  Incarnate Godhead's sacred shrine:
Round her there swelled no din of war:
  The peace that girt her was divine.

The deep foundations of that fane
  Were laid ere lived the hills and seas
In many a dread, unquarried vein
  Of God's deep Will, and fixed Decrees.

High Queen of Peace! Her God possessed,
  Her heart could feel no earthly want:
His kingdom, 'stablished in her breast,
  Triumphant was, not militant:

And day by day more amply played
  His love about its raptured thrall
Like some eternal sunset stayed
  On cliff rich-veined, or mountain wall.

*QUASI CEDRUS EXALTATA SUM IN LIBANO.**

XVIII.

Behold! I sought in all things rest:
  My Maker called me: I obeyed:
On me He laid His great behest:
  In me His tabernacle made.

The world's Creator thus bespake
  'My Salem be thy heritage:
Thy rest within mine Israel make:
  In Sion root thee, age by age.'

Within the City well-beloved
  Thenceforth I grew from flower to fruit:
And in an ancient race approved
  Behold thenceforth I struck my root.

Like Carmel's cedar, or the palm
  That gladdens 'mid Engaddi's dew
Or Plane-tree set by waters calm
  I stood, and round my fragrance threw.

Behold! I live where dwells not sin:
  I breathe in climes no foulness taints:
I reign in God's fair Court, and in
  The full assembly of His Saints.

* Ecclesiasticus xxiv.

SAPIENTIA.*

XIX.

My flowers are flowers of gladness : mine
    The boughs of honour and of grace :
Pure as the first bud of the vine
    My fragrance freshens all the place.

The Mother of fair Love am I :
    With me is Wisdom's name and praise :
With me are Hope, and Knowledge high,
    And sacred Fear, and peaceful days.

Through garden plots my course I took
    To bathe the beds of herb and tree :
Then to a river swelled my brook :
    Anon that river was a sea.

More high that sea shall rise and shine
    Far off, a prophet-beam of morn ;
Because my doctrine is not mine
    But light of God for Seers unborn.

BEATI MITES.

XX.

Thy song is not the song of morn
    O thrush, but calmer and more strong ;
While sunset woods around thee burn
    And echoing stems thy strain prolong.

* Ecclesiasticus xxiv.

O songstress of the thorn whereon
  As yet the white but streaks the green
Sing on! sing on! Thou sing'st as one
  That sings of what his eyes have seen!

In thee some Seraph's rapture tells
  Of joys we guess not! Heaven draws near:
I hear the immortal City's bells:
  The triumph of the Blest I hear.

The whole wide earth, to God heart-bare
  Basks like some happy Umbrian vale
By Francis trodden and by Clare
  When anthems sweetened every gale

When Greatness thirsted to be good
  When faith was meek and love was brave
When hope by every cradle stood
  And rainbows spanned each new-made grave.

SINE LABE ORIGINALI CONCEPTA.

XXI.

Her foot is on the Lord of Night:
  On Heaven, not him, are fixed her eyes:
That foot is, as a lily, light;
  Not less that Serpent writhes and dies!

O Eve, he dies, that tempter fell!
  O Earth, that pest whose poison-spume
Exasperate with the fires of hell
  Thy blood envenomed, meets his doom!

But whence the conquering puissance ? Lo !
    That Woman clasps the 'Woman's Seed:'
That Infant quells the infernal foe :
    Messiah triumphs : His the deed !

The weight she feels not she transmits :
    The weight of worlds her arms sustain :
Who made the worlds—in heaven Who sits—
    Through her that foe hath touched and slain !

SINE LABE ORIGINALI CONCEPTA.

XXII.

COULD she, that Destined One, could she
    On whom His gaze was stayed for aye
Transgress like Eve, partake that Tree
    Become, like her, the Dragon's prey ?

Had He no Pythian shaft that hour
    Her Son—her God—to pierce that Foe
Which strove her greatness to devour,
    Eclipse her glories ? Deem not so !

He saw her in that First Decree :
    He saw the Assailant ; sent the aid : —
Filial it was, His love for thee
    Ere thou wert born ; ere worlds were made.

SINE LABE ORIGINALI CONCEPTA.

XXIII.

When man gives up the ghost, behold,
　Honouring his God's Decree august
His body melts : the mortal mould
　Revisiteth its native dust.

The bulwarks of the breast give way :
　Those eyes that glorying watched the sun :
Each atom-speck of mortal clay
　Foregoes its nature—all save one.

A something—germ or power—survives,
　That seed which linked, from birth to death,
The structure's myriad cyclic lives
　That remnant never perisheth !

That seed reserved, too fine, too small
　For eye to scan, for chance to mar
Shall soar to meet God's trumpet-call,
　Re-clad, and glittering like a star.

With Man so fared it at the Fall :
　The Race lay dead : She did not die :
One seed survived—the hope of all—
　Thy pledge, Redeemed Humanity !

SINE LABE ORIGINALI CONCEPTA.

XXIV.

Met in a point* the circles twain
    Of temporal and eternal things
Embrace, close linked. Redemption's chain
    Drops thence to earth its myriad rings.

In either circle, from of old
    That point of meeting stood decreed;
Twin mysteries cast in one deep mould
    'The Woman,' and 'the Woman's Seed.'

Mary, long ages ere thy birth
    Resplendent with Salvation's Sign
In thee a stainless hand the earth
    Put forth, to meet the Hand Divine!

The Word made Flesh; the Way; the Door;
    The link that dust with Godhead blends!
Through Him the worlds their God adore:
    Through thee that God to man descends.

SINE LABE ORIGINALI CONCEPTA.

XXV.

A soul-like sound, subdued yet strong,
    A whispered music, mystery-rife,
A sound like Eden airs among
    The branches of the Tree of Life—

* The Incarnation.

At first no more than this; at last
    The voice of every land and clime
It swept o'er Earth a clarion blast:
    Earth heard, and shook with joy sublime.

Mary! thy triumph was Earth's own!
    In thee she saw her prime restored:
She saw ascend a spotless Throne
    For Him, her Saviour, and her Lord.

First trophy of all-conquering Grace
    First victory of that Blood all pure
Of man's once fair, but fallen Race,
    Thou stood'st, the monument secure.

The Church had spoken. She that dwells
    Sun-clad with beatific light,
From Truth's uncounted citadels
    From Sion's Apostolic height

Had stretched her sceptred hands, and pressed
    The seal of Faith, defined and known,
Upon that Truth till then confessed
    By Love's instinctive sense alone.

FREMUERUNT GENTES.

XXVI.

The sordid World, insane through pride
    Masking her sin in virtue's name
Rejects, usurps, self-deified,
    The Immaculate Mother's sacred claim.

'The Earth is mine, and Earth's desires:
  My Science reigns from zone to zone:
I warm my hands o'er Nature's fires;
  I reap the fields those hands have sown:

'From depths unknown I crept unseen
  Through worm and beast to Man's estate:
My hands are clean: *I* rule, a Queen
  Immortal and Immaculate.'

Thus boasteth Pride with brazen brow;
  That Pride which still 'believes a lie':—
The counter-boast of Grace art thou,
  Immaculate Humility!

Therefore, like Western hill that flings
  O'er sunset vales its gradual shade
Thy power shall wax while sensuous things
  Dissolve, and earthly grandeurs fade.

In the world's eve thy Star shall flash
  Through reddening skies that cease to weep
While kings to earth their sceptres dash
  And angel bands the harvest reap.

THE RAINBOW.

XXVII.

ALL-GLORIOUS shape that fleet'st wind-swept
  Athwart the empurpled pine-girt steep,
That, sinless, from thy birth hast wept,
  All-gladdening, till thy death must weep;

That in eterne ablution still
    Thine innocence in shame dost shroud
And, washed where stain was none, dost fill
    With light thy penitential cloud;

Illume with peace our glooming glen
    O'er-arch with hope yon distant sea
To angels whispering and to men
    Of her whose lowlier sanctity

In God's all-cleansing freshness shrined
    Renounced all pureness of her own,
And aye her lucent brow inclined
    God's 'Handmaid' meek, before His throne.

ANCILLA DOMINI.

XXVIII.

THE crown of Creatures, first in place,
    Was, of all creatures, creature most:
By nature nothing; all by grace;
    Redemption's first and loftiest boast.

Handmaid of God in heart and will
    Without His life she seemed a death
A void that He alone could fill
    A word suspended on His breath.

Yet—void and nothing—she in Him
    The Creature's sole perfection found;
She was the great Rock's shadow dim;
    She was the silence not the sound.

On golden airs, by Him upheld,
    She knelt, a soft Subjection mute
A hushed Dependance, tranced and spelled,
    Still yearning towards the Absolute.

She was a sea-shell from the deep
    Of God; her function this alone
Of Him to whisper as in sleep,
    In everlasting undertone.

This hour on Him her eyes are set!
    And those who tread the earth she trod
Like her themselves in her forget
    And her remember but in God.

XXIX.

Brow-bound with myrtle and with gold
    Spring, sacred now from blasts and blights,
Lifts high in firm, untrembling hold
    Her chalice of fulfilled delights.

Confirmed around her queenly lip
    The smile late wavering, on she moves;
And seems through deepening tides to step
    Of steadier joys and larger loves.

The stony Ash itself relents,
    Into the blue embrace of May
Sinking, like old impenitents
    Heart-touched at last; and, far away,

The long wave yearns along the coast
    With sob suppressed, like that which thrills,
Whilst o'er the altar mounts the Host,
    Some chapel on the Irish hills.

CORPUS CHRISTI.

XXX.

REJOICE, thou Church of God! be glad,
   This day triumphant here below!
He cometh, in lowliest emblems clad;
   Himself He cometh to bestow!

That Body which thou gav'st, O Earth
   He gives thee back—that Flesh, that Blood—
Born of the Altar's mystic birth;
   At once thy Worship and thy Food.

He who of old on Calvary bled
   On all thine altars lies to-day
A bloodless Sacrifice, but dread
   The Lamb in heaven adored for aye.

His Godhead on the Cross He veiled;
   His Manhood here He veileth too:
But Faith has eagle eyes unsealed,
   And Love to Him she loves is true.

'I will not leave you orphans. Lo!
   While lasts the world with you am I.'
Saviour! we see Thee not; but know
   With burning hearts that Thou art nigh!

He cometh! Blue Heaven, thine incense breathe
   O'er all the consecrated sod;
And thou, O Earth, with flowers enwreathe
   The steps of thine advancing God!

CORPUS CHRISTI.

XXXI.

What music swells on every gale?
  What heavenly Herald speedeth past?
Vale sings to vale, 'He comes; all hail!'
  Sea sobs to sea, 'He comes at last.'

The Earth bursts forth in choral song;
  Aloft her 'Lauda Sion' soars;
Her myrtle boughs at once are flung
  Before a thousand Minster doors.

Far on the white processions wind
  Through wood and plain and street and court:
The kings and prelates pace behind
  The King of kings in seemly sort.

The incense floats on Grecian air
  Old Carmel echoes Calpè's chant,
In every breeze the torches flare
  That curls the waves of the Levant.

On Ramah's plain in Bethlehem's bound
  Is heard to-day a gladsome voice:
'Rejoice,' it cries, 'the Lost is found!
  With Mary's joy, O Earth, rejoice!'

THE TWO LAST GIFTS.

XXXII.

'Behold thy Mother!' From the Cross
　He gave her—not to one alone :
We are His Brethren ; unto us
　He gave a Mother as to John.

Behold the greatest gift of Christ
　Save that wherein Himself He gives,
The wonder-working Eucharist,
　Sole life of each that truly lives :

Mysterious Bread not joined and knit
　With him that eats, like mortal food,
But, fire-like, joining him with It
　And blending with the Church of God !

Mary ! from thee the Saviour took
　That Flesh He gives ! The mercies twain
Like streams of a divided brook
　But separate to meet again.

DOMUS AUREA.

XXXIII.

'Wisdom hath built herself a House,
　And hewn her out her pillars seven :' *
Her wine is mixed : her guests are those
　Who share the harvest-home of heaven.

* Proverbs ix. 1.

The fruits upon her table piled
  Are gathered from the Tree of Life:
Around are ranged the undefiled,
  And those that conquered in the strife.

Who tends the guests? Who smiles away
  Sad memories? bids misgiving cease?
A crowned one countenanced like the day
  The Mother of the Prince of Peace!

XXXIV.

Pleasant the swarm about the bough;
  The meadow-whisper round the woods;
And for their coolness pleasant now
  The murmur of the falling floods.

Pleasant beneath the thorn to lie
  And let a summer fancy loose;
To hear the cuckoo's double cry;
  To make the noontide sloth's excuse.

Panting, but pleased, the cattle stand
  Knee-deep in water-weed and sedge
And scarcely crop that greener band
  Of osiers round the river's edge.

But hark! Far off the south wind sweeps
  The golden-foliaged groves among
Renewed or lulled, with rests and leaps—
  Ah! how it makes the spirit long

To drop its earthly weight and drift
  Like yon white cloud, on pinions free
Beyond that Mountain's purple rift
  And o'er that scintillating sea!

FEST. ASSUMPTIONIS.

XXXV.

The mother of the heavenly Child
    Who made the worlds, and who redeemed,
The maid and mother undefiled
    She died: or else to die she seemed.

Once more above the late-entombed
    They bent. What found they? Vacant space:
To heaven had Mary been assumed
    And only flowers were in the place.

O happy earth! Elected sphere!
    Hope of that starry host above!
Thou too thy Maker's voice shalt hear;
    Thou too thy great Assumption prove!

The earth shall be renewed: the skies
    Shall bloom with glories unrevealed:
Each season new but typifies
    The wonders then to be unsealed.

Revives, each spring, a world that died:
    A world by summer's store increased
Shall hear ere long that mandate wide
    'Prepare the glad Assumption Feast!'

ELIAS AND ENOCH.

XXXVI.

O THOU that rodest up the skies,
    Assumed ere death, on steeds of fire
That, rapt from earth in mortal guise
    Some air immortal dost respire;

That, ambushed in the enshrouding sheen,
    In quiet lulled of soul and flesh,
With one great thought of Him, the Unseen,
    Thy ceaseless vigil dost refresh;

Old lion of Carmelian steeps!
    Upon God's mountain, where, O where,
Or couchant by His unknown deeps,
    Mak'st thou thine everlasting lair?

Hast thou, that earlier Seer beside
    Who 'walked with God, and was not,' him
By contemplation glorified
    When faith, in shallower hearts, grew dim,

Hast thou—despite corporeal bars—
    A place among those Hierarchies,
Who fix on Mary's Throne, like stars,
    The light of never-closing eyes?

Behold, there is a debt to pay!
    With Enoch hid thou art on high:
Yet both shall back return one day,
    To gaze once more on earth, and die.

FEST. DE MONTE CARMELO.

XXXVII.

Carmel, with Alp and Apennine
   Low whispers in the wind that blows
Beneath the Eastern stars, ere shine
   The lights of morning on their snows.

Of thee, Elias, Carmel speaks,
   And that white cloud so small at first
Her Type, that neared the mountain peaks
   To quench a dying nation's thirst.

On Carmel like a sheathed sword
   Thy monks abode till Jesus came;
On Carmel then they served their Lord;
   Then Carmel rang with Mary's name.

Blow over all the garden; blow
   O'er all God's garden of the West
Balm-breathing Orient! Whisper low
   The secret of thy spicy nest!

' Who from the Desert upward moves
   Like cloud of incense onward borne?
Who moving, rests on Him she loves?
   Who mounts from regions of the Morn?

' Behold! The apple-tree beneath—
   There where of old thy Mother fell,
I raised thee up. More strong than Death
   Is Love; more strong than Death or Hell.' *

       * Cant. viii. 5, iii. 6.

VAS SPIRITUALE.

XXXVIII.

Hail, wingèd Heart, and crowned with fire!
  O wingèd with pinions of the morn
O crowned with flames whose every spire
  Bears witness to that crown of thorn!

Fair Dove of God, that, still at rest,
  On speed'st in never wavering flight
Winging the illimitable Breast —
  The Omnipresent Infinite;

We stagnate as in seas of lead,
  Ice-cold, or warmed with earthly fires:
O that like thine our souls were fed
  With sun-like yet serene desires!

A vase of quenchless love thou art
  Drawn from that boundless Breast divine:—
O that in thee, on-rushing Heart,
  Might rest, one hour, this heart of mine!

XXXIX.

Sing on, wide winds, your anthem vast!
  Man's ear is richer than his eye:
Upon the eye no shape can cast
  Such impress of Infinity.

And thou, my Soul, thy wings of might
  Put forth: thou too, one day shalt soar
And, onward borne in heavenward flight,
  The starry universe explore;

Breasting that breeze which waves the bowers
    Of Heaven's bright forest never mute
Whereof perchance this earth of ours
    Is but the feeblest forest-fruit.

Of all those worlds unnumbered none
    There lives but from that Blood all pure
Ablution, or its crown, hath won;
    Its state redeemed, or state secure.

'The Spirit bloweth where He wills'—
    O Effluence of that Life Divine
Which wakes the Universe, and stills,
    In Thy strong refluence make us Thine!

CŒLI ENARRANT.

XL.

Sole Maker of the Worlds! They lay
    A barren blank a void a nought
Beyond the ken of solar ray
    Or reach of archangelic thought.

Thou spak'st; and they were made! Forth sprang
    From every region of the abyss
Whose deeps, fire-clov'n, with anthems rang,
    The spheres new-born and numberless.

Thou spak'st: upon the winds were found
    The astonished Eagles. Awed and hushed
Subsiding seas revered their bound;
    And the strong forests upward rushed.

Before that Vision angels fell
   As though the Face of God they saw;
And all the panting Miracle
   Found rest within the arms of Law.

Perfect, O God, Thy primal plan,
   That scheme frost-bound by Adam's sin:
Create, within the heart of Man,
   Worlds meet for Thee; and dwell therein.

From Thy bright realm of Sense and Nature
   Which flowers enwreathe and stars begem,
Shape Thou Thy Church; the crownèd Creature;
   The Bride; the New Jerusalem!

CARO FACTUS EST.

XLI.

When from beneath the Almighty Hand
   The suns and systems rushed abroad
Like coursers which have burst their band
   Or torrents when the ice is thawed;

When round in luminous orbits flung
   The great stars gloried in their might;
Still, still a bridgeless gulf there hung
   'Twixt Finite things and Infinite.

That crown of light Creation wore
   Was girdled by the abysmal black;
And all of natural good she bore
   Confessed her supernatural lack.

For what is Nature at the best?
　An arch suspended in its spring;
An altar step without a priest;
　A throne whereon there sits no king.

As one stone-blind that fronts the morn
　The World before her Maker stood
Uplifting suppliant hands forlorn,
　God's creature yet how far from God!

O Shepherd Good! The trackless deep
　He pierced, that Lost One to restore!
His Universe, a wildered sheep,
　Upon His shoulder home He bore!

That Universe His Priestly robe,
　The Kingly Pontiff raised on high
The worship of the starry globe :—
　The gulf was bridged, and God was nigh.

CONDESCENSIO.

XLII.

When was it that in act began
　That Condescension from on high
Consummated in God made Man,
　Its shrine for all eternity?

'Twas when the Eternal Father spake,
　The Eternal Son in act replied:
When sudden forth from darkness brake
　The new-shaped worlds on every side.

Instant that All-Creative Power
  A meek, sustaining Power became,
A Ministration hour by hour
  From death preserving Nature's frame.

Instant into Creation's breast
  Nor merged nor mixed He passed, and gave
Continuance to the quivering guest
  That else had found at birth its grave.

In finite mansions He, the Immense,
  In service reigning, made abode,
Bore up—a Law, a Providence—
  The weight of worlds, 'His people's load.'

He came once more—not then to reign ;
  In servant's form to serve, and die
The 'Lamb before the ages slain,'
  'The Woman's Seed' of prophecy.

THE CREATED WISDOM.*

XLIII.

CREATED Wisdom at the gate
  Of Heaven's eternal House, I played :
The Eternal Wisdom Uncreate
  Beheld me ere the worlds were made.

I danced the void abyss above :
  Of lore unwrit the characters
I traced with wingèd feet, and wove
  The orbits of the unshaped stars.

* Proverbs viii. 27—34.

I flashed—a Thought in light arrayed—
    Beneath the Eternal Wisdom's ken :
When came mine hour I lived, and played
    Among the peopled fields of men.

Blessed is he that keeps my ways,
    That stands in reverence on my floor,
That seeks my praise, my word obeys,
    That waits and watches by my door.

REGINA ANGELORUM.

(Evangelism in Cœla.)

XLIV.

ERE yet mankind was made ; ere yet
    The sun and she that rules the night
Were in their heavenly stations set,
    God's Sons were playing in His sight.

Age after age those armies vast
    In winding line had upward flown
Yet ne'er their shadows higher cast
    Than on the first step of the Throne

And downward through the unsounded space
    If those had sunk who soared above
They ne'er had found the buried base
    Of Godhead's Condescending Love.

Then He, the God Who made them, proved :
    For, high and higher as they soared
Hymning the Eternal Son beloved
    The God from God, and Lord from Lord,

He showed them, in that Form decreed,
  Their God made man—man's hope and trust—
'The Woman,' and 'The Woman's Seed,'
  He showed; the Unbounded bound in dust.

As when from some world-conquering height
  The shepherd sees, ere risen the sun,
His advent clothe the cloud with light
  Before them thus that Vision shone:

And while, in wonder half half fear,
  That Child, that Mother fixed their eye,
He bade those heavenward hosts revere
  Their God in His Humility.

Set was that Infant as a sign:—
  In endless bliss confirmed were they
Who hailed that hour the Babe Divine;
  Self-sentenced those who turned away.

REGINA ANGELORUM.

(Spes Cœlestis.)

XLV.

Their Trial past, more near the Throne,
  And rapt thenceforth to holier skies,
Still on that Maid and Babe foreshown
  The Elect of Angels fixed their eyes.

A Spirit-galaxy they hung;
  A Cross unmeasured, limned in fire
And instinct-shaped, that swayed and swung
  On winds of unfulfilled desire.

They worshipped Him, that God made Man;
  To Him they spread their hands in power:
Unmarked the exhausted centuries ran:
  That trance millennial seemed an hour.

'Twixt Finite things and Infinite
  They saw the Patriarch's Ladder thrown;
Saw One Who o'er it moved in light:
  They saw, and knelt with foreheads prone.

Make answer, sinless Angels, say
  Ye who that hour your God adored
Less strong, less dear, is she this day,
  That Mother of your destined Lord!

REGINA ANGELORUM.

(In Cœlo Coronata.)

XLVI.

Angelic City in the skies
  Not built of stones but Spirits pure
Irradiate by the Eternal Eyes,
  And in the Eternal Love secure;

Angelic City, selfless chaste
  By Him thou watch'st upholden still,
That neither Future know'st, nor Past
  Tranced in thy God's all-present Will;

Thy mind a mirror sphered of gold
  Wherein alone His splendours shine;
Thy heart a vase His Hand doth hold
  That yields to Him alone its wine;

For one brief moment proved and tried;
　Thenceforth man's help in trial's stress;
Bright Sister of the Church—the Bride—
　The elder Sister, yet the less:

O like, unlike! O crownèd Twain!
　Celestial both, yet one terrene;
Behold, ye sing the same glad strain;
　Ye glory in the self-same Queen!

MULIER AMICTA SOLE.

XLVII.

A Woman 'clothèd with the sun,' *
　Yet fleeing from the Dragon's rage!
The strife in Eden-bowers begun
　Swells upward to the latest age.

That Woman's Son is throned on high; †
　The angelic hosts before Him bend:
The sceptre of His empery
　Subdues the worlds from end to end.

Yet still the sword goes through her heart
　For still on earth His Church survives:
In her that Woman holds a part:
　In her she suffers, and she strives.

Around her head the stars are set;
　A dying moon beneath her wanes:
By Death hath Death been slain: and yet
　The Power accurst awhile remains.

---

* Rev. xii. 1.
† 'And her Child was caught up 'unto God, and to His Throne' (Apoc. xiv. 5).

Break up, strong Earth, thy stony floors
   And snatch to penal caverns dun
That Dragon from the pit that wars
   Against the Woman and her Son!

XLVIII.

Regent of Change, thou waning Moon
   Whom they, the sons of night, adore
Her foot is on thee! Late or soon
   Heap up upon the expectant shore

The tides of Man's Intelligence;
   Or backward to the blackening deep
Remit them! Knowledge won from Sense
   But sleeps to wake and wakes to sleep.

Where are the hands that reared on high
   Heaven-threat'ning Babel? where the might
Of them, that giant progeny
   The Deluge dealt with? Lost in night.

The child who knows his creed doth stretch
   A sceptred hand o'er Space and hold
The end of all those threads that catch
   In wisdom's net the starry fold.

The Sabbath comes: the work-days six
   Go by. Meantime, of things to be
O Salutary Crucifix
   We clasp the burning heart in thee:

We clasp the end that knows no end;
   The Love that fears no lessening moon;
The Truth wherein all mysteries blend;
   His Truth, His word—the One Triune.

OTHER SHEEP I HAVE.

XLIX.

Fire-breathing concourse of the Stars
   That tremble as with Love's delight
How dungeon-girt by custom's bars
   How wrapped and swathed in error's night

His soul must be who nightly lifts
   On you his wide and wandering eyes
Yet doubts that ye partake the gifts
   Bequeathed by Calvary's Sacrifice!

Lift up your heads, Eternal Gates
   Of God's great Temple in the sky!
That Blood your lintels consecrates :—
   The Avenging Angel passes by!

The King of Glory issues forth :
   The King of Glory enters in :
That Blood which cleansed from sin our earth
   Or cleansed your spheres, or kept from sin.

L.

Is this, indeed, our ancient earth?
   Or have we died in sleep and risen?
Has earth, like man, her second birth?
   Rises the palace from the prison?

Hills beyond hills ascend the skies ;
   O'er winding valleys heaven-suspended,
Huge forests rich as sunset's dyes
   With rainbow-braided clouds are blended.

What means it?   Glory, sweetness, might?
　　Not these but something holier far;
Shadows of Him, that Light of Light
　　Whose priestly vestment all things are.

The veil of sense transparent grows:
　　God's Face shines out that veil behind
Like yonder sea-reflected snows—
　　Here man must worship, or be blind.

LI.

No ray of all their silken sheen
　　The leaves first fledged have lost as yet:
Unfaded, near the advancing queen
　　Of flowers, abides the violet.

The rose succeeds; her month is come;
　　The flower with sacred passion red:
She sings the praise of martyrdom
　　And Him for whom His martyrs bled.

The perfect work of May is done:
　　Hard by, a new perfection waits:
The twain, a sister and a nun,
　　A moment parley at the grates.

The whiter Spirit turns in peace
　　To hide her in the cloistral shade:
'Tis time that you should also cease,
　　Slight carols in her honour made.

EPILOGUE.

THE SON OF MAN.

I gazed—it was the Paschal night—
    In vision on the starry sphere:
Like suns the stars made broad their light:
    Then knew I Earth to Heaven drew near.

The Thrones of Darkness down were hurled;
    The veil was rent; the bond was riven:
Then knew I that Man's little world
    Had reached its home—the heart of heaven.

Made strong by God, mine eyes with awe
    Still roved from star-changed sun to sun
That ringed the earth in ranks, and saw
    A Spirit o'er each, that stood thereon.

And, clasped by every Spirit, stood
    More high, the Venerable Sign:
Then knew I that the Atoning Blood
    Had reached that sphere; the Blood Divine.

From orb to orb an anthem passed;
    'The Blessing of the Lord of All
Hath reached us from the least and last
    Of stars that light the Heavenly Hall;

'For He, that Greatest, loves the Least;
    Puts down the mighty; lifts the low:
On Earth began His Bridal Feast:
    Our Triumph is its overflow!'

Then Earth, that great 'New Earth'* foretold,
    Assumed those glories long her due:
Or were they hers indeed of old
    Though veiled till then from mortal view?

While—with her changing—far and wide
    Those worlds around her, blent in one,
Became that 'City of the Bride'
    Which needs no light of moon or sun.

Their splendour had not suffered change
    As, kenned through myriad senses new,
Self-radiant street, and columned range
    To one unmeasured Temple grew.

Ere long through all that throbbing frame
    Of things beheld and things unseen
Rolled forth that Name which none can name
    Save those that breathe not clime terrene.

And down that luminous Infinite
    I saw an Altar and a Throne;
And, near to each, a Form, all light
    That, resting, moved, and moved Alone:

But if He filled that Throne or knelt
    That Altar nigh, or Lamb-like lay,
I saw not. This I saw and felt
    That Son of Man was God for aye.

That Son of God was Man and stood,
    And from His Vest, more white than snow,
Slowly there dawned a Cross of Blood
    That through the glory seemed to grow:

   * 'There shall be New Heavens, and a New Earth,'

Above the heavens His Hands He raised
  To bless those Worlds whose race was run ;
And lo ! in either palm there blazed
  The blood-red sign of Victory won ;

That Blood the Bethlehem Shepherds eyed
  Warming His cheek Who slept apart :
That Blood He drew—the Crucified—
  Far-fountained from His Mother's Heart.

LEGENDS

OF

THE SAXON SAINTS.

TO THE
VENERABLE BEDE

'Mid quiet vale or city lulled by night
Well-pleased the wanderer, wakeful on his bed,
Hears from far Alps on fitful breeze the sound
Of torrents murmuring down their rocky glens,
Strange voice from distant regions, alien climes :—
Should these far echoes from thy legend-roll
Delight of loftier years, these echoes faint,
Thus waken, thus make calm, one restless heart
In our distempered day, to thee the praise
Voice of past times O Venerable Bede !

PREFACE.

MANY YEARS AGO my friend Miss Fenwick remarked to me on the strange circumstance that the chief event in a nation's history, its conversion to Christianity, largely as it is often recorded in national legends, has never been selected as a theme for poetry. That event may indeed not supply the materials necessary for an Epic or a Drama, yet it can hardly fail to abound in details significant and pathetic, which especially invite poetic illustration. With the primary interest of that great crisis many others, philosophical, social, and political, generally connect themselves. Antecedent to a nation's conversion the events of centuries have commonly either conduced to it, or thrown obstacles in its way; while the history as well as the character of that nation in the subsequent ages is certain to have been in a principal measure modified by that event. Looking back consequently on that period in which the moral influences of ages, early and late, are imaged, a people recognises its own features as in a mirror, but sees them such as they were when their expression was still undetermined; and it may well be struck by the resemblance at once to what now exists, and also by the dissimilitude. Many countries have unhappily lost almost all authentic records connected with their conversion. Such would have been the fate of England also, had it not been for a single book, Bede's *Ecclesiastical History*. In the following poems my aspiration was to walk humbly in the footsteps of that great master. Their scope will best be indicated by some remarks upon the character of that wonderful age which he records.

St. Augustine landed in the Isle of Thanet A. D. 597, and Bede died A. D. 735. The intervening period, that of his chronicle, is the golden age of Anglo-Saxon sanctity. Notwithstanding some twenty or thirty years of pagan reaction, it was a time of rapid though not uninterrupted progress, and one of an interest the more touching when contrasted with the calamities which followed so soon. Between the death of Bede and the first Danish invasion, were eighty years, largely years of decline, moral and religious. Then followed eighty years of retribution, those of the earlier Danish wars, till, with the triumph of Alfred, England's greatest king, came the Christian restoration. Once more periods of relaxed morals and sacrilegious princes alternated with intervals of reform; for again and again the Northmen over-swept the land. The 460 years of Anglo-Saxon Christianity constituted a period of memorable achievements and sad vicissitudes; but that period included more than a hundred years of high sanctity, belonging for the most part to the seventh century, a century to England as glorious as was the thirteenth to Mediæval Europe.

Within that century the kingdoms of the Heptarchy successively became Christian, and those among them which had relapsed returned to the Faith. Sovereigns, many of whom had boasted a descent from Odin himself, stood as interpreters beside the missionaries when they preached, and rivalled each other in the zeal with which they built churches, some of which were founded on the sites of ancient temples, though, in other cases, with a charitable prudence, the existing fanes were spared, purified, and adapted to Christian worship. At Canterbury and York, cathedrals rose, and on many a site besides; and when the earlier had been destroyed by fire, or had fallen through decay, fabrics on a vaster scale rose above their ruins, and maintained a succession which lasts to this day. Monasteries unnumbered lifted their towers above the forests of a land in which the streams still ran unstained and the air of which had not yet been dimmed by smoke—imparting a dignity to fen and flat morass. Round them ere long cities gathered, as at St. Albans, Malmesbury, Sherborne, and Wimborne; the most memorable of those monasteries being that at Canterbury, and that at Westminster, dedicated to St. Peter, as the cathedral church near it had been dedicated to St. Paul. In the North they were at least as numerous. The University of Oxford is also associated with that early age. It was beside the Isis that St. Frideswida raised her convent, occupied at a later date by canons regular, and ultimately transformed into Christ Church by Cardinal Wolsey—becoming thus the chief, as it had been the earliest, among the schools in that great seat of learning which within our own days has exercised a religious influence over England not less remarkable than that which belonged to its most palmy preceding period.

During that century England produced most of

those saintly kings and queens whose names still enrich the calendar of the Anglo-Saxon Church, sovereigns who ruled their kingdoms with justice, lived in mortification, went on pilgrimages, died in cloisters. The great missionary work had also begun. Within a century from the death of St. Augustine, apostles from England had converted multitudes in Germany, and St. Wilfrid had preached to the inhabitants of Friesland. Something, moreover, had been done to retrieve the past. The Saxon kings made amends for the wrongs inflicted by their ancestors upon the British Celts, endowing with English lands the churches and convents founded by them in Brittany. King Kenwalk of Wessex showed thus also a royal munificence to the Celtic monastery of Glastonbury, only stipulating in return that the British monks there, condoning past injuries, should offer a prayer for him when they knelt at the tomb of King Arthur.

The England of the seventh century had been very gradually prepared for that drama of many ages which had then its first rehearsal. In it three races had a part. They were those of the native Britons, the Saxons who had over-run the land, and the Irish missionaries. Rome, the last and greatest of the old-world empires, had exercised more of an enfeebling and less of an elevating influence among the British than among her other subject races; but her great military roads still remained the witnesses of her military genius; and many a city, some in ruin, were records of her wealth and her arts. The Teutonic race in England, which for centuries had maintained its independence against Rome, could not forgive the Britons for having submitted to their hated foe, and trampled on them the more ruthlessly because they despised them. Yet they at least might well have learned to respect that race. It has been well remarked that if the Britons submitted easily to Rome, yet of all her subject races they made far the most memorable fight against that barbaric irruption which swept over the ruins of her empire. For two centuries that race had fought on. It still retained the whole of Western Britain, Cornwall, Wales, and Strathclyde; while in other parts of England it possessed large settlements. On the other hand, in matters of spiritual concern the British race contrasted unfavourably with the other races subjected by the barbarians. In France, Spain, and Italy, the conquered had avenged a military defeat by a spiritual victory, bringing over their conquerors to Christianity; and, as a consequence, they had often risen to equality with them. In those parts of England, on the contrary, where the British had submitted to the Pagan conquerors, they by degrees abandoned their Christian faith; * and where they retained their independence, they hated the Saxon conquerors too much to share their Christianity with them. Far from desiring their conversion, they resisted all the overtures made to them by the Roman missionaries who ardently desired their aid; and as a consequence of that refusal, they eventually lost their country. The chief cause of that refusal was hatred of the invader. The Irish as well as the British had a

* See Montalembert's *Moines de l'Occident*, vol. iii. p. 343; and also Burke: 'On the Continent the Christian religion, after the northern irruptions, not only remained but flourished. . . . In England it was so entirely extinguished that when Augustine undertook his mission, it does not appear that among all the Saxons there was a single person professing Christianity.'

passionate devotion to their own local traditions in a few matters not connected with doctrine; but they notwithstanding worked cordially with the Benedictines from St. Gregory's convent for the spread of the Christian Faith. Had the Britons converted the Anglo-Saxon race they would probably have blended with them, as at a later time that race blended with their Norman conquerors. Three successive waves of the Teuton-Scandinavian race swept over their ancient land, the Anglo-Saxon, the Danish, and the Norman: against them all the British Celts fought on. They fell back toward their country's western coasts, like the Irish of a later day; and within their Cambrian mountains they maintained their independence for eight centuries.

Yet the Anglo-Saxons' victory was not an unmixed one. Everywhere throughout England they maintained during the seventh century two different battles, a material and a spiritual one, and with opposite results. Year by year that race pushed further its military dominion; but yearly the Christian Faith effected new triumphs over that of Odin. For this there were traceable causes. The character of the Teutonic invader included two very different elements, and the nobler of these had its affinities with Christianity. If, on the one hand, that character was fierce, reckless, and remorseless, and so far in natural sympathy with a religion which mocked at suffering and till the ninth century offered up human sacrifices, it was marked no less by robustness, simplicity, honesty, sincerity, an unexcitable energy and an invincible endurance. It possessed also that characteristic which essentially contradistinguishes the *ordo equestris* from the *ordo pedestris* in human character, viz., the spirit of reverence. It had aspirations; and, as a background to all its musings and all its hopes there remained ever the idea of the Infinite. As a consequence, it retained a large measure of self-respect, purity, and that veneration for household ties attributed to it by the Roman historian * at a time when that virtue was no longer a Roman one. Such a character could not but have its leanings toward Christianity; and, when brought under its influences, it put forth at once new qualities, like a wild flower which, on cultivation, acquires for the first time a perfume. Its spirit of reverence developed into humility, and its natural fortitude into a saintly patience; while its fierceness changed into a loyal fervour; and the crimes to which its passions still occasionally hurried it were voluntarily expiated by penances as terrible. Even King Penda, the hater of Christianity, hated an insincere faith more. 'Of all men,' he said, ' he that I have ever most despised is the man who professes belief in some God and yet does not obey his laws.' Such was that character destined to produce under the influences of faith such noble specimens of Christian honour and spiritual heroism. From the beginning its greatness was one

> True to the kindred points of Heaven and Home;

and in later ages it became yet more eminently domestic, combining household ties with the pursuit of letters and science in colleges which still preserved a family life. Its monks had no vocation to the life of the desert; in this unlike the Irish saints, who,

* Tacitus. The German's wife might well be called his 'helpmate.' His wedding gift to his bride consisted of a horse, a yoke of oxen, a lance and a sword.

like those of Eastern lands, delighted in the forest hermitage and the sea-beat rock.

The Anglo-Saxon race was but a branch of that great Teuton-Scandinavian race, generically one whether it remained in the German forests or wandered on to the remoter coasts of Denmark, Sweden and Norway. It was the race which the Romans called 'the Barbarians,' but which they could never conquer. A stern history had trained it for a wonderful destiny. Christianity in mastering the Greek had possessed itself of the intellect of the world, and in mastering Rome had found access to all those vast regions conquered by Roman arms, opened out by Roman roads, governed by Roman law, and by it helped to the conception of a higher law. But the Greek and the Roman civilisations had, each of them, corrupted its way, and yielded to the seductions of pride, sense, and material prosperity; and, as a consequence, both had become incapable of rendering full justice to much that is highest in Christianity. That which they lacked the 'Barbaric' race alone was capable of supplying. In its wanderings under darkened skies and amid pitiless climates it had preserved an innocence and simplicity elsewhere lost. Enriched by the union of the new element, thus introduced, with what it had previously derived from Greek thought and Roman law, that authentic Religion which had been prospectively sown within the narrow precinct of Judea extended its branches over the world. Had the Barbaric race shared in the Greek sciences and arts, and clothed itself in the Roman civilisation, it must have learned their corruptions. The larger destiny of man could thus, humanly speaking, never have been accomplished, and neither the mediaeval world, the modern world, nor that yet higher order of human society which doubtless lies beyond both, could have existed. It was necessary that in some region, exacting, yet beneficent, civilisation should be retarded, that a remedy might be found for the abuses of civilisation; and races whose present backward condition we are accustomed to deplore may likewise be intended for a similar purpose. Plants are thus kept in the dark in order to reserve their fruitage for a fitter season.

But what had been the earlier history of a race before which such destinies lay? What training had prepared it for its work—the last that might have been expected from it? On this subject there remains a tradition, the profoundly significant character of which ought to have made it more widely known. Mallet, in his *Northern Antiquities*, translated by Bishop Percy, to whom our ballad literature is so deeply indebted, records it thus:—'A celebrated tradition, confirmed by the poems of all the northern nations, by their chronicles, by institutions and customs, some of which subsist to this day, informs us that an extraordinary person named Odin formerly reigned in the north. . . . All their testimonies are comprised in that of Snorri, the ancient historian of Norway, and in the commentaries and explications which Torphæus added to his narrative. The Roman Commonwealth was arrived at the highest pitch of power, and saw all the then known world subject to its laws, when an unforeseen event raised up enemies against it from the very bosom of the forests of Scythia and on the banks of the Tanais. Mithridates by flying had drawn Pompey after him into those deserts. The King of Pontus sought there for refuge and new means of vengeance. He hoped to arm against the ambition of Rome all the barbarous nations his neighbours, whose liberty she threatened. He succeeded in this at first, but all those peoples, ill united as allies, ill armed as soldiers, and still worse disciplined, were forced to yield to the superior genius of Pompey. Odin is said to have been of their number. . . . Odin commanded the Æsir, whose country must have been situated between the Pontus Euxinus and the Caspian Sea. Their principal city was Asgard. The worship there paid to their supreme God was famous throughout the circumjacent countries. Odin, having united under his banners the youth of the neighbouring nations, marched towards the north and west of Europe, subduing, as we are told, all the races he found in his passage, and giving them to one or other of his sons for subjects. Many sovereign families of the North are said to be descended from these princes. Thus Horsa and Hengist, the chiefs of those Saxons who conquered Britain in the fifth century, counted Odin or Wodin in the number of their ancestors; it was the same with the other Anglo-Saxon princes as well as the greatest part of those of lower Germany and the North.' *

Gibbon refers to this ancient tradition, though not as accepting it for a part of ascertained history, yet in a spirit less sceptical than was usual to him. He writes thus: 'It is supposed that Odin was chief of a tribe of barbarians which dwelt on the banks of the lake Mæotis, till the fall of Mithridates and the arms

* Mallet's *Northern Antiquities*, pp. 79, 80. (Bell and Daldy, 1873.) Burke records this tradition with an entire credence. See note in p. 288.

of Pompey menaced the north with servitude. That Odin, yielding with indignant fury to a power which he was unable to resist, conducted his tribe from the frontiers of the Asiatic Sarmatia into Sweden, with the great design of forming, in that inaccessible retreat of freedom, a religion and a people which, in some remote age, might be subservient to his immortal revenge; when his invincible Goths, armed with martial fanaticism, should issue in numerous swarms from the neighbourhood of the Polar circle to chastise the oppressors of mankind. . . . Notwithstanding the mysterious obscurity of the Edda, we can easily distinguish two persons confounded under the name of Odin; the god of war, and the great legislator of Scandinavia. The latter, the Mahomet of the north, instituted a religion adapted to the climate and to the people. Numerous tribes on either side of the Baltic were subdued by the invincible valour of Odin, by his persuasive eloquence, and by the fame which he acquired of a most skilful magician. The faith that he had propagated during a long and prosperous life he confirmed by a voluntary death. Apprehensive of the ignominious approach of disease and infirmity, he resolved to expire as became a warrior. In a solemn assembly of the Swedes and Goths he wounded himself in nine mortal places, hastening away (as he asserted with his dying voice) to prepare the feast of heroes in the palace of the great god of war.'*

In a note Gibbon adds, referring to the Roman and Oriental part of the legend: 'This wonderful expedition of Odin, which, by deducing the enmity of the Goths and Romans from so memorable a cause,

---

* *Decline and Fall of the Roman Empire*, chap. x.

might supply the noble groundwork of an epic poem, cannot safely be received as authentic history. According to the obvious sense of the Edda, and the interpretation of the most skilful critics, Asgard, instead of denoting a real city of the Asiatic Sarmatia, is the fictitious appellation of the mystic abode of the gods, the Olympus of Scandinavia.' Whether the emigration of the Barbaric race from the East be or be not historical, certainly the grounds upon which Gibbon bases his distrust of it are slender. He forgot that there might well have been both an earthly Asgard and also, according to the religion of the north, an Asgard in heaven, the destined abode of warriors faithful to Odin. Those who after his death changed their king into a god would, by necessity, have provided him with a celestial mansion; nor could they have assigned to it a name more acceptable to a race which blended so closely their religion with their patriotic love than that of their ancient capital, from which their great deliverer and prophet had led them forth in pilgrimage. Let us hope that Gibbon's remark as to the fitness of this grand legend for the purposes of epic poetry may yet prove prophecy. It has had one chance already: for we learn from the first book of *The Prelude* that the theme was one of those on which the imagination of Wordsworth rested in youth, when he was seeking a fit subject for epic song.

It is difficult to imagine a historical legend invested with a greater moral weight or dignity than belongs to this one. The mighty Republic was soon to pass into an Empire mightier and more ruthless still, the heir of all those ancient empires which from the earliest had represented a dominion founded on the pride of this world, and had trampled upon human right. A race is selected to work the retribution. It is qualified for its work by centuries of adversity, only to be paralleled by the prosperity of its rival. Yet when at last that retribution comes, it descends more in mercy than in judgment! Great changes had prepared the world for a new order of things. The centre of empire had moved eastward from Rome to Constantinople: the spiritual centre had moved westward from Jerusalem to Rome. The empire had herself become Christian, and was allowed after that event nearly a century more of gradual decline. The judgment was not thus averted; but it was ennobled. Her children were enabled to become the spiritual instructors of those wild races by which the '*State Universal*' had been overwhelmed. That empire indeed, was not so much destroyed as transformed and extended, a grace rendered possible by her having submitted to the yoke of Christ; the new kingdoms which constituted the Christian '*Orbis Terrarum*' being, for the most part, fragments of it, while its laws made way into regions wider far, and exercised over them a vast though modified authority not yet extinct. Here, if anywhere, we catch glimpses of a hand flashing forth between the clouds, pointing their way to the nations, and conducting Humanity forward along its arduous and ascending road. There is a Providence or there could be no Progress.

For the fulfilment of that part assigned to the 'Barbarians' in this marvellous drama of the ages, it was necessary that many things should combine; an exemption from the temptations which had materialised the races of the south; the severe life that perfects strength; a race endowed with the physical strength needed to render such sufferings endurable; and lastly, an original spiritual elevation inherent in that race, and capable of making them understand the lesson, and accept their high destiny. The last and greatest of these qualifications had not been wanting. Much as the religion of the Barbaric race had degenerated by the time when it deified its great deliverer, it had inherited the highest traditions of the early world. Mallet thus describes their religion in its purity: 'It taught the being of a "Supreme God, master of the universe, to whom all things are submissive and obedient." Such, according to Tacitus, was the supreme God of the Germans. The ancient Icelandic mythology calls him "the Author of everything that existeth; the eternal, the ancient, the living and awful Being, the searcher into concealed things, the Being that never changeth." This religion attributed to the Supreme Deity "an infinite power, a boundless knowledge, an incorruptible justice," and forbade its followers to represent Him under any corporeal form. They were not even to think of confining Him within the enclosure of walls, but were taught that it was within woods and consecrated forests that they could serve Him properly. There He seemed to reign in silence, and to make Himself felt by the respect which He inspired.* . . . From this Supreme God were sprung (as it were emanations from His divinity) an infinite number of subaltern deities and genii, of which every part of the visible world was the seat and the temple. . . . To serve this divinity with sacrifices and prayers, to do no wrong to others, and to be brave and intrepid in themselves, were all the moral consequences they

* Mallet's *Northern Antiquities*, pp. 88, 89.

derived from these doctrines. Lastly, the belief of a future state cemented and completed the whole building.* ... Perhaps no religion ever attributed so much to a Divine Providence as that of the northern nations.' †

It was not among the Scandinavians only that the religion of the North retained long these vestiges of its original purity, and elevation. 'All the Teutonic nations held the same opinions, and it was upon these that they founded the obligation of serving the gods, and of being valiant in battle. ... One ought to regard in this respect the Icelandic mythology as a precious monument, without which we can know but very imperfectly this important part of the religion of *our fathers.*' ‡

The earlier and purer doctrine seems to have long survived the incrustations of later times in the case of a select few. Harold Harfraga, the first king of all Norway, thus addressed an assembly of his people: 'I swear and protest in the most sacred manner that I will never offer sacrifice to any of the gods adored by the people, but to Him only who hath formed this world, and everything we behold in it.' A belief in the divine Love, as well as the divine power, knowledge and justice, though probably not held by the many at a later day, is yet distinctly expressed, as well as the kindred belief in an endless reign of peace, by the earliest and most sacred document of the Northern religion, viz. the 'Völuspá Prophecy.' That prophecy, after foretelling the destruction of all things, including the Odin gods themselves, by the Supreme God and His ministers,

* Mallet's *Northern Antiquities*, p. 89.
† P. 100. ‡ P. 103.

proceeds : 'There will arise out of the sea, another earth most lovely and verdant with pleasant fields where the grain shall grow unsown. Vidar and Vali, shall survive; neither the flood nor Surtur's fire shall harm them; they shall dwell on the plain of Ida *where Asgard formerly stood.* . . . Baldur and Hödur shall also repair thither from the abode of death. There they shall sit and converse together, and call to mind their former knowledge and the perils they underwent.' *

The similarity between the higher doctrines of the northern faith and the religion of ancient Persia is at once accounted for by the tradition of the Odin migration from the East. A writer the reverse of credulous expresses himself thus on that subject : 'We know that the Scandinavians came from some country of Asia. . . This doctrine was in many respects the same with that of the Magi. Zoroaster had taught that the conflict between Ormuzd and Ahriman (*i.e.* light and darkness, the Good and Evil Principle) should continue to the last day; and that then the Good Principle should be reunited to the Supreme God, from whom it had first issued; the Evil should be overcome and subdued; darkness should be destroyed; and the world, purified by a universal conflagration, should become a luminous and shining abode, into which evil should never be permitted to enter.' † The same writer continues thus : 'Odin and the Æsir may be compared to Ormuzd and the Amshaspands; Loki and his evil progeny, the Wolf Fenrir and the Midgard Serpent, together with the giants and monsters of Jötunheim

* *The Prose Edda.*
† *Northern Antiquities:* the Editor, T. A. Blackwell.

and Hvergelmir, to Ahriman and the Devs.* . . .
We will not deny that some of these doctrines may
have been handed down by oral tradition to the
pontiff-chieftains of the Scandinavian tribes, and that
the Skalds who composed the mystic poems of the
Edda may have had an obscure and imperfect knowledge of them. Be this as it may, we must not
forget that the higher doctrines of the Scandinavian
system were confined to the few, whereas those of
the Zendavesta were the religious belief of the whole
nation.† . . . The Persian system was calculated to
form an energetic, intellectual and highly moral
people; the Scandinavian a semi-barbarous troop of
crafty and remorseless warriors. . . . Yet, such as
they were, these Scandinavians seemed to have been
destined by the inscrutable designs of Providence to
invigorate at least one of the nations of which they
were for centuries the scourge, in order, as we
previously had occasion to observe, that the genial
blending of cognate tribes might form a people the
most capable of carrying on the great work of
civilisation, which in some far distant age may
finally render this world that abode of peace and
intellectual enjoyment dimly shadowed forth in
ancient myths as only to be found in a renovated
and fresh emerging universe.' ‡

The inferiority of the later Scandinavian to the
earlier Persian religion may be sufficiently accounted
for by the common process of gradual degeneration. That degeneration was not confined to the
great emigrant race. Centuries before Odin had left
the East, the Persian religion had degenerated upon

---

* T. A. Blackwell. See Mallet's *Northern Antiquities*, p. 474.
† P. 475. ‡ P. 476.

its native soil. Its Magi retained a pure doctrine, which led them later to the Bethlehem crib; but its vulgar had in part yielded to the seduction of Greek poets, and worshipped in temples like theirs. It is remarkable that that 'one of the nations' with which the hopes of the future are so singularly connected is that one upon which the discipline of adversity had fallen with double force. When the ancient enemy of the 'Barbaric races,' Rome, had passed away, a new enemy, and one to it more formidable, rose up against England in her own kinsfolk, the Scandinavian branch of the same stock. The Danish invaders expected to set kingdom against kingdom throughout the Heptarchy, and subject them all to the sceptre of Odin. On the contrary, it united them in one; and that union was facilitated by the bond of a common Christianity.*

That the belief of the Anglo-Saxons, though less developed by poetry and romance, was substantially the same as that recorded in the Scandinavian Edda, appears to be certain. It is thus that Mr. Kemble speaks:

'On the Continent as well as in England, it is only by the collection of minute and isolated facts —often preserved to us in popular superstitions, legends and even nursery tales—that we can render probable the prevalence of a religious belief identical in its most characteristic features with that which we know to have been entertained in Scandinavia. Yet whatsoever we can thus recover proves that, in all main points, the faith of the Island

---

* 'This (Christianity), as it introduced great mildness into the tempers of the people, made them less warlike, and consequently prepared the way to their forming one body.'—Burke, *An Abridgment of English History*, book ii. chap. iii.

Saxons was that of their Continental brethren.' 'The early period at which Christianity triumphed in England, adds to the difficulties which naturally beset the subject. Norway, Sweden, and Denmark, had entered into public relations with the rest of Europe long before the downfall of their ancient creed; here the fall of heathendom, and the commencement of history were contemporaneous. We too had no Iceland to offer a refuge to those who fled from the violent course of a conversion.' *

Among the proofs of identity between the Anglo-Saxon and the Scandinavian religion, Mr. Kemble refers to the fact that 'genealogies of the Anglo-Saxon kings contain a multitude of the ancient gods, reduced indeed into the family relations, but still capable of identification with the deities of the North, and of Germany. In this relation we find Odin, Boldeg, Géat, Wig, and Frea. The days of the week, also dedicated to gods, supply us further with the names of Tiw, Dunor, Friege, and Sætere; and the names of places in all parts of England attest the wide dispersion of the worship.' †

Mr. Kemble shows also that among the Anglo-Saxons and the Scandinavians there existed a common belief respecting monsters, especially the wolf Fenrir, the Midgard snake, evil spirits and giants; respecting Loki, the accursed spirit, and Hela, the queen of Hades. To the same effect Mr. Sharon Turner speaks: 'The Voluspá and the Edda are the two great repositories of the oldest and most venerated traditions of pagan Scandinavia. The Voluspá opens abruptly, and most probably represents many of the

* *Saxons in England*, vol. i. p. 330.
† *Ibid.* p. 335.

ancient *Saxon* traditions or imaginations.'* The authority of these eminent writers accounts for and justifies the frequent references to the Scandinavian mythology in the following 'Saxon Legends.'

We have thus seen that in the religion of the 'Barbaric' race there were blended two different elements: a higher one derived from its eastern origin, and a lower one the result of gradual degeneration. We had previously seen that a remarkable duality was to be found in the character of that race; and without understanding this duality and its root in their religion, no just conception can be formed of the relations of that race with Christianity. Had the 'Barbarians' possessed nothing deeper than is indicated by their fiercer traits, the history of the seventh century in England must have been very different. It was characterised by rapid conversions to Christianity on a large scale, and often, after the lapse of a few years, by sanguinary revolts against the Faith. The chief reason of such fluctuation seems to have been this, viz. because all that was profound, and of venerable antiquity in the Northern religion, was in sympathy with Christianity, as the religion of sanctity and self-sacrifice; while all that was savage in it opposed itself to a religion of humility and of charity. The Northern religion was an endless warfare, and so was that early Persian religion from which its higher element was derived; but by degrees that warfare had, for the many, ceased to be the warfare between light and darkness, between Good and Evil. To the speculative it had become a conflict between all the wild and illimitable forces of Nature

* *History of the Anglo-Saxons*, vol. i. p. 241.

and some unknown higher Law; but to the common herd it meant only an endless feud between race and race. Thus understood it could have no affinities with Christianity, either in her militant character, or as the religion of peace.

In explanation of the frequent outbreaks against Christianity on the part of the Anglo-Saxons, after their conversion, Montalembert assigns another cause, viz. that the Roman missionaries had sometimes relied too much upon the converted kings, and their authority over their subjects. The work had in such cases to be done again; and it was largely done by Irish missionaries, who had left Iona only to seek as lonely a retreat in Lindisfarne. They shunned cities, drew the people to them, and worked upwards through that people to the great.

The Irish mission in England during the seventh century was one among the great things of history, and has met with an inadequate appreciation. The ancient name of the Irish, 'Scoti,' commemorative of their supposed Scythian origin, the name by which Bede always designates them, had been frequently translated 'Scottish' by modern historians; and those who did not know that an Irish immigrant body had entered Scotland, then called Alba, about the close of the second century, had conquered its earlier inhabitants, the Picts, after a war of centuries, and had eventually given to that heroic land, never since subdued, its own name and its royal house, naturally remained ignorant that those 'Scottish' missionaries were Irish. A glance at Bede,* or such

---

* 'In process of time, Britain, besides the Britons and Picts, received a third nation, the Scots, who migrating from Ireland, under their leader Reuda, either by fair means or by force of

well-known recent works as Sir W. Scott's *History of Scotland*,* makes this matter plain; yet the amount of work done in England by those Irish missionaries is still known to few.

They came from a country the fortunes, the character, and the institutions of which were singularly unlike those of England; one in which ancient Rome had had no part; which, in the form of clan-life, retained as its social type the patriarchal customs of its native East, all authority being an expansion of domestic authority, and the idea of a family, rather than that of a state, ruling over the hearts of men. About two centuries previously, Ireland had become Christian; and an image of its immemorial clan-

---

arms secured to themselves those settlements among the Picts which they still possess.'—Bede's *Ecclesiastical Hist.* book. i. cap. i.

* 'In the fifth century there appear in North Britain two powerful and distinct tribes, who are not before named in history. These are the Picts and the Scots. . . . The Scots, on the other hand, were of Irish origin; for, to the great confusion of ancient history, the inhabitants of Ireland, those at least of the conquering and predominating caste, were called Scots. A colony of these Irish Scots distinguished by the name of Dalriads, or Dalreudini, natives of Ulster, had early attempted a settlement on the coast of Argyleshire; they finally established themselves there under Fergus, the son of Eric, about the year 503, and, recruited by colonies from Ulster, continued to multiply and increase until they formed a nation which occupied the western side of Scotland.'—Sir Walter Scott's *History of Scotland*, vol. i. p. 7. Scott proceeds to record the eventual triumph of the Irish or Scotic race over the Pictish in the ninth century. 'So complete must have been the revolution that the very language of the Picts is lost. . . The country united under his sway (that of Kenneth Mac Alpine) was then called for the first time Scotland.' The same statement is made by Burke: 'The principal of these were the Scots, a people of ancient settlement in Ireland, and who had thence been transplanted into the northern part of Britain, which afterwards derived its name from that colony.'—Burke, *Abridgment of English History*, book i. cap. iv.

system was reproduced in the vast convents which ere long covered the land, and sent forth their missionaries over a large part of Europe. It might well have been thought doubtful whether these were likely to work successfully among a race so dissimilar as the Anglo-Saxon; but the event proved that in this instance dissimilar qualities meant qualities complemental to each other, and that sympathy was attracted by unlikeness.

The Irish mission in England began at a critical time, just when the reaction against the earlier successes of the Roman mission had set in. At York, under Paulinus, Christianity had triumphed; but eight years after that event Edwin, the Christian king of Deira, perished in battle, and northern England was forced back by king Penda into paganism. Southern England, with the exception of Canterbury and a considerable part of Kent, had also lost the Gospel, after possessing it for thirty years. Nearly at the same time East Anglia and Essex, at the command of pagan-kings, had discarded it likewise. It was then that Oswald, on recovering his kingdom of Northumbria, besought the Irish monks of Iona to reconvert it, or rather to complete a conversion which had been but begun. Their work prospered; by degrees the largest kingdom of the Heptarchy became solidly and permanently Christian, its See being fixed in the Island of Lindisfarne, whence the huge diocese of the north was ruled successively by three of St. Columba's order, Aidan, Finan, and Colman. But the labours of St. Columba's sons were not confined to the north. In East Anglia an Irish monk, St. Fursey, founded on the coast of Suffolk the monastery of Burghcastle, in which King

Sigebert became a monk. An Irish priest, Maidulphus, built that of Malmesbury in Wessex. Glastonbury was an older Celtic monastery inhabited partly by Irish monks, and partly by British. Peada, king of Mercia, son of the terrible Penda, was baptized by St. Finan close to the Roman Wall, as was also Sigebert, king of the East Saxons. Diama, an Irish monk, was first bishop of all Mercia, its second, Céoloch, being Irish also, and also its fourth.

Montalembert, in his *Moines d'Occident*, has given us the most delightful history that exists of the conversion of Anglo-Saxon England, a work combining the depth of a Christian philosopher with the sagacity of a statesman, and a dramatist's appreciation of character, while in it we miss nothing of that picturesque vividness and engaging simplicity which belong to our early chroniclers; thus conferring upon England a boon if possible greater than that bestowed upon Ireland in his lives of St. Columba, St. Columbanus and other saints. It is thus that he apportions the share which the Irish missionaries and the Roman had in that great enterprise.

'En résumant l'histoire des efforts tentés pendant les soixante ans écoulés depuis le débarquement d'Augustin jusqu'à la mort de Penda, pour introduire le Christianisme en Angleterre, on constate les résultats que voici. Des huit royaumes de la confédération Anglo-Saxonne, celui de Kent fut seul exclusivement conquis et conservé par les moines romains, dont les premières tentatives, chez les Est-Saxons et les Northumbriens, se terminèrent par un échec. En Wessex et en Est-Anglie les Saxons à l'ouest et les Angles à l'est furent convertis par l'action combinée de missionnaires continentaux et de moines celtiques. Quant aux deux royaumes North-umbriens' (Dëira and Bernicia), 'à l'Essex et à la Mercie, comprenant à eux seuls plus de deux tiers du territoire occupé par les conquérants germains, ces quatre pays durent leur conversion définitive exclusivement à l'invasion pacifique des moines celtiques, qui n'avaient pas seulement rivalisé de zèle avec les moines romains, mais qui, une fois les premiers obstacles surmontés, avaient montré bien plus de persévérance et obtenu bien plus de succès.'* The only effort made at that early period to introduce Christianity into the kingdom of the South-Saxons was that of an Irish monk, Dicul, who founded a small monastery at Bosham. It did not however prove successful.

There is something profoundly touching in the religious ties which subsisted between England and Ireland during the seventh century, when compared with the troubled relations of those two countries during many a later age. If the memory of benefits received produces a kindly feeling on the part of the recipient, that of benefits conferred should exert the same influence on the heart of the bestower. To remember the past, however disastrous or convulsed, is a nation's instinct, and its duty no less, since a tribute justly due is thus paid to great actions and to great sufferings in times gone by; nor among the wise and the generous can the discharge of that patriotic duty ever engender an enmity against the living: but there is a special satisfaction in turning to those recollections with which no human infirmity can connect any feeling save that of good will; and it is

* *Moines d'Occident*, vol. iv. pp. 127-8. Par le Comte de Montalembert.

scarcely possible to recall them in this instance without a hope that the sacred bonds which united those two countries at that remote period may be a pledge for reciprocated benefits in the ages yet before us. For both countries that early time was a time of wonderful spiritual greatness. In noble rivalry with Ireland England also sent her missionaries to far lands: and a child of Wessex, St. Boniface, brought the Faith to Germany, by which it was eventually diffused over Scandinavia, thus, by anticipation, bestowing the highest of all gifts on that terrible race the Northmen, in later centuries the scourge of his native land.

At home both islands were filled with saints whose names have ever since resounded throughout Christendom. Both islands, as a great writer * has told us, 'had been the refuge of Christianity, for a time almost exterminated in Christendom, and the centres of its propagation in countries still heathen. Secluded from the rest of Europe by the stormy waters in which they lay, they were converted just in time to be put in charge with the sacred treasures of Revelation, and with the learning of the old world, in that dreary time which intervened between Gregory and Charlemagne. They formed schools, collected libraries, and supplied the Continent with preachers and teachers.' He remarks also that 'There was a fitness in the course of things that the two peoples who had rejoiced in one prosperity should drink together the same cup of suffering: *Amabiles, et decori in vitâ suâ, in morte non divisi;*' and he proceeds to remind us that, immediately after their

* Cardinal Newman's *Historical Sketches*, vol. i. p. 226: *The Northmen and Normans in England and Ireland*.

participation in that common religious greatness, they partook also a tragic inheritance. In England for two centuries and a half, in Ireland for a longer period, the Northmen were repulsed but to reappear. Again and again the sons of Odin blackened the river-mouths of each land with their fleets; whenever they marched they left behind them the ashes of burned churches and monasteries, till, in large parts of both, Christianity and learning had well-nigh perished, and barbarism had all but returned. In both countries domestic dissensions had favoured the invader; eventually in both the Danish power broke down; but in both and in each case claiming a spiritual sanction—another branch of the same Scandinavian stock succeeded to the Dane, viz. the only one then Christianised, the Norman. In that seventh century how little could Saxon convert or Irish missionary have foreseen that the destinies of their respective countries should be at once so unlike yet so like, so antagonistic yet so interwoven!

The aim of the 'Legends of Saxon Saints,' as the reader will perhaps have inferred from the preceding remarks, is to illustrate England, her different races and predominant characteristics, during the century of her conversion to Christianity, and in doing this to indicate what circumstances had proved favourable or unfavourable to the reception of the Faith. It became desirable thus to revert to the early emigration of that 'Barbaric' race of which the Anglo-Saxon was a scion, making the shadow of Odin pass in succession over the background of the several pictures presented (the Heroic being thus the unconscious precursor of the Spiritual), and to show how the religion which bore his name was fitted at once to predispose its nobler votaries to Christianity and to infuriate against it those who but valued their faith for what it contained of degenerate. It seemed also expedient to select for treatment not only those records most abounding in the picturesque and poetic, but likewise others useful as illustrating the chief representatives of a many-sided society; the pagan king and the British warrior, the bard of Odin and the prophetess of Odin, the Gaelic missionary and the Roman missionary, the poet and the historian of Anglo-Saxon Christianity. In a few instances, as in the tales of Oswald and of Oswy, where the early chronicle was copious in detail, it has been followed somewhat closely; but more often, where the original record was brief, all except the fundamental facts had to be supplied. On these occasions I found encouragement in the remark of a writer at once deep and refined. 'Stories to be versified should not be already nearly complete, having the beauty in themselves, and gaining from the poet but a garb. They should be rough, and with but a latent beauty. The poet should have to supply the features and limbs as well as the dress.' *

Bede has been my guide. His records are, indeed, often 'rough,' as rough as the crab-tree, but, at the same time, as fresh as its blossom. Their brief touches reveal all the passions of the Barbaric races; but the chief human affections, things far deeper than the passions, are yet more abundantly illustrated by them.† It was a time when those affections were not

* Sara Coleridge.
† As the illustration of an Age, Bede's *History* has been well compared by Cardinal Manning with the *Fioretti di S. Francesco*, that exquisite illustration of the thirteenth century.

frozen by conventionalities and forced to conceal themselves until they forgot to exist. In the narrative of Bede we find also invaluable illustrations of a higher but not less real range of human affections, viz. the affections of 'Christianised Humanity,' affections grounded on divine truths and heavenly hopes, and yet in entire harmony with affections of a merely human order, which lie beneath them in a parallel plane. Occasionally the two classes enter into conflict, as in the case of the monks of Bardency who found it so difficult to reconcile their reverence for a Saint with their patriotic hatred of a foreign invader; but almost invariably the earthly and the heavenly emotions are mutually supplemental, as in those tender friendships of monk with monk, of king and bishop, grounded upon religious sympathy and co-operation; so that the lower sentiment without the higher would present, compared with the pictures now bequeathed to us, but an unfinished and truncated image of Humanity. Here, again, the semi-barbaric age described by Bede rendered the delineation more vivid. In ages of effeminate civilisation the Christian emotions, even more than those inherent in unassisted human nature, lose that ardour which belongs to them when in a healthy condition—an ardour which especially reveals itself during that great crisis, a nation's conversion, when beside a throng of new feelings and new hopes, a host of new Truths has descended upon the intelligence of a whole people, and when a sense of new knowledge and endless progress is thus communicated to it, far exceeding that which is the boast of nations devoted chiefly to physical science. The sense of progress, indeed, when such a period reaches its highest, is a rapture. It is as though the motion of the planet which carries us through space, a motion of which we are cognisant but which we yet cannot feel, could suddenly become, like the speed of a racehorse, a thing brought home to our consciousness.

Such ardours are scarcely imaginable in the later ages of a nation; but in Bede's day a people accepting the 'glad tidings' was glad; and, unambitious as his style is of the ornamental or the figurative, it is brightened by that which it so faithfully describes. His chronicle is often poetry, little as he intended it to be such; nay, it is poetry in her 'humanities' yet more than in her distinctively spiritual province, and better poetry than is to be found in the professed poetry of a materialistic age, when the poet is tempted to take refuge from the monotony of routine life, either amid the sensational accidents to be found on the byeways, not the highways, of life, or in some sickly dreamland that does not dare to deal with life, and belongs neither to the real nor to the ideal. In nothing is Bede's history of that great age, to which our own owes all that it possesses of real greatness, more striking than in that spirit of unconscious elevation and joyousness which belongs to the Christian life it records, a joyousness often so strikingly contrasted with the sadness—sometimes a heroic sadness—to be found in portions of his work describing pagan manners. With all its violences and inconsistencies, the seventh century was a noble age—an age of strong hearts which were gentle as well as strong, of a childhood that survived in manhood, of natures that had not lost their moral unity, of holy lives and of happy deaths. Bede's picture of it is a true one; and for that reason it comes home to us.

To some it may seem a profaneness to turn those old legends into verse. I should not have attempted the enterprise if they were much read in prose. The verse may at least help to direct the attention of a few readers to them. From them the thoughtful will learn how to complete a 'half-truth' often reiterated. Those who have declared that 'the wars of the Heptarchy are as dull as the battles of kites and crows,' have not always known that the true interest of her turbulent days belonged to peace, not to war, and that it is to be found in the spiritual development of the Anglo-Saxon race.

PROLOGUE.

ODIN THE MAN.

Odin, a Prince who reigned near the Caspian Sea, after a vain resistance to the Roman arms, leads forth his people to the forests north of the Danube, that, serving God in freedom on the limits of the Roman Empire, and being strengthened by an adverse climate, they may one day descend upon that empire in just revenge; which destiny was fulfilled by the sack of Rome, under Alaric, Christian King of the Goths, a race derived, like the Saxon, from that Eastern people.

FORTH with those missives, Chiron, to the Invader!
Hence, and make speed: they scathe mine eyes like
    fire:
Pompeius, thou hast conquered! What remains?
Vengeance! Man's race has never dreamed of such;
So slow, so sure. Pompeius, I depart:
I might have held these mountains yet four days:
The fifth had seen them thine—
I look beyond the limit of this night:
Four centuries I need; then comes mine hour.

    What saith the Accursed One of the Western
        World?
I hear even now her trumpet! Thus she saith:
'I have enlarged my borders: iron reaped
Earth's field all golden. Strenuous fight we fought:

I left some sweat drops on that Carthage shore,
Some blood on Gallic javelins. That is past!
My pleasant days are come: my couch is spread
Beside all waters of the Midland Sea;
By whispers lulled of nations kneeling round;
Illumed by light of balmiest climes; refreshed
By winds from Atlas and the Olympian snows:
Henceforth my foot is in delicious ways;
Bathe it, ye Persian fountains! Syrian vales,
All roses, make me sleepy with perfumes!
Caucasian cliffs, with martial echoes faint
Flatter light slumbers; charm a Roman dream!
I send you my Pompeius; let him lead
Odin in chains to Rome!' Odin in chains!
Were Odin chained, or dead, that God he serves
Could raise a thousand Odins—
Rome's Founder-King beside his Augur standing
Noted twelve ravens borne in sequent flight
O'er Alba's crags. They emblem'd centuries twelve,
The term to Rome conceded. Eight are flown;
Remain but four. Hail, sacred brood of night!
Hencefore my standards bear the Raven Sign,
The bird that hoarsely haunts the ruined tower;
The bird sagacious of the field of blood
Albeit far off. Four centuries I need:
Then comes my day. My race and I are one.

O Race beloved and holy! From my youth
Where'er a hungry heart impelled my feet,
Whate'er I found of glorious, have I not
Claimed it for thee, deep-musing? Ignorant, first,
For thee I wished the golden ingots piled
In Susa and Ecbatana:—ah fool!
At Athens next, treading where Plato trod,
For thee all triumphs of the mind of man,

And Phidian hand inspired! Ah fool, that hour
Athens lay bound, a slave! Later to Rome
In secrecy by Mithridates sent
To search the inmost of his hated foe,
For thee I claimed that discipline of Law
Which made her State one camp. Fool, fool once
    more!
Soon learned I what a heart-pollution lurked
Beneath that mask of Law. As Persia fell,
By softness sapped, so Rome. Behold, this day,
Following the Pole Star of my just revenge,
I lead my people forth to clearer fates
Through cloudier fortunes. They are brave and
    strong:
'Tis but the rose-breath of their vale that rots
Their destiny's bud unblown. I lead them forth,
A race war-vanquished, not a race of slaves;
Lead them, not southward to Euphrates' bank,
Not Eastward to the realms of rising suns,
Nor West to Rome, and bondage. Hail, thou North!
Hail, boundless woods, by nameless oceans girt,
And snow-robed mountain islets, founts of fire!
    Four hundred years! I know that awful North:
I sought it when the one flower of my life
Fell to my foot. That anguish set me free:
It dashed me on the iron side of life:
I woke, a man. My people too shall wake:
They shall have icy crags for myrtle banks,
Sharp rocks for couches. Strength! I must have
    strength;
Not splenetic sallies of a woman's courage,
But hearts to which self-pity is unknown:
Hard life to them must be as mighty wine
Gladdening the strong: the death on battle-fields

Must seem the natural, honest close of life;
Their fear must be to die without a wound
And miss Life's after-banquet. Wooden shield
Whole winter nights shall lie their covering sole:
Thereon the boy shall stem the ocean wave;
Thereon the youth shall slide with speed of winds
Loud-laughing down the snowy mountain-slope:
To him the Sire shall whisper as he bleeds,
'Remember the revenge! Thy son must prove
More strong, more hard than thou!'
                                  Four hundred years!
Increase is tardy in that icy clime,
For Death is there the awful nurse of Life:
Death rocks the cot. Why meet we there no wolf
Save those huge-limbed? Because weak wolf-cubs die.
'Tis thus with man; 'tis thus with all things strong:—
Rise higher on thy northern hills, my Pine!
That Southern Palm shall dwindle.
                                House stone-walled—
Ye shall not have it! Temples cedar-roofed—
Ye shall not build them! Where the Temple stands
The City gathers. Cities ye shall spurn:
Live in the woods; live singly, winning each,
Hunter or fisher by blue lakes, his prey:
Abhor the gilded shrine: the God Unknown
In such abides not. On the mountain's top
Great Persia sought Him in her day of strength:
With her ye share the kingly breed of Truths,
The noblest inspirations man hath known,
Or can know—ay, unless the Lord of all
Should come, Man's Teacher. Pray as Persia prayed;
And see ye pray for Vengeance! Leave till then
To Rome her Idol fanes and pilfered Gods.

I see you, O my People, year by year
Strengthened by sufferings ; pains that crush the weak,
Your helpers. Men have been that, poison-fed,
Grew poison-proof : on pain and wrong feed ye !
The wild-beast rage against you ! frost and fire
Rack you in turn ! I'll have no gold among you ;
With gold come wants ; and wants mean servitude.
Edge, each, his spear with fish-bone or with flint,
Leaning for prop on none. I want no Nations !
A Race I fashion, playing not at States :
I take the race of Man, the breed that lifts
Alone its brow to heaven : I change that race
From clay to stone, from stone to adamant
Through slow abrasion, such as leaves sea-shelves
Lustrous at last and smooth. To *be*, not *have*,
A man to be ; no heritage to clasp
Save that which simple manhood, at its will,
Or conquers or re-conquers, held meanwhile
In trust for Virtue ; this alone is greatness.
Remain ye Tribes, not Nations ; led by Kings,
Great onward-striding Kings, above the rest
High towering, like the keel-compelling sail
That takes the topmost tempest. Let them die,
Each for his people ! I will die for mine
Then when my work is finished ; not before.
That Bandit King who founded Rome, the Accursed,
Vanished in storm. My sons shall see me die,
Die, strong to lead them till my latest breath,
Which shall not be a sigh ; shall see and say,
'This Man far-marching through the mountainous
    world,
No God, but yet God's Prophet of the North,
Gave many crowns to others : for himself
His people were his crown.'

                                  Four hundred years—
Ye shall find savage races in your path:
Be ye barbaric, ay, but savage not:
Hew down the baser lest they drag you down;
Ye cannot raise them: they fulfil their fates:
Be terrible to foes, be kind to friend:
Be just; be true. Revere the Household Hearth;
This knowing, that beside it dwells a God:
Revere the Priest, the King, the Bard, the Maid,
The Mother of the heroic race—five strings
Sounding God's Lyre. Drive out with lance for goad
That idiot God by Rome called Terminus,
Who standing sleeps, and holds his reign o'er fools.
The earth is God's, not Man's: that Man from Him
Holds it whose valour earns it. Time shall come,
It may be, when the warfare shall be past,
The reign triumphant of the brave and just
In peace consolidated. Time may come
When that long winter of the Northern Land
Shall find its spring. Where spreads the black morass
Harvest all gold may glitter; cities rise
Where roamed the elk; and nations set their thrones;
Nations not like those empires known till now,
But wise and pure. Let such their temples build
And worship Truth, if Truth should e'er to Man
Show her full face. Let such ordain them laws
If Justice e'er should mate with laws of men.
Above the mountain summits of Man's hope
There spreads, I know, a land illimitable,
The table land of Virtue trial-proved,
Whereon one day the nations of the world
Shall race like emulous Gods. A greater God
Served by our sires, a God unknown to Rome,
Above that shining level sits, high-towered:

Millions of Spirits wing His flaming light,
And fiery winds among His tresses play:
When comes that hour which judges Gods and men
That God shall plague the Gods that filched His name
And cleanse the Peoples.
                      When ye hear, my sons,
That God uprising in His judgment robes
And see their dreadful crimson in the West,
Then know ye that the knell of Rome is nigh
Then stand, and listen! When His Trumpet sounds
Forth from your forests and your snows, my sons,
Forth over Ister, Rhenus, Rhodonus,
To Mœsia forth, to Thrace, Illyricum,
Iberia, Gaul; but, most of all, to Rome!
Who leads you thither leads you not for spoil:
A mission hath he, fair though terrible;
He makes a pure hand purer, washed in blood:
On, Scourge of God! the Vengeance Hour is come.
  I know that hour, and wait it. Odin's work
Stands then consummate. Odin's name thenceforth
Goes down to darkness.
                  Farewell, Ararat!
How many an evening, still and bright as this,
In childhood, youth, or manhood's sorrowing years,
Have I not watched the sunset hanging red
Upon thy hoary brow! Farewell for ever!
A legend haunts thee that the race of man
In earliest days, a sad and storm-tossed few,
From thy wan heights descended making way
Into a ruined world. A storm-tossed race,
But not self-pitying, once again thou seest
Into a world all ruin making way
Whither they know not, yet without a fear.
This hour—lo, there, they pass yon valley's verge!—

In sable weeds that pilgrimage moves on,
Moves slowly like thy shadow, Ararat,
That eastward creeps. Phantom of glory dead!
Image of greatness that disdains to die
Move Northward thou! Whate'er thy fates decreed
At least that shadow shall be shadow of Man,
And not of beast gold-weighted! On, thou Night
Cast by my heart! Thou too shalt meet thy morn!

LEGENDS.

KING ETHELBERT OF KENT AND SAINT AUGUSTINE.

Ethelbert, King of Kent, converses first with his Pagan Thanes, and next with Saint Augustine, newly landed on the shores of Thanet Island. The Saint, coming in sight of Canterbury, rejoices greatly, and predicts the future greatness of that city.

Far through the forest depths of Thanet Isle
That never yet had heard the woodman's axe,
Rang the glad clarion on the May-day morn
Blent with the cry of hounds. The rising sun
Flamed on the forest's dewy jewelry,
While, under rising mists, a host with plumes
Rode down a broad oak alley t'wards the sea.

King Ethelbert rode first : he reigned in Kent
Least kingdom of the Seven yet Head of all
Through his desert. That morn the royal train,
While sang the invisible lark her song in heaven,
Pursued the flying stag. At times the creature
As though he too had pleasure in the sport,
Vaulted at ease through sunshine and through shade,
Then changed his mood, and left the best behind him.
Five hours they chased him ; last, upon a rock
High up in scorn he held his antlered front,
Then took the wave and vanished.
                    Many a frown
Darkened that hour on many a heated brow ;
And many a spur afflicted that poor flank

Which panted hard and smoked. The King alone
Laughed at mischance. 'The stag, with God to aid,
Has left our labour fruitless! Give him joy!
He lives to yield us sport some later morn:
So be it! Waits our feast, and not far off:
On to the left 'twixt yonder ash and birch!'

  He spake, and anger passed: they praised their sport;
And many an outblown nostril seemed to snuff
That promised feast. They rode through golden furze
So high the horsemen only were descried;
And glades whose centuried oaks their branches laid
O'er violet banks; and fruit trees, some snow-veiled
Like bridesmaid, others like the bride herself
Behind her white veil blushing. Glad, the thrush
Carolled; more glad, the wood-dove moaned; close by
A warbling runnel led them to the bay:
Two chestnuts stood beside it snowy-coned:
The banquet lay beneath them.
                              Feasting o'er
The song succeeded. Boastful was the strain
Each Thane his deeds extolling, or his sire's;
But one, an aged man, among them scoffed:
'When I was young; when Sigbert on my right
To battle rode, and Sefred on my left;
That time men stood not worsted by a stag!
Not then our horses swerved from azure strait
Scared by the ridged sea-wave!' Next spake a chief,
Pirate from Denmark late returned: 'Our skies,
Good friends, are all too soft to build the man!
We fight for fame: the Northman fights for sport;
Their annals boast they fled but once:—'twas thus:
In days of old, when Rome was in her pride,

Huge hosts of hers had fallen on theirs, surprised,
And way-worn: long they fought: a remnant spent,
Fled to their camp. Upon its walls their wives
Stood up, black-garbed, with axes heaved aloft,
And fell upon the fugitives and slew them;
Slew next their little ones; slew last themselves,
Cheating the Roman Triumph. Never since then
Hath Northman fled the foemen.'
                                Egfrid rose:
'Who saith our kinsfolk of the frozen North
One stock with us, one faith, one ancient tongue
Pass us in valour? Three days since I saw
Crossing the East Saxon's border and our own
Two boys that strove. The Kentish wounded fell;
The East Saxon on him knelt; then made demand:
"My victim art thou by the laws of war!
Yonder my dagger lies;—till I return
Wilt thou abide?" The vanquished answered, "Yea!"
A minute more, and o'er that dagger's edge
His life-blood rushed.' The pirate chief demurred;
'A gallant boy! Not less I wager this,
The glitter of that dagger ere it smote
Made his eye blink. Attend! Three years gone by,
Sailing with Hakon on Norwegian fiords
We fought the Jomsburg Rovers, at their head
Sidroc, oath-pledged to marry Hakon's child
Despite her father's best. In mist we met:
Instant each navy at the other dashed
Like wild beast, instinct-taught, that knows its foe;
Chained ship to ship, and clashed their clubs all day,
Till sank the sun: then laughed the white peaks forth,
And reeled, methought, above the reeling waves!
The victory was with us. Hakon, next morn,
Bade slay his prisoners. Thirty on one bench

Waited their doom: their leader died the first;
He winked not as the sword upon him closed!
No, nor the second! Hakon asked the third
"What think'st thou, friend, of Death?" He tossed
    his head:
"My Father perished; I fulfil my turn."
The fourth, "Strike quickly, Chief! An hour this
    morn
We held contention if, when heads are off
The hand can hold its dagger: I would learn."
The dagger and the head together fell.
The fifth, "One fear is mine—lest yonder slave
Finger a Prince's hair! Command some chief
Thy best beloved, to lift it in his hands;
Then strike and spare not!" Hakon struck. That
    youth,
Sigurd by name, his forehead forward twitched,
Laughing, so deftly that the downward sword
Shore off those luckless hands that raised his hair.
All laughed; and Hakon's son besought his sire
To loosen Sigurd's bonds: but Sigurd cried,
"Unless the rest be loosed I will not live!"
Thus all escaped save four.'
                              In graver mood
That chief resumed: 'A Norland King dies well!
His bier is raised upon his stateliest ship;
Piled with his arms; his lovers and his friends
Rush to their monarch's pyre, resolved with him
To share in death, and with becoming pomp
Attend his footsteps to Valhalla's Hall.
The torch is lit: forth sails the ship, black-winged,
Facing the midnight seas. From beach and cliff
Men watch all night that slowly lessening flame:
Yet no man sheds a tear.'

                        Earconwald,
An aged chief, made answer, 'Tears there be
Of divers sorts: a wise and valiant king
Deserves that tear which praises, not bewails
Greatness gone by.' The pirate shouted loud
'A land it is of laughter, not of tears!
Know ye the tale of Harald? He had sailed
Round southern coasts and eastern; sacked or burned
A hundred Christian cities. One he found
So girt with giant walls and brazen gates
His sea-kings vainly dashed their ships against them;
And died beneath them, frustrate. Harald sent
A herald to that city proffering terms:
"Harald is dead: Christian was he in youth:
He sends you spoils from many a city burnt
And craves interment in your chiefest church."
Next day the masked procession wound in black
Through streets defenceless. When the church was reached
They laid their chief before the altar-lights:
Anon to heaven rang out the priestly dirge,
And incense-smoke upcurled. Forth from its cloud
Sudden upleaped the dead man, club in hand,
Spurning his coffin's gilded walls, and smote
The hoary pontiff down, and brake his neck;
And all those maskers doffed their weeds of woe
And showed the mail beneath, and raised their swords
And drowned that pavement in a sea of blood,
While raging rushed their mates through portals wide,
And, since that city seemed but scant of spoil
Fired it and sailed. Ofttimes old Harald laughed
That tale recounting.'
                        Many a Kentish chief
Re-echoed Harald's laugh;—not Ethelbert:

The war-scar reddening on his brow he rose
And spake: 'My Thanes, ye laugh at deeds accurst!
An old King I, and make my prophecy
One day that northern race which smites and laughs,
Our kith and kin albeit, shall smite our coasts:
That day ye will not laugh!' Earconwald
Not rising, likewise answer made, heart-grieved:
'Six sons had I: all these are slain in war;
Yet I, an unrejoicing man forlorn,
Find solace ofttimes thinking of their deeds:
They laughed not when they smote. No God, be sure,
Smiles on the jest red-handed.' Egfrid rose,
And three times cried with lifted sword unsheathed,
'Behold my God! No God save him I serve!'

While thus they held discourse, where blue waves danced
Not far from land, behold, there hove in sight
Seen 'twixt a great beech silky yet with Spring
And pine broad-crested, round whose head old storms
Had wov'n a garland of his own green boughs,
A bark both fair and large; and hymn was heard.
Then laughed the King, 'The stag-hunt and our songs
So drugged my memory, I had nigh forgotten
Why for our feast I chose this heaven-roofed hall:
Missives I late received from friends in France;
They make report of strangers from the South
Who, tarrying in their coasts have learned our tongue
And northward wend with tidings strange and new
Of some celestial Kingdom by their God
Founded for men of Faith. Nor churl am I
To frown on kind intent, nor child to trust
This sceptre of Seven Realms to magic snare
That puissance hath—who knows not?—greater thrice
In house than open field. I therefore chose

For audience hall this precinct.'
                    Muttered low
Murdark, the scoffer with the cave-like mouth
And sidelong eyes, ' Queen Bertha's voice was that!
A woman's man!   Since first from Gallic shores
That dainty daughter of King Charibert
Pressed her small foot on England's honest shore
The whole land dwindles!'
                    Mid seraphic hymns
Ere long that serpent hiss was lost: for soon
In raiment white, circling a rocky point
O'er sands still glistening with a tide far-ebbed,
On drew, preceded by a silver Cross,
A long Procession.   Music as it moved
Floated on sea-winds inland, deadened now
By thickets, echoed now from cliff or cave:
Ere long before them that Procession stood.
The King addressed them: ' Welcome, Heralds sage!
If sent from God I welcome you the more,
Since great is God, and therefore great His gifts:
God grant He send them daily, heaped and huge!
Speak without fear, for him alone I hate
Who brings ill news, or makes inept demand
Unmeet for Kings.   I know the Cross ye bear;
And in my palace sits a Christian wife,
Bertha, the sweetest lady in this land;
Most gracious in her ways, in heart most leal.
I knew her yet a child: she knelt whene'er
The Queen, her mother, entered: then I said,
A maid so reverent will be reverent wife,
And wedded her betimes.   Morning and eve
She in her wood-girt chapel sings her prayer,
Which wins us kindlier harvest, and, some think,
Success in war.   She strives not with our Gods:

Confusion never wrought she in my house,
Nor minished Hengist's glory. Had her voice,
Clangorous or strident, drawn upon my throne
Deserved opprobrium'—here the monarch's brows
Flushed at the thought, and fire was in his eyes—
'The hand that clasps this sceptre had not spared
To hunt her forth an outcast in the woods,
Thenceforth with beasts to herd! More lief were I
To take the lioness to my bed and board
Than house a rebel wife.' Remembering then
The mildness of his Queen, King Ethelbert
Resumed, appeased, for placable his heart;
'But she no rebel is, and this I deem
Fair auspice for her Faith.'
      A little breeze
Warm from the sea that moment softly waved
The standard from its staff, and showed thereon
The Child Divine. Upon His mother's knee
Sublime He stood. His left hand clasped a globe
Crowned with a golden Cross; and with His right
Two fingers heavenward raised, o'er all the earth
He sent His blessing.
     Of that band snow-stoled
One taller by the head than all the rest
Obeisance made; then, pointing to the Cross,
And forward moving t'ward the monarch's seat,
Opened the great commission of the Faith:
'Behold the Eternal Maker of the worlds!
That hand which shaped the earth and blesses earth
Must rule the race of man!'
      Majestic then
As when, far winding from its mountain springs,
City and palm-grove far behind it left,
Some Indian river rolls while mists dissolved

Leave it in native brightness unobscured,
And kingly navies share its sea-ward sweep,
Forward on-flowed in Apostolic might
Augustine's strong discourse. With God beginning
He showed the Almighty all-compassionate
Down drawn from distance infinite to man
By the Infinite of Love. Lo, Bethlehem's crib!
There lay the Illimitable in narrow bound:
Thence rose that triumph of a world redeemed!
Last, to the standard pointing, thus he spake:
'Yon standard tells the tale! Six hundred years
Westward it speeds from subject realm to realm;
First from the bosom of God's Race Elect,
His people, till they slew Him, mild it soared:
Rejected, it returned. Above their walls
While ruin rocked them, and the Roman fire,
Dreadful it hung. When Rome had shared that guilt
Mocking that Saviour's Brethren and His Bride,
Above the conquered conqueror of all lands
In turn this Standard flew. Who raised it high?
A son of this your island, Constantine!
In these, thine English oakwoods, Helena,
'Twas thine to nurse thy warrior. He had seen
Star-writ in heaven the words this Standard bears,
"Through Me is victory." Victory won, he raised
High as his empire's queenly head, and higher,
This Standard of the Eternal Dove thenceforth
To fly where eagle standard never flew,
God's glory in its track, goodwill to man.
Advance for aye, great Emblem! Light as now
Famed Asian headlands, and Hellenic isles!
O'er snow-crowned Alp and citied Apennine
Send forth a breeze of healing! Keep thy throne
For ever on those western peaks that watch

The setting sun descend the Hesperean wave,
Atlas and Calpe!   These, the old Roman bound,
Build but the gateway of the Rome to be—
Till Christ returns thou Standard, hold them fast:
But never till the North, that, age by age,
Dashed back the Pagan Rome, with Christian Rome
Partakes the spiritual crown of man restored
From thy strong flight above the world surcease,
And fold thy wings in rest!'
       Upon the sod
He knelt, and on that standard gazed, and spake,
Calm-voiced, with hand to heaven: 'I promise thee,
Thou Sign, another victory, and thy best—
This island shall be thine!'
        Augustine rose
And took the right hand of King Ethelbert,
And placed therein the Standard's staff, and laid
His own above the monarch's, speaking thus:
'King of this land, I bid thee know from God
That kings have higher privilege than they know,
The standard-bearers of the King of kings.'
  Long time he clasped that royal hand; long time
The King, that patriarch's hand at last withdrawn,
His own withdrew not from that Standard's staff
Committed to his charge.   His hand he deemed
Thenceforth its servant vowed.   With large, meek eyes
Fixed on that Maid and Babe, he stood as child
That, gazing on some reverent stranger's face
Nor loosening from that stranger's hold his palm,
Listens his words attent.
       The Man of God
Meantime as silent gazed on Thanet's shore
Gold-tinged, with sunset spray to crimson turned
In league-long crescent.   Love was in his face,

That love which rests on Faith. He spake: 'Fair
    land,
I know thee what thou art, and what thou lack'st!
The Master saith, " I give to him that hath : "
Thy harvest shall be great.' Again he mused,
And shadow o'er him crept. Again he spake:
' That harvest won, when centuries have gone by,
What countenance wilt thou wear? How oft on
    brows
Brightened by Baptism's splendour, sin more late
Drags down its cloud! The time may come when thou
This day, though darkling, yet so innocent,
Barbaric, not depraved, on greater heights
May'st sin in malice—sin the great offence,
Changing thy light to darkness, knowing God,
Yet honouring God no more: that time may come
When, rich as Carthage, great in arms as Rome,
Keen-eyed as Greece, this isle, to sensuous gaze
A sun all gold, to angels may present
Aspect no nobler than a desert waste,
Some blind and blinding waste of sun-scorched sands,
Trod by a race of pigmies not of men,
Pigmies by passions ruled!'
                            Once more he mused;
Then o'er his countenance passed a second change;
And from it flashed the light of one who sees,
Some hill-top gained, beyond the incumbent night
The instant foot of morn. With regal step,
Martial yet measured, to the King he strode,
And laid a strong hand on him, speaking thus:
' Rejoice, my son, for God hath sent thy Land
This day Good Tidings of exceeding joy,
And planted in her Breast a Tree divine
Whose leaves shall heal far nations. Know besides

Should sickness blight that Tree, or tempest mar it,
The strong root shall survive : the winter past,
Heavenward once more shall rush both branch and
　　bough,
And over-vault the stars.'
　　　　　　　　　　　　He spake, and took
The sacred Standard from that monarch's hand,
And held it in his own, and fixed its point
Deep in the earth, and by it stood. Then lo !
Like one disburthened of some ponderous charge,
King Ethelbert became himself again,
And round him gazed well pleased. Throughout his
　　train
Sudden a movement thrilled : remembrance had
Of those around, his warriors and his thanes,
That ever on his wisdom waiting hung,
Thus he replied discreet : 'Stranger and friend,
Thou bear'st good tidings ! That thou camest thus far
To fool us, knave and witling may believe :
I walk not with their sort ; yet, guest revered,
Kings are not as the common race of men ;
Counsel they take, lest honour heaped on one
Dishonour others. Odin holds on us
Prescriptive right, and special claims on me,
Of Hengist's race—thence Odin's. Preach your Faith !
The man who wills I suffer to believe :
The man who wills not, let him moor his skiff
Where anchorage likes him best. The day declines :
This night with us you harbour, and our Queen
Shall lovingly receive you.'
　　　　　　　　　　　Staid and slow
The King rode homewards, while behind him paced
Augustine and his Monks. The ebb had left
'Twixt Thanet and the mainland narrow space

Marsh-land more late; beyond the ford there wound
A path through flowery meads; and, as they passed,
Not herdsmen only, but the broad-browed kine
Fixed on them long their meditative gaze;
And oft some blue-eyed boy with flaxen locks
Ran, fearless, forth, and plucked them by the sleeve,
Some boy clear-browed as those Saint Gregory
    marked,
Poor slaves, new-landed from the quays of Rome,
That drew from him that saying, '" Angli " !—nay,
Call them henceforward " Angels " !'
                                From a wood
Issuing, before them lustrous they beheld
King Ethelbert's chief city Canterbury,
Strong-walled, with winding street, and airy roofs,
And high o'er all the monarch's palace pile
Thick-set with towers. Then fire from God there fell
Upon Augustine's heart: and thus he sang
Advancing; and the brethren sang 'Amen':

  'Hail, City loved of God, for on thy brow
Great Fates are writ. Thou cumberest not His earth
For petty traffic reared, or petty sway;
I see a heavenly choir descend, thy crown
Henceforth to bind thy brow. Forever hail!

  'I see the basis of a kingly throne
In thee ascending! High it soars and higher,
Like some great pyramid o'er Nilus kenned
When vapours melt—the Apostolic Chair!
Doctrine and Discipline thence shall hold their course,
Like Tigris and Euphrates, through all lands
That face the Northern Star. Forever hail!

  'Where stands yon royal keep, a church shall rise

Like Incorruption clothing the Corrupt
On the resurrection morn! Strong House of God,
To him exalt thy walls, and nothing doubt
For lo! from thee like lions from their lair
Abroad shall pace the Primates of this land:
They shall not lick the hand that gives and smites
Doglike, nor snakelike on their bellies creep
In indirectness base. They shall not fear
The people's madness nor the rage of kings
Reddening the temple's pavement. They shall lift
The strong brow mitred, and the crosiered hand
Before their presence sending Love and Fear
To pave their steps with greatness. From their
    fronts
Stubborned with marble from Saint Peter's Rock
The sunrise of far centuries forth shall flame:
He that hath eyes shall see it, and shall say,
" Blessed who cometh in the name of God!"'

  Thus sang the Saint, advancing; and, behold,
At every pause the brethren sang ' Amen!'
While down from window and from roof the throng
Eyed them in silence. As their anthem ceased
Before them stood the palace clustered round
By many a stalwart form. Midway the gate
On the first step, like angel newly lit
Queen Bertha stood. Back from her forehead meek
The meeker for its crown, a veil descended,
While streamed the red robe to the foot snow-white
Sandalled in gold. The morn was on her face,
The star of morn within those eyes upraised
That flashed all dewy with the grateful light
Of many a granted prayer. O'er that sweet shape
Augustine signed the Venerable sign;

The lovely vision sinking, hand to breast,
Received it; while, by sympathy surprised
Or taught of God, the monarch and his thanes
Knelt as she knelt, and bent like her their heads,
Sharing her blessing. Like a palm the Faith
Thenceforth o'er England rose, those saintly men
Preaching by life severe, not words alone,
The doctrine of the Cross. Some Power divine
Stronger than patriot love, more sweet than Spring,
Made way from heart to heart, and daily God
Joined to His Church the souls that should be saved,
Thousands, where Medway mingles with the Thames,
Rushing to Baptism. In his palace cell
High-nested on that Vaticanian Hill
Which o'er the Martyr-gardens kens the world
Gregory, that news receiving, or from men
Or haply from that God with whom he walked
The Spirit's whisper ever in his ear,
Rejoiced that hour, and cried aloud, 'Rejoice,
Thou Earth! that North which from its cloud but
    flung
The wild beasts' cry of anger or of pain
Redeemed from wrath, its Hallelujahs sings;
Its waves by Roman galleys feared, this day
Kiss the bare feet of Christ's Evangelists;
That race whose oak-clubs brake our Roman swords
Glories now first in bonds—the bond of Truth:
At last it fears; but fears alone to sin,
Striving through Faith for Virtue's heavenly crown.'

THE CONSECRATION OF WESTMINSTER ABBEY.

Sebert, King of the East Saxons, having built the great church of Saint Peter at Westminster, Mellitus the Bishop prepares to consecrate it, but is warned in a vision that it has already been consecrated by one greater than he.

As morning brake, Sebert, East Saxon king,
Stood on the winding shores of Thames alone,
And fixed a sparkling eye upon Saint Paul's:
The sun new-risen had touched its roofs that laughed
Their answer back.   Beyond it London spread;
But all between the river and that church
Was slope of grass and blossoming orchard copse
Glittering with dews dawn-reddened.   Bertha here,
That church begun had thus besought her Lord
'Spare me this bank which God has made so fair!
Here let the little birds have leave to sing
The bud to blossom!   Here, the vespers o'er,
Lovers shall sit; and here, in later days,
Children shall question, "Who was he—Saint Paul?
What taught, what wrought he that his name should shine
Thus like the stars in heaven?"'
                                    As Sebert stood
The sweetness of the morning more and more
Made way into his heart.   The pale blue smoke
Rising from hearths by woodland branches fed,
Dimmed not the crystal matin air; not yet

From clammy couch had risen the mist sun-warmed:
All things distinctly showed; the rushing tide
The barge, the trees, the long bridge many-arched,
And countless huddled gables, far away,
Lessening, yet still descried.
      A voice benign
Dispersed the Prince's trance: 'I marked, my King,
Your face in yonder church; you took, I saw,
A blessing thence; and Nature's here you find:
The same God sends them both.' The man who spake
Though silver-tressed, was countenanced like a child;
Smooth-browed, clear-eyed. That still and luminous
  mien
Predicted realms where Time shall be no more;
Where gladness, like some honey-dew divine,
Freshens an endless present. Mellitus,
From Rome late missioned and the Cœlian Hill
Made thus his greeting.
      Westward by the Thames
The King and Bishop paced, and held discourse
Of him whose name that huge Cathedral bore,
Israel's great son, the man of mighty heart,
The man for her redemption zealous more
Than for his proper crown. Not task for her
God gave him: to the Gentiles still he preached
And won them to the Cross. 'That Faith once
  spurned,'
Thus cried the Bishop with a kindling eye,
'Lo, how it raised him as on eagle's wings
And past the starry gates; The Spirit's Sword
He wielded well! Save him who bears the Keys,
Save him who made confession, "Thou art Christ,"
Saint Paul had equal none! Hail, Brethren crowned!
Hail, happy Rome, that guard'st their mingled dust!'

Next spake the Roman of those churches twain
By Constantine beside the Tyber built
To glorify their names.   With sudden turn
Sebert, the crimson mounting to his brow,
Made question, 'Is your Tyber of the South
Ampler than this, our Thames?'   The old man smiled;
'Tyber to Thames is as that willow-stock
To yonder oak.'   The Saxon cried with joy:
'How true thy judgment is! how just thy tongue!
What hinders, O my Father, but that Thames,
Huge river from the forests rolled by God,
Should image, like that Tyber, churches twain,
Honouring those Princes of the Apostles' Band?
King Ethelbert, my uncle, built Saint Paul's;
Saint Peter's Church be mine!'

         An hour's advance
Left them in thickets tangled.   Low the ground,
Well-nigh by waters clipt, a savage haunt
With briar and bramble thick, and 'Thorny Isle'
For that cause named.   Sebert around him gazed,
A maiden blush upon him thus he spake:
'I know this spot; I stood here once, a boy:
'Twas winter then: the swoll'n and turbid flood
Rustled the sallows.   Far I fled from men:
A youth had done me wrong, and vengeful thoughts
Burned in my heart: I warred with them in vain:
I prayed against them; yet they still returned:
O'erspent at last, I cast me on my knees
And cried, "Just God, if Thou despise my prayer,
Faithless, thence weak, not less remember well
How many a man in this East Saxon land
Stands up this hour, in wood, or field, or farm,
Like me sore tempted, but with loftier heart:
To these be helpful—yea, to one of these!"

And lo, the wrathful thoughts, like routed fiends,
Left me, and came no more!'
                              Discoursing thus,
The friends a moment halted in a space
Where stood a flowering thorn. Adown it trailed
In zigzag curves erratic here and there
Long lines of milky bloom, like rills of foam
Furrowing the green back of some huge sea wave
Refluent from cliffs.   Ecstatic minstrelsy
Swelled from its branches. Birds as thick as leaves
Thronged them; and whether joy was theirs that hour
Because the May had come, or joy of love,
Or tenderer gladness for their young new-fledged,
So piercing was that harmony, the place
Eden to Sebert looked, while brake and bower
Shone like the Tree of Life.   'What minster choir,'
The Bishop cried, ' could better chant God's praise ?
Here shall your church ascend :—its altar rise
Where yonder thorn tree stands!' The old man
      spake ;
Yet in him lived a thought unbreathed : 'How oft
Have trophies risen to blazon deeds accursed !
Angels this church o'er-winging, age on age
Shall see that boy at prayer !'
                                In peace, in war,
Daily the work advanced. The youthful King
Kneeling, himself had raised the earliest sod,
Made firm the corner stone. Whate'er of gold
Sun-ripened harvests of the royal lands
Yielded from Thames to Stour, or tax and toll
From quays mast-thronged to loud-resounding sea,
Save what his realm required by famine vexed
At times, or ravage of the Mercian sword,
Went to the work. His Queen her jewels brought,

Smiling, huge gift in slenderest hands up-piled;
His thanes their store; the poor their labour free.
Some clave the quarry's ledges: from its depths
Some haled the blocks; from distant forests some
Dragged home the oak-beam on the creaking wain:
Alas, that arms in noble tasks so strong
Should e'er have sunk in dust! Ere ten years passed
Saint Peter's towers above the high-roofed streets
Smiled on Saint Paul's. That earlier church had risen
Where stood, in Roman days, Apollo's fane:
Upon a site to Dian dedicate
Now rose its sister. Erring Faith had reached
In those twin Powers that ruled the Day and Night,
To Wisdom witnessing and Chastity,
Her loftiest height, and perished. Phœnix-like,
From ashes of dead rites and Truth abused
Now soared unstained Religion.
                                What remained?
The Consecration. On its eve, the King
Held revel in its honour, solemn feast,
And wisely-woven dance, where beauty and youth,
Through loveliest measures moving, music-winged,
And winged not less by gladness, interwreathed
Brightness with brightness, glance turned back on
    glance,
And smile on smile—a courtseying graciousness
Of stateliest forms that, winding, sank or rose
As if on heaving seas. In groups apart
Old warriors clustered. Eadbald discussed
And Snorr, that truce with Wessex signed, and said,
'Fear nought: it cannot last!' A shadow sat
That joyous night upon one brow alone,
Redwald's East Anglia's King. In generous youth
He, guest that time with royal Ethelbert,

Had gladly bowed to Christ. From shallowest soil
Faith springs apace, but springs to die. Returned
To plains of Ely, all that sweetness past
Seemed but a dream while scornful spake his wife,
Upon whose brow beauty from love divorced
Made beauty's self unbeauteous: 'Lose—why not?—
Thwarting your liegeful subjects, lose at will
Your Kingdom; you that might have reigned ere now
Bretwalda of the Seven!' In hour accursed
The weak man with his Faith equivocated:
Fraudful, beneath the self-same roofs he raised
Altars to Christ and idols. By degrees
That Truth he mocked forsook him. Year by year
His face grew dark, and barbed his tongue though
 smooth,
Manner and mind like grass-fields after thaw,
Silk-soft above, yet iron-hard below:
Spleenful that night at Sebert's blithe discourse
He answered thus, with seeming-careless eye
Wandering from wall to roof:

                      'I like your Church:
Would it had rested upon firmer ground,
Adorned some airier height: its towers are good,
Though dark the stone: three quarries white have I;
You might have used them gratis had you willed:
At Ely, Elmham, and beside the Cam
Where Felix rears even now his cloistral Schools,
I trust to build three churches soon: my Queen,
That seconds still my wishes, says, "Beware
Lest overhaste, your people still averse,
Frustrate your high intent." A woman's wit—
Yet here my wife is wiser than her wont.
I miss your Bishop: grandly countenanced he,
Save for that mole. He shuns our revel:—ay!

Monastic virtue never feels secure
Save when it skulks in corners!' As he spake,
Despite that varnish on his brow clear-cut,
Stung by remembrance, from the tutored eye
Forth flashed the fire barbaric: race and heart
A moment stood confessed.
      Old Mellitus,
That night how fared he? In a fragile tent
Facing that church expectant, low he knelt
On the damp ground. More late, like youthful knight
In chapel small watching his arms untried,
He kept his consecration vigil still,
With hoary hands screening a hoary head,
And thus made prayer: 'Thou God to Whom all
  worlds
Form one vast temple: Thou Who with Thyself,
Ritual eterne, dost consecrate *that* Church,
For aye creating, hallowing it forever;
Thou Who in narrowest heart of man or child
Makest not less Thy dwelling, turn Thine eyes
To-morrow on our rite. The work we work
Work it Thyself! Thy storm shall try it well;
Consummate first its strength in righteousness;
So shall beginning just, whate'er befall,
Or guard it, or restore.'
      So prayed the man,
Nor ever raised his head—saw nought—heard
  nought—
Nor knew that on the night had come a change,
Ill Spirits, belike, whose empire is the air,
Grudging its glories to that pile new raised,
And, while they might, assailing. Through the
  clouds
A panic-stricken moon stumbled and fled,

And wildly on the waters blast on blast
Ridged their dark floor. A spring-tide from the sea
Breasted the flood descending. Woods of Shene
And Hampton's groves had heard that flood all day,
No more a whisperer soft; and meadow banks
Not yet o'er-gazed by Windsor's crested steep
Or Reading's tower, had yielded to its wave
Blossom and bud. More high, near Oxenford,
Isis and Cherwell with precipitate stream
Had swelled the current. Gathering thus its strength
Far off and near, allies and tributaries
That night by London onward rolled the Thames
Beauteous and threatening both.
      Its southern bank
Fronting the church had borne a hamlet long
Where fishers dwelt. Upon its verge that night
Perplexed the eldest stood: his hand was laid
Upon the gunwale of a stranded boat;
His knee was crooked against it. Shrinking still
And sad, his eye pursued that racing flood,
Here black like night, dazzled with eddies there,
Eddies by moonshine glazed. In doubt he mused:
Sudden a Stranger by him stood and spake:
'Launch forth, and have no fear.' The fisher gazed
Once on his face; and launched. Beside the helm
That Stranger sat. Then lo! a watery lane
Before them opening, through the billows curved,
Level, like meadow-path. As when a weed
Drifts with the tide, so softly o'er that lane
Oarless the boat advanced, and instant reached
The northern shore, dark with that minster's shade;—
Before them close it frowned.
      'Where now thou stand'st
Abide thou:' thus the Stranger spake; anon

Before the church's southern gate he stood :—
Then lo ! a marvel. Inward as he passed,
Its threshold crossed, a splendour as of God
Forth from the bosom of that dusky pile
Through all its kindling windows streamed, and blazed
From wave to wave, and spanned that downward tide
With many a fiery bridge. The moon was quenched;
But all the edges of the headlong clouds
Caught up the splendour till the midnight vault
Shone like the noon. The fisher knew, that hour,
That with vast concourse of the Sons of God
That church was thronged; for in it many a head
Sun-bright, and hands lifted like hands in prayer,
High up he saw : meantime harmonic strain,
As though whatever moves in earth or skies,
Winds, waters, stars, had joined in one their song,
Above him floated like a breeze from God
And heaven-born incense. Louder swelled that strain;
And still the Bride of God, that church late dark,
Glad of her saintly spousals, laughed and shone
In radiance ever freshening. By degrees
That vision waned. At last the fisher turned :
The matin star shook on the umbered wave;
Along the East there lay a pallid streak,
That streak which preludes dawn.
      Beside the man
Once more that Stranger stood :—' Seest thou yon tent ?
My Brother kneels within it. Thither speed
And bid him know I sent thee, speaking thus,
" He whom the Christians name ' the Rock ' am I :
My Master heard thy prayer : I sought thy church,
And sang myself her Consecration rite :
Close thou that service with thanksgiving psalm." '

Thus spake the Stranger, and was seen no more:
But whether o'er the waters, as of old
Footing that Galilean Sea, with faith
Not now infirm he reached the southern shore,
Or passed from sight as one whom crowds conceal
The fisher knew not.   At the tent arrived,
Before its little door he bent, and lo!
Within, there knelt a venerable man
With hoary hands screening a hoary head,
Who prayed, and prayed.   His tale the fisher told:
With countenance unamazed, yet well content
That kneeler answered, 'Son, thy speech is true!
Hence, and announce thy tidings to the King,
Who leaves his couch but now.'
                        'How beautiful'—
That old man sang, as down the Thames at morn
In multitudinous pomp the barges dropped,
Following those twain that side by side advanced,
One royal, one pontific, bearing each
The Cross in silver blazoned or in gold—
'How beautiful, O Sion, are thy courts!
Lo, on thy brow thy Maker's name is writ:
Fair is this place and awful; porch of heaven:
Behold, God's Church is founded on a rock:
It stands, and shall not fall: the gates of Hell
Shall not prevail against it.'
                        From the barge
Of Sebert and his Queen, antiphonal
Rapturous response was wafted: 'I beheld
Jerusalem, the City sage and blest;
From heaven I saw it to the earth descending
In sanctity gold-vested, as a Bride
Decked for her Lord.   I heard a voice which sang,
Behold the House where God will dwell with men:

And God shall wipe the tears from off their face;
And death shall be no more.'
                      Old Thames that day
Brightened with banners of a thousand boats
Winnowed by winds flower-scented. Countless hands
Tossed on the brimming river chaplets wov'n
On mead or hill, or branches lopped in woods
With fruit-bloom red, or white with clustering
    cone,
Changing clear stream to garden. Mile on mile
Now song was heard, now bugle horn that died
Gradual 'mid sedge and reed. Alone the swan
High on the western waters kept aloof;
Remote she eyed the scene with neck thrown back,
Her ancient calm preferring, and her haunt
Crystalline still. Alone the Julian Tower
Far down the eastern stream, though tap'stries waved
From every window, every roof o'er-swarmed
With anthem-echoing throngs, maintained, unmoved,
Roman and Stoic, her Cæsarean pride:
On Saxon feasts she fixed a cold, grey gaze;
'Mid Christian hymns heard but the old acclaim—
'Consul Romanus.'
                  When the sun had reached
Its noonday height, a people and its king
Around their minster pressed. With measured tread
And Introit chanted, up the pillared nave
Reverent they moved: then knelt. Between their
    ranks
Their Bishop last advanced with mitred brow
And in his hand the Cross, at every step
Signing the benediction of his Lord.
The altar steps he mounted. Turning then
Westward his face to that innumerous host,

Thus spake he unastonished: 'Sirs, ere now
This Church's Consecration rite was sung :—
Be ours to sing thanksgiving to our God,
" Ter-Sanctus," and " Te Deum." '

THE PENANCE OF SAINT LAURENCE.

Eadbald, King of Kent, persecuting the Church, Laurence the Bishop deems himself the chief of sinners because he has consented, like the neighbouring bishops, to depart; but, being consoled by a wonderful reprimand, faces the King, and offers himself up to death. The King reproves them that gave him evil counsel.

THE day was dying on the Kentish downs
And in the oakwoods by the Stour was dead.
While sadly shone o'er snowy plains of March
Her comfortless, cold star. The daffodil
That year was past its time. The leaden stream
Had waited long that lamp of river-beds
Which, when the lights of Candlemas are quenched,
Looks forth through February mists. A film
Of ice lay brittle on the shallows: dark
And swift the central current rushed: the wind
Sighed through the tawny sedge.
                              'So fleets our life—
Like yonder gloomy stream; so sighs our age—
Like yonder sapless sedge!' Thus Laurence mused
Standing on that sad margin all alone,
His twenty years of gladsome English toil
Ending at last abortive. 'Stream well-loved,
Here on thy margin standing saw I first,
My head by chance uplifting from my book,

King Ethelbert's strong countenance; he is dead;
And, next him, riding through the April gleams,
Bertha, his Queen, with face so lit by love
Its lustre smote the beggar as she passed
And changed his sigh to song. She too is dead;
And half their thanes that chased the stag that day,
Like echoes of their own glad bugle-horn,
Have passed and are not. Why must I abide?
And why must age, querulous and coward both,
Past days lamenting, fear not less that stroke
Which makes an end of grief? Base life of man!
How sinks thy slow infection through our bones;
Then when you fawned upon us, high-souled youth
Heroic in its gladness, spurned your gifts,
Yearning for noble death. In age, in age
We kiss the hand that nothing holds but dust,
Murmuring, "Not yet!"'

                    A tear, ere long ice-glazed,
Hung on the old man's cheek. 'What now remains?'
Some minutes passed; then, lifting high his head,
He answered, 'God remains.' His faith, his heart,
Were unsubverted. 'Twas the weight of grief,
The exhausted nerve, the warmthless blood of age,
That pressed him down like sin, where sin was none—
Not sin, but weakness only. Long he mused,
Then slowly walked, and feebly, through the woods
Towards his house monastic. Vast it loomed
Through ground-fog seen; and vaster, close beside,
That convent's church by great Augustine reared
Where once old woodlands clasped a temple old,
Vaunt of false Gods. To Peter and to Paul
That church was dedicate, albeit so long
High o'er the cloudy rack of fleeting years
It bore, and bears, its founder's name, not theirs.

Therein that holy founder slept in Christ,
And Ethelbert, and Bertha. All was changed:
King Eadbald, new-crowned and bad of life
Who still, whate'er was named of great or good,
Made answer, 'Dreams! I say the flesh rules all!'
Hated the Cross. His Queen, that portent crowned,
She that with name of wife was yet no wife,
Abhorred that Cross and feared. A Baptist new
In that Herodian court had Laurence stood,
Commanding, 'Put the evil thing away!'
Since then the woman's to the monarch's hate
Had added strength—the serpent's poison-bag
Venoming the serpent's fang. 'Depart the realm!'
With voice scarce human thus the tyrant cried,
'Depart or die!' and gave the Church's goods
To clown and boor.
     Upon the bank of Thames
Settled like ruin. Holy Sebert dead,
In that East Saxon kingdom monarch long,
Three sons unrighteous now their riot held.
Frowning upon the Christian Church they strode,
Full-armed, and each, with far-stretched foot firm set
Watching the Christian rite. 'Give us,' they cried,
While knelt God's children at their Paschal Feast,
'Give us those circlets of your sacred bread:
Ye feed therewith your beggars; kings are we!'
The Bishop answered, 'Be, like them, baptized,
Sons of God's Church, His Sacrament with man,
For that cause Mother of Christ's Sacraments,
So shall ye share her Feast.' With lightning speed
Their swords leaped forth; contemptuous next they
  cried,
'For once we spare to sweep a witless head
From worthless shoulders. Ere to-morrow's dawn

Hence, nor return!'   He sped to Rochester:
Her bishop, like himself, was under ban:
The twain to Canterbury passed, and there
Resolved to let the tempest waste its wrath,
And crossed the seas.   By urgency outworn,
'Gainst that high judgment of his holier will
Laurence to theirs deferred, but tarried yet
For one day more to cast a last regard
On regions loved so long.
                              As compline ceased
He reached the abbey gates, and entered in:
Sadly the brethren looked him in the face,
Yet no one said, 'Take comfort!'   Sad and sole
He passed to the Scriptorium: round he gazed,
And thought of happy days, when Gregory,
One time their Abbot, next their Pope, would send
Some precious volume to his exiled sons,
While they in reverence knelt, and kissed its edge,
And, kissing, heard once more, as if in dream,
Gregorian chants through Roman palm trees borne
With echoes from the Coliseum's wall
Adown that Cœlian Hill; and saw God's poor
At feast around that humble board which graced
That palace senatorial once.   He stood:
He raised a casket from an open chest,
And from that casket drew a blazoned scroll,
And placed it on the window-sill up-sloped
Breast-high, and faintly warmed by sinking sun;
Then o'er it bent a space.
                              With sudden hands
The old man raised that scroll; aloud he read:
'I, Ethelbert the King, and all my Thanes,
Honouring the Apostle Peter, cede to God
This Abbey and its lands.   If heir of mine

Cancel that gift, when Christ with angels girt
Makes way to judge the Nations of this world,
His name be cancelled from the Book of Life.'
The old man paused; then read the signatures,
'I, Ethelbert, of Kent the King.' Who next?
'I, Eadbald, his son;' to these succeeding,
'I, Hennigisil, Duke;' 'I, Hocca, Earl.'—
'Can such things be?' Around the old man's brow
The veins swelled out; dilated nostril, mouth
Working as mouth of him that tasteth death,
With what beside is wiselier unrevealed,
Witnessed that agony which spake no more;
He dashed the charter on the pavement down;
Then on it gazed a space.
                          Remembering soon
Whose name stood first on that dishonoured list,
Contrite he raised that charter to his breast,
And pressed it there in silence. Hours went by;
Then dark was all that room, and dark around
The windy corridors and courts stone-paved;
And bitter blew the blast: his unlooped cloak
Fell loose: the cold he noted not. At last
A brother passed the door with lamp in hand:
Dazzled, he started first: then meekly spake,
'Beseech the brethren that they strew my bed
Within the church. Until the second watch
There must I fast, and pray.'
                            The brethren heard,
And strewed his couch within the vast, void nave,
A mat and deer-skin, and, more high, that stone
The old head's nightly pillow. Echoes faint
Ere long of their receding footsteps died
While from the dark fringe of a rainy cloud
An ice-cold moon, ascending, streaked the church

With gleam and gloom alternate. On his knees
Meantime that aged priest was creeping slow
From stone to stone, as when on battle-plain,
The battle lost, some warrior wounded sore
By all forsaken, or some war-horse maimed
Drags a blind bulk along the fields in search
Of thirst-assuaging spring. Glittered serene
That light before the Sacrament of Love:
Thither he bent his way, and long time prayed:
Thence onward crept to where King Ethelbert
Slept, marble-shrined—his ashes, not the King,
Yet ashes kingly since God's temple once,
And waiting God's great day. Before that tomb,
Himself as rigid, with lean arms outspread,
Thus made the man his moan:

      'King Ethelbert!
Hear'st thou in glory? Ofttimes on thy knees
Thou mad'st confession of thine earthly sins
To me, a wounded worm this day on earth:
Now comforted art thou, and I brought low:
Yet, though I see no more that beaming front
And haply for my sins may see it never
Yet inwardly I gladden, knowing this
That thou art glad. Perchance thou hear'st me not
For thou wert still a heedless man of mirth,
Though sage as strong at need. If this were so,
Not less thy God would hear my prayer to thee
And grant it in thy reverence. Ethelbert!
Thou had'st thy trial time, since, many a year
All shepherdless thy well-loved people strayed
What time thyself, their shepherd, knew'st not Christ,
Sole shepherd of man's race. King Ethelbert!
Rememberest thou that day in Thanet Isle?
That day the Bride of God on English shores

Set her pure foot; and thou didst kneel to kiss it:
Thou gav'st her meat and drink in kingly wise;
Gav'st her thy palace for her bridal bower;
This Abbey build'dst—her fortress! O those days
Crowned with such glories, with such sweetness winged!
Thou saw'st thy realm made one with Christ's: thou
    saw'st
Thy race like angels ranging courts of Heaven:
This day, behold, thou seest the things thou seest!
If there be any hope, King Ethelbert
Help us this day with God!'
                      Upon his knees
Then crept that exile old to Bertha's tomb,
And there made moan: 'Thou tenderest Queen and
    sweetest,
Whom no man ever gazed on save with joy
Or spake of, dead, save weeping! Well I know
That on thee in thy cradle Mary flung
A lily whiter from her hand, a rose
Warm from her breath and breast, for all thy life
Was made of Chastities and Charities:
This hour thine eyes are on that Vision bent
Whereof the radiance, ere by thee beheld,
Gave thee thine earthly brightness. Mirrored there,
Seest thou, like mote in sunbeam well-nigh lost,
Our world of temporal anguish? See it not!
For He alone, the essential Peace Eterne
Could see it unperturbed. In Him rejoice!
Yet, 'mid thy heavenly triumph, plead, O plead
For hearts that break below!'
                      Upon the ground
Awhile that man sore tried his forehead bowed;
Then raised it till the frore and foggy beam
Mixed with his wintry hair. Once more he crept

Upon his knees through shadow; reached at length
His toilsome travel's last and dearest bourn,
The grave of Saint Augustine.   O'er it lay
The Patriarch's statued semblance as in sleep:
He knew it well, and found it, though to him
In darkness lost and veil beside of tears,
With level hands grazing those upward feet
Oft kissed, yet ne'er as now.

       'Farewell forever!
Farewell, my Master, and farewell, my friend!
Since ever thou in heaven abid'st—and I——
Gregory the Pontiff from that Roman Hill
Sent thee to work a man's work far away,
And manlike didst thou work it.   Prince, yet child,
Men saw thee, and obeyed thee.   O'er the earth
Thy step was regal, meekness of thy Christ
Weighted with weight of conquerors and of kings:
Men saw a man who toiled not for himself
Yet never ceased from toil; who warred on Sin;
Had peace with all beside.   In happy hour
God laid his holy hand upon thine eyes:
I knelt beside thy bed: I leaned mine ear
Down to thy lips to catch their last; in vain:
Yet thou perchance wert murmuring in thy heart
"I leave my staff within no hireling's hand;
Therefore my work shall last."   Ah me!   Ah me!
There was a Laurence once on Afric's shore:
He with his Cyprian died.   I too, methinks,
Had shared—how gladly shared—my Bishop's doom.
Father, with Gregory pray this night!   That God
Who promised, "for my servant David's sake,"
Even yet may hear thy prayer.'

       Thus wept the man,
Till o'er him fell half slumber.   Soon he woke

And, from between that statue's marble feet
Lifting a marble face, in silence crept
To where far off his bed was strewn, and drew
The deer-skin covering o'er him. With its warmth
Deep sleep, that solace of lamenting hearts
Which makes the waking bitterer, o'er him sank,
Nor wholly left him, though in sleep he moaned
When from the neighbouring farm, an hour ere dawn,
The second time rang out that clarion voice
Which bids the Christian watch.
       As thus he lay
T'wards him there moved in visions of the Lord
A Venerable Shape, compact of light,
And loftier than our mortal. Near arrived,
That mild, compassionate Splendour shrank his beam,
Or healed with strengthening touch the gazer's eyes
Made worthier of such grace ; and Laurence saw
Princedom not less than his, the Apostles' Chief,
To whom the Saviour answered, ' Rock art thou,'
And later—crowning Love, not less than Faith—
' Feed thou My Sheep, My Lambs ! ' He knew that
  shape
For oft, a child 'mid catacombs of Rome
And winding ways girt by the martyred dead
His eyes had seen it. Pictured on those vaults
Stood Peter, Moses of the Christian Law,
Figured in one that by the Burning Bush
Unsandalled knelt, or drew with lifted hand
The torrent from the rock, yet wore not less
In aureole round his head the Apostle's name
'Petros,' and in his hand sustained the Keys:
Such shape once more he saw.
       ' And comest thou then
Long-waited, or with sceptre-wielding hand

Earthward to smite the unworthiest head on earth,
Or with the darker of those Keys thou bearest
Him from the synod of the Saints to shut
Who fled as flies the hireling? Let it be!
Not less in that bright City by whose gate
Warder thou sitt'st, my Master thou shalt see
Pacing the diamond terraces of God
And bastions jacinth-veined, my great Augustine,
When all who wrought the ill have passed to doom,
And all who missed the good. Nor walks he sole:
By him forever and forever pace
My Ethelbert, my Bertha! Who can tell
But in the on-sweeping centuries thrice or twice
These three may name my name?' He spake and wept.

  To whom the Apostolic Splendour thus:
'Live, and be strong: for those thou lovest in Christ
Not only in far years shall name thy name;
This day be sure that name they name in Christ:
Else wherefore am I here? Not thou alone
Much more in grief's bewilderment than fear
Hast from the right way swerved. Was I not strong?
I, from the first Elect and named anew?
I who received at first divine command
The Brother-band to strengthen; last to rule?
I who to Hebrew and to Gentile both
Flung wide the portals of the heavenly realm?
Was I not strong? Behold, thou know'st my fall!
A second fall was near. At Rome the sword
Against me raged. Forth by the Appian Way
I fled; and, past the gateway, face to face,
Him met Who up the steep of Calvary bare
For man's behoof the Cross. "Where goest Thou,
    Lord?"
I spake; then He: "I go to Rome, once more

To die for him who fears for Me to die."
To Rome returned I; and my end was peace.
Return thou too. Thy brethren have not sinned:
They fled, consentient with the Will Supreme:
Their names are written in the Book of Life:
Enough that He Who gives to each his part
Hath sealed thy sons and thee to loftier fates
Therefore more sternly tries. Be strong; be glad:
For strength from joyance comes.'
       The Vision passed:
The old man, seated on his narrow bed,
Rolled thrice his eyes around the vast, dim church,
Desiring to retain it. Vain the quest!
Yet still within his heart that Radiance lived:
The sweetness of that countenance fresh from God
Would not be dispossessed, but kindled there
Memorial dawn of brightness, more and more
Growing to perfect day: inviolate peace,
Such peace as heavenly visitants bequeath,
O'er-spread his spirit, gradual, like a sea:
Forth from the bosom of that peace upsoared
Hope, starry-crowned, and winged, that liberates oft
Faith, unextinct, though bound by Powers accursed
That o'er her plant the foot, and hold the chain—
Terror and Sloth. To noble spirits set free
Delight means gratitude. Thus Laurence joyed:
But soon, remembering that unworthy past,
Remorse succeeded, sorrow born of love,
Consoled by love alone. 'Ah! slave,' he cried,
'That, serving such a God, could'st dream of flight:
How many a babe too weak to lift his head
Is strong enough to die!' While thus he mused
The day-dawn reaching to his pallet showed
That Discipline, wire-woven, in ancient days

Guest of monastic bed.   He snatched it thence:
Around his bending neck and shoulders lean
In dire revenge he hurled it.   Spent at last,
Though late, those bleeding hands down dropped: the cheek
Sank on the stony pillow.   Little birds,
Low-chirping ere their songs began, attuned
Slumber unbroken.   In a single hour
He slept a long night's sleep.
       The rising sun
Woke him: but in his heart another sun,
New-risen serene with healing on its wings,
Outshone that sun in brightness.   'Mid the choir
His voice was loudest while they chanted lauds:
Brother to brother whispered, issuing forth,
'He walks in stature higher by a head
Than in the month gone by!'
       That day at noon
King Eadwald, intent to whiten theft
And sacrilege with sanctitudes of law,
Girt by his warriors and his Witena,
Enthronèd sat.   'What boots it?' laughed a thane;
'Laurence has fled! we battle with dead men!'
'Ay, ay,' the King replied, 'I told you oft
Sages can brag; your dreamer weaves his dream:
But honest flesh rules all!'   While thus they spake
Confusion filled the hall: through guarded gates
A priest advanced with mitre and with Cross,
A monk that seemed not monk, but prince disguised:
It was Saint Laurence.   As he neared the throne
The fashion of the tyrant's face was changed:
'Dar'st thou?' he cried, 'I deemed thee fled the realm—
What seek'st thou here?'   The Saint made answer,
  'Death.'

Calmly he told his tale; then ended thus:
'To me that sinful past is sin of one
Buried in years gone by. All else is dream
Save that last look the Apostle on me bent
Ere from my sight he ceased. I saw therein
The reflex of that wondrous last Regard
Cast by the sentenced Saviour of mankind
On one who had denied Him, standing cold
Beside the High Priest's gate. Like him, I wept;
His countenance wrought my penance, not his hand:
I scarcely felt the scourge.'
     King Eadbald
Drave back the sword half drawn, and round him stared;
Then sat as one amazed. He rose; he cried,
'Ulf! Kathnar! Strip his shoulders bare? If true
His tale, the brand remains!'
     Two chiefs stepped forth:
They dragged with trembling hand, and many a pause,
The external garb pontific first removed,
Dark, blood-stained garment from the bleeding flesh,
The old man kneeling. Once, and only once,
The monarch gazed on that disastrous sight,
Muttering, 'and yet he lives!' A time it was
Of swift transitions. Hearts, how proud soe'er,
Made not that boast—consistency in sin,
Though dark and rough accessible to Grace
As earth to vernal showers. With hands hard-
 clenched
The King upstarted: thus his voice rang out:
'Beware, who gave ill counsel to their King!
The royal countenance is against them set,
Ill merchants trafficking with his lesser moods!
Does any say the King wrought well of late,
Warring on Christ, and chasing hence His priests?

The man that lies shall die! This day, once more
I ratify my Father's oath, and mine,
To keep the Church in peace: and though I sware
To push God's monks from yonder monastery
And lodge therein the horses of the Queen,
Those horses, and the ill-persuading Queen,
Shall flee my kingdom, and the monks abide!
Brave work ye worked, my loose-kneed Witena,
This day, Christ's portion yielding to my wrath!
See how I prize your labours!' With his sword
He clave the red seal from the statute scroll
And stamped it under foot. Once more he spake,
Gazing with lion gaze from man to man:
'The man that, since my Father, Ethelbert,
Though monarch, stooped to common doom of men,
Hath filched from Holy Church fee-farm, or grange,
Sepulchral brass, gold chalice, bell or book,
See he restore it ere the sun goes down;
If not, he dies! Not always winter reigns;
May-breeze returns, and bud-releasing breath,
When hoped the least:—'tis thus with royal minds!'
He spake: from that day forth in Canterbury
Till reigned the Norman, crowned on Hastings' field,
God's Church had rest. In many a Saxon realm
Convulsion rocked her cradle: altars raised
By earlier kings by later were o'erthrown:
One half the mighty Roman work, and more,
Fell to the ground: Columba's Irish monks
The ruin raised. From Canterbury's towers,
'Rome of the North' long named, from them alone
Above sea-surge still shone that vestal fire
By tempest fanned, not quenched; and at her breast
For centuries six were nursed that Cœlian race,
The Benedictine Primates of the Land.

KING SIGEBERT OF EAST ANGLIA, AND HEIDA THE PROPHETESS.

Sigebert, King of East Anglia, moved by what he has heard from a Christian priest, consults the Prophetess Heida. In the doctrine he reports Heida recognises certain sacred traditions from the East, originally included in the Northern religion, and affirms that the new Faith is the fulfilment of the great Voluspá prophecy, the earliest record of that religion, which foretold the destruction both of the Odin-Gods and the Giant race, the restoration of all things, and the reign of Love.

Long time upon the late-closed door the King
Kept his eyes fixed. The wondrous guest was gone;
Yet, seeing that his words were great and sage
Compassionate for the sorrowful state of man
Yet sparing not man's sin, their echoes lived
Thrilling large chambers in the monarch's breast
Silent for many a year. Exiled in France
The mystery of the Faith had reached his ear
In word but not in power. The westering sun
Lengthened upon the palace floor its beam
Yet the strong hand which propped that thoughtful head
Sank not, nor moved. Sudden, King Sigebert
Arose and spake: 'I go to Heida's Tower:
Await ye my return.'
    The woods ere long
Around him closed. Upon the wintry boughs
An iron shadow pressed; and as the wind
Increased beneath their roofs an iron sound

Clangoured funereal.   Down their gloomiest aisle
With snow flakes white, the monarch strode till now
Before him, and not distant, Heida's Tower,
The Prophetess by all men feared yet loved
Smit by a cold beam from the yellowing west,
Shone like a tower of brass.   Her ravens twain
Crested the turrets of its frowning gate
Unwatched by warder.   Sigebert passed in:
Beneath the stony vault the queenly Seer
Sat on her ebon throne.
                            With pallid lips
The King rehearsed his tale; how one with brow
Lordlier than man's, and visionary eyes
Which, wander where they might, saw Spirits still
Had told him many marvels of some God
Mightier than Odin thrice.   He paused awhile:
A warning shadow came to Heida's brow:
Nathless she nothing spake.   The King resumed:
'He spake—that stranger—of the things he saw:
For he, his body tranced, it may be dead,
In spirit oft hath walked the Spirit-Land:
Thence, downward gazing, once he saw our earth
A little vale obscure; above it hung,
Those four great Fires that desolate mankind:
The Fire of Falsehood first; the Fire of Lust,
Ravening for weeds and scum; the Fire of Hate,
Hurling on war-fields brother-man 'gainst man;
The Fire of tyrannous Pride.   While yet he gazed,
Behold, those Fires, widening, commixed, then soared
Threatening the skies.   A Spirit near him cried
"Fear nought; for breeze-like pass the flames o'er him
In whom they won no mastery there below:
But woe to those who, charioted therein
Rode forth triumphant o'er the necks of men,

And had their day on earth. Proportioned flames
Of other edge shall try their work and them!"
Thus spake my guest: the frost wind smote his brows,
While on that moonlit crag we sat ice-cold
Yet down them, like the reaper's sweat at noon,
The drops of anguish streamed. Till then, methinks,
That thing Sin is I knew not.
       Calm of voice
Again he spake. He told me of his God:
That God, like Odin, is a God of War:
Who serve Him wear His armour day and night:
The maiden, nay, the child, must wield the sword;
Yet none may hate his neighbour. Thus he spake
That Prophet from far regions: "Wherefore wreck
Thy brother man? upon his innocent babes
Drag down the ruinous roof? Seek manlier tasks!
The death in battle is the easiest death:
Be yours the daily dying; lifelong death;
Death of the body that the soul may live.
War on the Spirits unnumbered and accurst
Which, rulers of the darkness of this world,
Drive, hour by hour, their lances through man's soul
That wits not of the wounding!"'
        Heida turned
A keen eye on the King: 'Whence came your guest?
Not from those sun-bright southern shores, I ween?'
He answered, 'Nay, from western isle remote
That Prophet came.' Then Heida's countenance fell:
'The West! the West! it should have been the East!
Conclude your tale: what saith your guest of God?'
The King replied: 'His God so loved mankind
That, God remaining, He became a man;
So hated sin that, sin to slay, He died.
One tear of His had paid the dreadful debt:—

Not so He willed it: thus He willed, to wake
In man, His lost one, quenchless hate of sin
Proportioned to the death-pang of a God;
Nor chose He lonely majesty of death:
'Twixt Sinners paired He died.'
       In Heida's eye
Trembled a tear. 'A dream was mine in youth,
When first the rose of girlhood warmed my cheek,
A dream of some great Sacrifice that claimed
Not praise—not praise—it only yearned to die
Helping the Loved. A maid alone, I thought,
Such sacrifice could offer.' As she spake,
She pressed upon the pale cheek, warmed once more,
Her cold, thin hand a moment.
       'Maiden-born
Was He, my guest revealed,' the King replied:
'Then from that Angel's "Hail," and her response,
"So be it unto me," when sinless doubt
Vanished in world-renewing, free consent,
He told the tale;—the Infant in the crib;
The shepherds o'er Him bowed'—with widening eyes
Heida, bent forward, saw like them that Child—
'The Star that lead the Magians from the East:'
'The East, the East! It should have been the East!'
Once more she cried; 'our race is from the East:
The Persian worshipped t'ward the rising sun:
You said, but now, the West.' The King resumed:
'God's priest was from the West; but in the East
The great Deliverer sprang.' Next, step by step,
Like herald panting forth in leaguered town
Tidings unhoped for of deliverance strange
Through victory on some battle-field remote,
The King rehearsed his theme, from that first Word,
'The Woman's Seed shall bruise the Serpent's head,'

Prime Gospel, ne'er forgotten in the East,
To Calvary's Cross, the Resurrection morn,
Lastly the great Ascension into heaven:
And ever as he spake on Heida's cheek
The red spot, deepening, spread; within her eyes
An unastonished gladness waxed more large:
Back to the marble woman came her youth:
Once more within her heaving breast it lived,
Once more upon her forehead shone, as when
The after-glow returns to Alpine snows
Left death-like by dead day. Question at times
She made, yet seemed the answer to foreknow.
That tale complete, low-toned at last she spake:
'Unhappy they to whom these things are hard!'
Then silent sat, and by degrees became
Once more that dreaded prophet, stern and cold.
The silence deeper grew: the sun, not set,
Had sunk beneath the forest's western ridge;
And jagged shadows tinged that stony floor
Whereon the monarch knelt. Slowly therefrom
He raised his head; then slowly made demand:
'Is he Apostate who discards old Faith?'

Long time in musings Heida sat, then spake:
'Yea, if that Faith discarded be the Truth:
Not so, if it be falsehood. God is Truth;
God-taught, true hearts discern that Truth, and
    guard it;
Whom God forsakes forsake it. O thou North,
That beat'st thy brand so loud against thy shield
Hearing nought else, what Truth one day was thine!
Behold within corruption's charnel vaults
It sleeps this day. What God shall lift its head?
We came from regions of the rising sun:

Scorning the temples built by mortal hand,
We worshipp'd God—one God—the Immense, All-
 Just:
That worship was the worship of great hearts:
Duty was worship then: that God received it:
I know not if benignly He received it;
If God be Love I know not. This I know,
God loves not priest that under roofs of gold
Lifts, in his right hand held, the Sacrifice;
The left, behind him, fingering for the dole.
King of East Anglia's realm, the primal Truths
Are vanished from our Faith: the ensanguined rite,
The insane carouse survive!'
       Thus Heida spake,
Heida, the strong one by the strong ones feared;
Heida the sad one by the mourners loved,
Heida, the brooder on the sacred Past,
The nursling of a Prophet House, the child
Of old traditions sage!
      She paused, and then
Milder, resumed: 'What moved thee to believe?'
And Sigebert made answer thus: 'The Sword:
For as a sword that Truth the stranger preached
Ran down into my heart.' Heida to him,
'Well saidst thou "as a Sword:" a Sword is Truth;—
As sharp a sword is Love: and many a time
In youth, but not the earliest, happiest youth,
When first I found that grief was in the world
Had learned how deep its root, an infant's wail
Went through me like a sword. Man's cry it seemed
The blindfold, crownèd creature's cry for Truth
His spirit's sole deliverer.'
        Once again
She mused and then continued, 'Truth and Love

Are gifts too great to give themselves for nought,
Exacting Gods. Within man's bleeding heart,
If e'er to man conceded, both shall lie
Crossed, like two swords—
Behold thine image, crowned Humanity!
Better such dower than life exempt from woe:
Our Fathers knew to suffer; joyed in pain;
They knew not this—how deep its root!'
                                        Once more
The Prophetess was mute: again she spake:
'How named thy guest his God?' The King replied:
'The Warrior God Who comes to judge the world;
The Lord of Love; the God Who wars on Sin,
And ceases not to war.' 'Ay, militant'
Heida rejoined, with eyes that shone like stars:
'The Persian knew Him. Ormuzd was His name:
Unpitying Light against the darkness warred;
Against the Light the Darkness. Could the Light
Remit, one moment's length, to pierce that gloom,
Himself in gloom were swallowed.'
                                    Yet again
In silence Heida sat; then cried aloud
'Odin, and all his radiant Æsir Gods
Forth thronging daily from the golden gates
Of Asgard City, their supernal house
War on that giant brood of Jötunheim,
Lodged 'mid their mountains of eternal ice
Which circles still that sea surrounding earth
Man's narrow home. I know that mystery now!
That warfare means the war of Good on Ill:
We shared that warfare once! This day, depraved,
Warring, we war alone for rage and hate;
Men fight as fight the lion and the pard:
For them the sanctity of war is lost

Lost like that kindred sanctity of Love,
Our household boast of old. The Father-God
Vowed us to battle but as Virtue's proof,
High test of softness scorned. *His* warrior knew
'Twas Odin o'er the battle field who sent
Pure-handed maiden Goddesses, the Norns,
Not vulture-like, but dove-like, mild as dawn,
To seal the foreheads of his sons elect
Seal them to death, the bravest with a kiss :
His warrior, arming, cried aloud, "This day
I speed five Heroes to Valhalla's Hall :
To-morrow night in love I share their Feast !"
He honoured whom he slew.'
       To her the King:
'That Stranger with severer speech than thine,
Sharp flail and stigma, charged the world with sin,
The vast, wide world, and not one race alone :
Each nation, he proclaimed, from Man's great stem
Issuing, had with it borne one Word divine
Rapt from God's starry volume in the skies,
Each word a separate Truth, that, angel-like,
Before them winging, on their faces flung
Splendour of destined morn, and led man's race
Triumphant long on virtue's road. Themselves
Had changed that True to False. The Judge had come ;
That Power Who both beginning is and end
Had stooped to earth to judge the earth with fire ;
A fire of Love, He came to cleanse the just ;
A fire of Vengeance, to consume the impure :
His fan is in His hand : the chaff shall burn ;
The grain be garnered. " Fall, high palace roofs "
He cried, "for ye have sheltered dens of sin :
Fall, he that, impious, scorned the First and Last ;
Fall, he that bowed not to the hoary head ;

Fall, he that loosed by fraud the maiden zone;
Fall, he that lusted for the poor man's field;
Fall, rebel Peoples; fall, disloyal Kings;
And fall" dread Mother, is the word offence?—
" False Gods, long served; for God Himself is nigh."'

The monarch ceased: on Heida's face that hour
He feared to look; but when she spake, her voice
Betrayed no passion of a soul perturbed:
Austere it was; not wrathful; these her words:
'Son, as I hearkened to thy tale this day
Memory returned to me of visions three
That lighted three great junctures of my life:
And thrice thy words were echoes strange of words
That shook my tender childhood slumbering half
Half-waked by matin beams—"The Gods must die."
Three times that awful sound was in mine ear:
Later I learned that voice was nothing new.
My Son, the earliest record of our Faith,
So sacred that on Runic stave or stone
None dared to grave it, lore from age to age
Transmitted by white lips of trembling seers
Spared not to wing, like arrow sped from God
That word to man, " Valhalla's Gods must die!"
The Gods and Giant Race that strove so long,
Met in their last and mightiest battle-field,
Must die, and die one death. That prophet-voice
The Gods have heard. Therefore they daily swell
Valhalla's Hall with heroes rapt from earth
To aid them in that fight.'
                              On Heida's face
At last the King, his head uplifting, gazed.
There where the inviolate calm had dwelt alone
A million thoughts, each following each, on swept,

That calm beneath them still, as when some grove
O'er-run by sudden gust of summer storm
With inly-working panic thrills at first,
Then springs to meet the gale while o'er it rush
Shadows with splendours mixed.   Upon her breast
Came down the fire divine.   With lifted hands
She stood: she sang a death-song centuries old
The dirge prophetic both of Gods and men:

'The iron age shall make an iron end:
The men who lived in hate, or impious love,
Shall meet in one red battle-field.   That day
The forests of the earth, blackening, shall die;
The stars down-fall; the Wingèd Hound of Heaven
That chased the Sun from age to age shall close
O'er it at last; the Ash Tree, Ygdrasil
Whose boughs o'er-roof the skies, whose roots descend
To Hell, whose leaves are lives of men, whose boughs
Are destined empires that o'er-awe the world,
Shall drop its fruit unripe.   The Midgard Snake
Circling that sea which girds the orb of earth,
Shall wake, and turn, and ocean in one wave
O'er-sweep all lands.   Thereon shall Naglfar ride,
The skeleton ship all ribbed with bones of men,
Whose sails are woven of night, and by whose helm
Stand the Three Fates.   When heaves that ship in sight
Then know the end draws nigh.'
                            She ceased; then spake:
'If any doubt, the Voluspá tells all,
The song the mystic maiden, Vola, sang,
Our first of prophets she, as I the last:
She sang that song no Prophet dared to write.'
   But Sigebert made answer where he knelt,

Old Faith back rushing blindly on his heart:
'Though man's last nation lay a wreath of dust,
Though earth were sea, not less in heaven the Gods
Would hold their revels still; Valhalla's Halls
Resound the Heroes' triumph!'
       Once again
Heida arose: once more her pallid face
Shone lightning-like, wan cheeks and flashing eyes;
Once more she sang: 'The Warder of the Gods,
Soundeth the Gjallar Trumpet, never heard
Before by Gods or mortals: from their feast
The everlasting synod of the Gods
Rush forth, gold-armed, with chariot and with horse:
First rides the Father of the flock divine,
Odin, our King, and, at his right hand, Thor
Whose thunder hammer splits the mountain crags
And level lays the summits of the world;
Heimdall and Bragi, Uller, Njord, and Tyr,
Behind them throng; with these the concourse huge
Of lesser Gods, and Heroes snatched from earth
Since man's first battle, part to bear with Gods
In this their greatest. From their halls of ice
To meet them stride the mighty Giant-Brood
The moving mountains of old Jötunheim,
Strong with all strengths of Nature, flood or fire,
Glacier, or stream volcanic from red hills
Cutting its way through billows;—on they throng
Topping the clouds, and, leagues before them, flinging
Huge shade, like shade of mountains cast o'er wastes
When sets the sun.' A little time she ceased;
Then fiercelier sang: 'Flanking that Giant-Brood
I see two Portents terrible as Sin:—
The Midgard Snake primeval at the right
With demon-crest as haughtily upheaved

As though all ocean curled into one wave,
A million rainbows braid that glooming arch;
And Death therein is mirrored. At the left,
On moves that brother Terror, wolf in shape,
Which, bound till now by craft of prescient Gods,
Weltered in Hell's abyss. Till came the hour
A single hair inwoven by heavenly hand
Sufficed to chain that monster to his rock;
His fast is over now; his dusky jaws
At last the Eternal Hunger lifts distent
As far as heaven from earth.'
       The Prophetess
One moment pressed her palms upon her eyes
Then flung them wide. 'The Father of the Gods
Our Odin, at that Portent hurls his lance;
And Thor, though bleeding fast, with hammer raised
Deals with that Serpent's scales.'
        'The Gods shall win,'
Shouted the King, forgetting at that hour
All save the strife, while on his brow there burned
Hue of the battle at the battle's height
When no man staunches wound. With voice serene
(The storm had left her) Heida made reply:
'If any doubt, the Voluspá tells all.
Ere yet Valhalla's lower heaven was shaped
Muspell, the great Third Heaven immeasurable,
Above it towered, throne of that God Supreme
Who knew beginning none and knows no end:
High on its southern cliff that dread One sits,
Nor ever from the South withdraws His gaze,
Nor ever drops that bright, sky-pointing Sword
Whose splendour dims the noontide sun. That God—
He, and the Spirit-Host that wing His light
When shines the Judgment Sign, shall stand on earth

And judge the earth with fire. Nor men nor Gods
Shall face that fire and live.'
       As Heida spake
The broad full moon above the forest soared
And changed her form to light. With hands out-
  stretched
She sang her last of songs: 'The Hour is come:
Bifrost, the rainbow-bridge 'twixt heaven and earth
Shatters; the crystal walls of heaven roll in:
Above the ruins ride the Sons of Light.
That dread One first—
Forth from His helm the intolerable beam
Strikes to the battle-field; the Giant-Brood
Die in that flame; and Odin, and his Gods:
Valhalla falls, and with it Jötunheim,
Its ice-piled mountains melting into waves:
In fire are all things lost!'
       Then wept the King:
'Alas for Odin and his brethren Gods
That in their great hands stayed the Northern Land!
Alas for man!' But Heida, with fixed face
Whereon there sat its ancient calm, replied:
'Nothing that lived but shall again have life,
Such life as Virtue claims. Ill-working men
With Loki and with Hela, evil Gods,
Shall dwell far down in Nåströnd's death-black pile
Compact of serpent scales, whose thousand gates
Face to the North, blinded by endless storm;
But from the sea shall rise a happier earth,
Holier and happier. There the good and true
Secure shall gladden, and the fiery flame
Harm them no more. Another Asgard there
Where stood that earlier, ere our fathers left
Their native East, shall lift sublimer towers

Dawn-lighted by a loftier Ararat:
Just men and pure shall pace its palmy steeps
With him of race divine yet human heart,
Baldur upon whose beaming front the Gods
Gazing, exulted; from whose lips mankind
Shall gather counsel. Hand in hand with him
Shall stand the blind God, Hödur, now not blind,
That, witless, slew him with the mistletoe,
Yet loved him well. Others, both men and Gods
That dread Third Heaven attained, shall make abode
With Him Who ever is, and ever was,
Enthroned like Him upon its southern cliff,
Drinking the light immortal. From beneath
Like winds from flowery wildernesses borne,
The breath of all good deeds and virtuous thoughts
Their own, or others', since the worlds were made
All generous sufferings, o'er their hearts shall hang,
Fragrance perpetual; and, where'er they gaze
The Vision of their God shall on them shine.'

Thus Heida spake, and ceased; then added, 'Son,
Our Faith shall never suffer wreck: fear nought!
Fulfilment, not Destruction, is its end.
But thou return, and bid thy herald guest
Who sought thee, wandering from his westward Isle
Approach my gates at dawn, and in mine ear
Divulge his message to this land. Farewell!'

Then from his knees the monarch rose, and took
Through the huge moonlit woods his homeward way.

KING SIGEBERT OF ESSEX, OR A FRIEND AT NEED.

Sigebert, King of Essex, labours with Cedd the Bishop for the conversion of his people; but he feasts with a certain impious kinsman; and it is foretold to him that for that sin, though pardoned, he shall die by that kinsman's hand. This prophecy having been accomplished, Cedd betakes himself to Lastingham, there to pray with his three brothers for the King's soul. His prayer is heard, and in a few days he dies. Thirty of Cedd's monks, issuing from Essex to pray at his grave, die also, and are buried in a circle round it.

'At last, resolve, my brother, and my friend!
Fling from you, as I fling this cloak, your Gods
And cleave to Him the Eternal, One and Sole,
The All-Wise, All-Righteous and Illimitable,
Who made us, and will judge.' Thus Oswy spake
To Sigebert, his friend, of Essex King
Essex once Christian. Royal Sebert dead,
The church of God had sorrow by the Thames:
Three Pagan brothers in his place held sway:
They warred upon God's people; for which cause
God warred on them and by the Wessex sword
In one day hewed them down. King Sigebert
Throned in their place, to Oswy thus replied:
'O friend, I saw the Truth, yet saw it not!
'Twas like the light forth flashed from oar remote,
Now vivid, vanished now. Not less, methinks
Thy Christ ere now had won me save for this;
I feared that in my bosom love for thee
Not Truth alone, prevailed. I left thy court;

I counselled with my wisest; by degrees,
Though grieving thus to outrage loyal hearts
Reached my resolve: henceforth I serve thy God:
My kingdom may renounce me if it will.'
Then came the Bishop old, and nigh that Wall
Which spans the northern land from sea to sea
Baptized him to the God Triune. At night
The King addressed him thus: 'My task is hard;
Yield me four priests of thine from Holy Isle
To shape my courses.' Finan gazed around
And made election—Cedd and others three;
He consecrated Cedd with staff and ring;
And by the morning's sunrise Sigebert
Rode with them, face to south.
      The Spring, long checked,
Fell, like God's Grace, or fire, or flood, at once
O'er all the land: it swathed the hills in green;
It fringed with violets cleft and rock; illumed
The stream with primrose tufts: but mightier far
That Spring which triumphed in the monarch's breast,
All doubt dispelled. That smile which knew not
 cause
Looked like his angel's mirrored on his face:
At times he seemed with utter gladness dazed;
At times he laughed aloud. 'Father,' he cried,
'That darkness from my spirit is raised at last:
Ah fool! ah fool! to wait for proof so long!
Unseal thine eyes, and all things speak of God:
The snows on yonder thorn His pureness show;
Yon golden iris bank His love. But now
I marked a child that by its father ran:
Some mystery they seemed of love in heaven
Imaged in earthly love.' With sad, sweet smile
The old man answered: 'Pain there is on earth—

Bereavement, sickness, death.' The King replied:
'It was by suffering, not by deed, or word
God's Son redeemed mankind.' Then answered Cedd:
'God hath thee in His net; and well art thou!
That Truth thou seest this day and feelest, live!
So shall it live within thee. If, more late,
Rebuke should come, or age, remember then
This day-spring of thy strength and answer thus,
"With me God feasted in my day of youth:
So feast He now with others!"'
                                        Years went by,
And Cedd in work and word was mighty still
And throve with God. The strong East Saxon race
Grew gentle in his presence: they were brave
And faith is courage in the things divine,
Courage with meekness blent. The heroic heart
Beats to the spiritual cognate, paltering not
Fraudulent with Truth once known. Like winds from
     God
God's message on them fell. Old bonds of sin
Snapt by the vastness of the growing soul
Burst of themselves; and in the heart late bound
Virtue had room to breathe. As when that Voice
Primeval o'er the formless chaos rolled,
And, straight, confusions ceased, the greater orb
Ruling the day, the lesser, night; even so,
Born of that Bethlehem Mystery, Order lived:
Divine commandments fixed a firmament
Betwixt man's lower instincts and his mind:
From unsuspected summits of his Spirit
The morning shone. The nation with the man
Partook the joy: from duty freedom flowed;
And there where tribes had roved a People lived.
A pathos of strange beauty hung thenceforth

O'er humblest hamlet: he who passed it prayed
'May never sword come here!' Bishop and King
Together laboured: well that Bishop's love
Repaid that royal zeal. If random speech
Censured the King, though justly, sudden red
Circling the old man's silver-tressèd brow
Showed, though he spake not, that in saintly breast
The human heart lived on.
                              In Ithancester
He dwelt, and toiled: not less to Lindisfarne,
His ancient home in spirit oft he yearned
Longing for converse with his God alone;
And made retreat there often, not to shun
Labour allotted, but to draw from heaven
Strength for his task. One year, returning thence,
Deira's King addressed him as they rode:
'My father, choose the richest of my lands
And build thereon a holy monastery;
So shall my realm be blessed, and I, and mine.'
He answered: 'Son, no wealthy lands for us!
Spake not the prophet: "There where dragons roamed,
In later days the grass shall grow—the reed"?
I choose those rocky hills that, on our left
Drag down the skiey waters to the woods:
Such loved I from my youth; to me they said,
"Bandits this hour usurp our heights, and beasts
Cumber our caves: expel the seed accurst,
And yield us back to God!"'
                              The King gave ear;
And Cedd within those mountains passed his Lent,
Driving with prayer and fast the Spirits Accurst
With ignominy forth. Foundations next
He laid with sacred pomp. Fair rose the walls:
All day the March sea blew its thunder blasts

Through wide-mouthed trumpets of ravine or rift
On winding far to where in wooden cell
The old man prayed, while o'er him rushed the cloud
Storm borne from crag to crag. Serener breeze,
With alternation soft in Nature's course,
Following ere long, great Easter's harbinger,
Thus spake he; 'I must keep the Feast at home;
My children there expect me.' Parting thence,
He left his brothers three to consummate
His work begun, Celin, and Cynabil,
And Chad at Lichfield Bishop ere he died.
Thus Lastingham had birth.
                              Beside the Thames
Meantime dark deeds were done. There dwelt two
    thanes,
The kinsmen of the King, his friends in youth,
Of meanest friend unworthy. Far and wide
They ravined, and the laws of God and man
Despised alike. Three times, in days gone by,
A warning hand their Bishop o'er them raised;
The fourth like bolt from heaven on them it fell,
And clave them from God's Church. They heeded
    not:
And now the elder kept his birthday feast,
Summoning his friends around him, first the King.
Doubtful and sad, the o'er-gentle monarch mused:
'To feast with sinners is to sanction sin,
A deed abhorred; the alternative is hard:
Must then their sovereign shame with open scorn
Kinsman and friend? I think they mourn the past,
And, were our Bishop here, would pardon sue.'
Boding, yet self-deceived, he joined that feast:
Thereat he saw scant sign of penitence:
Ere long he bade farewell.

       That self-same hour
Cedd from his northern pilgrimage returned;
The monarch met him at the offenders' gate,
And, instant when he saw that reverend face,
His sin before him stood. Down from his horse
Leaping, he told him all, and penance prayed.
Long time the old man on that royal front
Fixed a sad eye. 'Thy sin was great, my son,
Shaming thy God to spare a sinner's shame:
That sin thy God forgives and I remit:
But those whom God forgives He chastens oft:
My son, I see a sign upon thy brow!
Ere yonder lessening moon completes her wane
Behold, the blood-stained hand late clasped in thine
Shall drag thee to thy death.' The King replied:
' A Sigebert there lived, East Anglia's King,
Whose death was glorious to his realm. May mine,
Dark and inglorious, strengthen hearts infirm,
And profit thus my land.'
       A time it was
When Christian mercy judged by Pagan hearts
Not virtue seemed but sin. That sin's reproach
The King had long sustained. Ere long it chanced
That, near the stronghold of that impious feast,
A vanquished rebel, long in forests hid
Drew near, and knelt to Sigebert for grace
And won his suit. The monarch's kinsmen twain,
Those men of blood, forth-gazing from a tower
Saw all; heard all. Upon them fury fell,
As when through cloudless skies there comes a blast
From site unknown, that, instant, finds its prey,
Circling some white-sailed bark or towering tree
And, with a touch, down-wrenching; all things
  else

Unharmed, though near. They snatched their daggers
    up,
And rushed upon their prey, and, shouting thus
'White-livered slave, that mak'st thy throne a jest
And mock'st great Odin's self, and us thy kin,
To please thy shaveling' struck him through the heart;
Then, spurring through the woodlands to the sea,
Were never heard of more.
                  Throughout the land
Lament was made; lament in every house,
As though in each its eldest-born lay dead;
Lament far off and near. The others wept:
Cedd, in long vigils of the lonely night,
Not wept alone, but lifted strength of prayer
And, morn by morn, that Sacrifice Eterne,
Mightier tenfold in impetrative power
Than prayers of all man's race, from Adam's first
To his who latest on the Judgment Day
Shall raise his hands to God. Four years went by:
That mourner's wound they staunched not. Oft in
    sleep
He murmured low, 'Would I had died for thee!'
And once, half-waked by rush of morning rains,
'Why saw I on his brow that fatal sign?—
He might have lived till now!' Within his heart
At last there rose a cry, 'To Lastingham!
Pray with thy brothers three, for saints are they:
So shall thy friend, who resteth in the Lord
With perfect will submiss, the waiting passed,
Gaze on God's Vision with an eye unsealed,
In glory everlasting.' At that thought
Peace on the old man settled. Staff in hand
Forth on his way he fared. Nor horse he rode
Nor sandals wore. He walked with feet that bled,

Paying, well pleased, that penance for his King;
And murmured ofttimes, 'Not my blood alone!
Nay, but my life, my life!'
                              Yet penance pain
Like pain of suffering Souls at peace with God,
Quelled not that gladness which, from secret source
Rising, o'erflowed his heart. Old times returned:
Once more beside him rode his King in youth
Southward to where his realm—his duty—lay,
Exulting captive of the Saviour Lord,
With face love-lit. As then, the vernal prime
Hourly with ampler respiration drew
Delight of purer green from balmier airs:
As then the sunshine glittered. By their path
Now hung the woodbine; now the hare-bell waved;
Rivulets new-swollen by melted snows, and birds
'Mid echoing boughs with rival rapture sang:
At times the monks forgat their Christian hymns,
By humbler anthems charmed. They gladdened more
Beholding oft in cottage doors cross-crowned
Angelic faces, or in lonely ways;
Once as they passed there stood a little maid,
Some ten years old, alone 'mid lonely pines,
With violet crowned and primrose. Who were those,
The forest's white-robed guests, she nothing knew;
Not less she knelt. With hand uplifted Cedd
Signed her his blessing. Hand she kissed in turn;
Then waved, yet ceased not from her song, 'Alone
Two lovers sat at sunset.'
                              Every eve
Some village gave the wanderers food and rest,
Or half-built convent with its church thick-walled
And polished shafts, great names in after times
Ely, and Croyland, Southwell, Medeshamstede,

Adding to sylvan sweetness holier grace
Or rising lonely o'er morass and mere
With bowery thickets isled where dogwood brake
Retained, though late, its red. To Boston near
Where Ouse, and Aire, and Derwent join with Trent,
And salt sea waters mingle with the fresh
They met a band of youths that o'er the sands
Advanced with psalm, cross-led. The monks rejoiced,
Save one from Ireland—Dicul. He, quick-eared
Had caught that morn a war-cry on the wind
And, sideway glancing from his Office-book,
Descried the cause. From Mercia's realm a host
Had crossed Northumbria's bound. His thin, worn face
O'er-flamed with sudden anger, thus he cried:
' In this, your land, men say, "Who worketh prayeth,"
In mine we say, " Well prays who fighteth well :"
A Pagan race treads down your homesteads! Slaves,
That close not with their throats ! '
        Advancing thus,
On the tenth eve they came to Lastingham :
Forth rushed the brethren, watching long far off
To meet them, first the brothers three of Cedd
Who kissed him, cheek and mouth. Gladly that night
Those foot-worn travellers laid them down and slept
Save one alone. Old Cedd his vigil made
And, kneeling by the tabernacle's lamp
Prayed for the man he mourned for, ending thus :
' Thou Lord of Souls, to Thee the Souls are dear !
Thou yearn'st toward them as they yearn to Thee ;
Behold, not prayer alone for him I raise :
I offer Thee my life.' When morning's light
In that great church commingled with its gloom,
The monks, slow-pacing, by that kneeler knelt,

And prayed for Sigebert, beloved of God;
And lastly offered Mass: and it befell
That when, the Offering offered, and the Dead
Rightly remembered, he who sang that Mass
Had reached the 'Nobis quoque famulis,'
There came to Cedd an answer from the Lord
Heard in his heart; and he beheld his King
Throned 'mid the Saints Elect of God who keep
Perpetual triumph, and who see that Face
Which to its likeness hourly more compels
Those faces t'ward It turned. That function o'er,
Thus spake the Bishop: 'Brethren, sing "Te Deum;"'
They sang it; while within him he replied,
' Lord, let Thy servant now depart in peace.'

A week passed by with gladness winged and prayer.
In wonder Cedd beheld those structures new
From small beginnings reared, though many a gift
Sent for that work's behoof, had fed the poor
In famine time laid low. Moorlands he saw
By cornfields vanquished; marked the all-beauteous
    siege
Of pasture yearly threatening loftier crags
Loud with the bleat of lambs. Their shepherd once
Had roved a bandit, next had toiled a slave,
Now with both hands he poured his weekly wage
Down on his young wife's lap, his pretty babes
Gambolling around for joy. A hospital
Stood by the convent's gate. With moistened eye
Musing on Him Who suffers in His sick,
The Bishop paced it. There he found his death:
That year a plague had wasted all the land:
It reached him. Late that night he said, ' 'Tis well!'
In three days more he lay with hands death-cold

Crossed on a peaceful breast.
                      Like winter cloud
Borne through dark air, that portent feared of man
Ill tidings, making way with mystic speed,
Shadowed ere long the troubled bank of Thames,
And spread a wailing round its Minsters twain
Saint Peter's and Saint Paul's. Saint Alban's caught
That cry, and northward echoed. Southward soon
Forlorn it rang 'mid towers of Rochester;
Then seaward died. But in that convent pile
Wherein so long the Saint had made abode
A different grief there lived, a deeper grief,
That grief which part hath none in sobs or tears—
Which needs must act. There thirty monks arose
And, taking each his staff, made vow thenceforth
To serve God's altar where their father died
Or share his grave. Through Ithancester's gate
As forth they paced between two kneeling crowds,
A little homeless boy, who heard their dirge
(Late orphaned, at its grief he marvelled not),
So loved them that he followed, shorter steps
Doubling 'gainst theirs. At first the orphan wept:
That mood relaxed: before them now he ran
To pluck a flower; as oft he lagged behind
The wild bird's song so aptly imitating
That, by his music drawn, or by his looks,
That bird at times forgat her fears, and perched
Pleased on his arm. As flower and bird to him
Such as those monks the child. Better each day
He loved them; yet, revering, still he mocked,
And though he mocked, he kissed. The westering sun
On the eighth eve from towers of Lastingham
Welcomed those strangers. In another hour,
Well-nigh arrived, they saw that grave they sought

Sole on the church's northern slope. As when,
Some father, absent long, returns at last,
His children rush loud-voiced from field to house,
And cling about his knees; and they that mark—
Old reaper, bent no more, with hook in hand,
Or ploughman leaning 'gainst the old blind horse
Beholding wonder not; so to that grave
Rushed they; so clung. Around that grave ere long
Their own were ranged. That plague which smote
    the sire
Spared not his sons. With ministering hand
From pallet still to pallet passed the boy,
Now from the dark spring wafting colder draught
Now moistening fevered lips, or on the brow
Spreading the new-bathed cincture. Him alone
The infection reached not. When the last was gone
He felt as though the earth, man's race—yea, God
Himself—were dead. Around he gazed and spake
'Why then do I remain?'
                      From hill to hill,
The monks on reverend offices intent,
All solitary oft that boy repaired,
From each in turn forth gazing, fain to learn
If friend were t'wards him nighing. Many a hearth
More late, bereavement's earlier anguish healed,
Welcomed the creature: many a mother held
The milk-bowl to his mouth in both hands stayed,
With smile the deeper for the draught prolonged,
And lodged, as he departed, in his hand
Her latest crust. With children of his age
Seldom he played. That convent gave him rest;
Nor lost he aught surviving thus his friends,
Since childhood's sacred innocence he kept
While life remained, unspotted. When mature

Five years he lived there monk, and reverence drew
To that high convent through his saintly ways;
Then died. Within that cirque of thirty graves
They laid him, close to Cedd. In later years,
Because they ne'er could learn his name or race,
Nor yet forget his gentle looks, the name
Of Deodatus graved they on his tomb.

KING OSWALD OF NORTHUMBRIA,
OR THE BRITON'S REVENGE.

    Northumbria having been subdued by Pagan Mercia, Oswald raises there again the Christian standard. Penda wages war against him, in alliance with Cadwallon, a Cambrian prince who hates the Saxon conquerors the more bitterly when become Christians. Encouraged by St. Columba in a vision, Oswald with a small force vanquishes the hosts of Cadwallon, who is slain. He sends to Iona for monks of St. Columba's order, converts his country to the Faith, and dies for her. The earlier British race expiates its evil revenge.

THE agony was over which but late
Had shook to death Northumbria's realm new-raised
By Edwin, dear to God. The agony
At last was over; but the tear flowed on:
The Faith of Christ had fallen once more to dust
That Faith which spoused with golden marriage ring
The land to God, when Coifli, horsed and mailed,
Chief Priest himself, hurled at the Temple's wall
His lance, and quivering left it lodged therein.
The agony had ceased; yet Rachael's cry
Still pierced the childless region. Penda's sword
Had swept it, Mercia's Christian-hating King;

Fiercelier Cadwallon's, Cambria's Christian Prince,
Christian in vain. The British wrong like fire
Burned in his heart. Well-nigh two hundred years
That British race, they only of the tribes
By Rome subdued, sustained unceasing war
'Gainst those barbaric hordes that, nursed long since
'Mid Teuton woods, when Rome her death-wound felt,
And '*Habet*' shrilled from every trampled realm,
Rushed forth in ruin o'er her old domain:—
That race against the Saxon still made head;
Large remnant yet survived. The Western coast
Was theirs; old sea-beat Cornwall's granite cliffs,
And purple hills of Cambria; northward thence
Strathclyde, from towered Carnegia's winding Dee
To Morecambe's shining sands, and those fair vales
Since loved by every muse, where silver meres
Slept in the embrace of yew-clad mountain walls;
With tracts of midland Britain and the East.
Remained the memory of the greatness lost;
The Druid circles of the olden age;
The ash-strewn cities radiant late with arts
Extinct this day; bath, circus, theatre
Mosaic-paved; the Roman halls defaced;
The Christian altars crushed. That last of wrongs
The vanquished punished with malign revenge:
Never had British priest to Saxon preached;
And when that cry was heard, 'The Saxon King
Edwin hath bowed to Christ,' on Cambrian hills
Nor man nor woman smiled.
                          They had not lacked
The timely warning. From his Kentish shores
Augustine stretched to them paternal hands:
Later, he sought them out in synod met,
Their custom, under open roof of heaven.

'The Mother of the Churches,' thus he spake
' Commands—implores you ! Seek from her, and win
The Sacrament of Unity Divine !
Thus strengthened, be her strength ! With her conjoined
Subdue your foe to Christ !' He sued in vain.
The British bishops hurled defiance stern
Against his head, while Cambrian peaks far off
Darkened, and thunder muttered. From his seat,
Slowly and sadly as the sun declined
At last, though late, that Roman rose and stretched
A lean hand t'ward that circle, speaking thus :
' Hear then the sentence of your God on sin !
Because ye willed not peace, behold the sword !
Because ye grudged your foe the Faith of Christ
Nor help to lead him on the ways of life,
For that cause from you by the Saxon hand
Your country shall be taken !'
       Edwin slain,
Far off in exile dwelt his nephews long
Oswald and Oswy. Alba gave them rest,
Alba, not yet called Scotland. Ireland's sons,
Then Scoti named, had warred on Alba's Picts :
Columba's Gospel vanquished either race ;
Won both to God. It won not less those youths
In boyhood Oswald, Oswy still a child.
That child was wild and hot, and had his moods,
Despotic now, now mirthful. Mild as Spring
Was Oswald's soul, majestic and benign ;
Thoughtful his azure eyes, serene his front ;
He of his ravished sceptre little recked ;
The shepherds were his friends : the mountain deer
Would pluck the ivy fearless from his hand :
In gladness walked he till Northumbria's cry

Smote on his heart. 'Why rest I here in peace,'
Thus mused he, 'while my brethren groan afar?'
By night he fled with twelve companion youths
Christians like him and reached his native land.
Too fallen it seemed to aid him. On he passed;
The ways were desolate, yet evermore
A slender band around his footsteps drew
Less seeking victory than an honest death.
Oft gazed their King upon them; murmured oft,
'Few hands—true hearts!' Sudden aloud he cried
'Plant here the royal Standard, friends, and hence
Let sound the royal trumpet.'
                              Stern response
Reached him ere long: not Mercia's realm alone;
Cambria that heard the challenge joined the war:
Cambria, upon whose heart the ancestral woe
For ever with the years, like letters graved
On growing pines, grew larger and more large;—
To Penda forth she stretched a hand blood-red;
Christian with Pagan joined, an unblest bond,
A league accursed. The indomitable hate
Compelled that league. Still from his cave the Seer
Admonished, 'Set the foe against the foe;
Slay last the conqueror!' and from rock and hill
The Bard cried, 'Vengeance!' In the bardic clan
That hatred of their country's ancient bane
Lived like a faith. One night it chanced a tarn
Secreted high 'mid cold and moonless hills
Bursting its bank down burst. That valley's Bard
Clomb to the church-roof from his buried house:
Thence rang his song,—'twas 'Vengeance!—Ven-
        geance' still!
That torrent reached the roof: he clomb the tower:
The torrent mounted: on the bleak hill-side

All night the dalesmen, wailing o'er their drowned
Amid the roar of winds and downward rocks
Still heard that war-song, 'Vengeance! Blood for
   blood!'
At last the tower fell flat, and winter morn
Shone on the waters only.
                       Three short weeks
Dinned with alarums passed; in Mercia still
Lay Penda, sickness-struck, when, face to face
The Cambrian host and Oswald's little band
Exulting met at sunset near a height
Then 'Heaven-Field' named, but later 'Oswald's Field,'
Backed by that Wall the Roman built of old
His fence from sea to sea. There Oswald stood:
There raised with hands outstretched a mighty Cross,
Strong-based, and deep in earth: his comrades twelve
Around it heaped the soil, while priests white-stoled
Chanted 'Vexilla Regis.' Work and rite
Complete, the King knelt down and made his prayer,
'True God Eternal, look upon this Cross,
The sole now standing on Northumbria's breast
And help Thine own, though few, who trust in Thee!'

That night before his tent the wanderer sate
Listening the circling sentinel, or bay
Of wakeful hound remote, or downward course
Of streams from moorland hills. Before his view
His whole life rose: his father's angry brow;
The eyes all-wondrous, and all-tender hand
Of her, his mother, striving evermore
To keep betwixt her husband and her sire
Unbroken bond: his exiled days returned,
The kind that pitied them, the rude that jeered;
Lastly, that monk whose boast was evermore

Columba of Iona, Columkille;
That monk who made him Christian. 'Come what
    may,'
Thus Oswald mused, 'I have not lived in vain:
Lose I or win, a kingdom there remains;
Though not on earth!' A tear the vision dimmed
As thus he closed, 'My mother will be there!'
Then sank his lids in slumber.
                      On his sleep
Was this indeed but dream?—a glory brake:
Columba, dear to Oswald from his youth
Columba, clad in glory as the sun
Beside him stood and spake: 'Be strong! On earth
There lives not who can guess the might of prayer:
What then is prayer on high?' The saintly Shape
Heavenward his hands upraised while rose to heaven
His stature, towering ever high and higher,
Warlike and priestly both. As morning cloud
Blown by a mighty wind his robe ran forth,
Then stood, a golden wall that severance made
'Twixt Oswald's band and that unnumbered host.
Again he spake, 'Put on thee heart of man
And fight: though few, thy warriors shall not die
In darkness of an unbelieving land
But live, and live to God.' The vision passed:
By Oswald's seat his warriors stood and cried
'The Bull-horn! Hark!' The monarch told them all:
They answered, 'Let thy God sustain thy throne:
Thenceforth our God is He.'
                      The sun uprose:
Ere long the battle joined. Three dreadful hours
Doubtful the issue hung. Fierce Cambria's sons
With chief and clan, with harper and with harp,
Though terrible yet mirthful in their mood,

Rushed to their sport. Who mocked their hope that
    day?
Did Angels help the just? Their falling blood,
Say, leaped it up once more, each drop a man
Their phalanx to replenish? Backward driven,
Again that multitudinous foe returned
With clangour dire; futile, again fell back
Down dashed, like hailstone showers from palace halls
Where princes feast secure. Astonishment
Smote them at last. Through all those serried ranks,
Compact so late, sudden confusions ran
Like lines divergent through a film of ice
Stamped on by armèd heel, or rifts on plains
Prescient of earthquake underground. Their chiefs
Sounded the charge;—in vain: Distrust, Dismay,
Ill Gods, the darkness lorded of that hour:
Panic to madness turned. Cadwallon sole
From squadron on to squadron speeding still
As on a wingèd steed—his snow-white hair
Behind him blown—a mace in either hand,
Stayed while he might the inevitable rout;
Then sought his death, and found. Some fated Power
Mightier than man's that hour dragged back his hosts
Against their will and his: as when the moon
Shrouded herself, drags back the great sea-tides
That needs must follow her receding wheels
Though wind and wave gainsay them, breakers wan
Thundering indignant down nocturnal shores,
And city-brimming floods against their will
Down drawn to river-mouths.
                      In after days
Who scaped made oath that in the midmost fight
The green earth sickened with a brazen glare
While darkness held the skies. They saw besides

On Heaven-Field height a Cross, and, at its foot,
A sworded warrior vested like a priest
Who still in stature high and higher towered
As raged the battle. Higher far that Cross
Above him rose, barring with black the stars
That bickered through the eclipse's noonday night,
And ever from its bleeding arms sent forth
Thick-volleyed lightnings, azure fork and flame,
Through all that headlong host.
                              At eventide,
Where thickest fight had mingled, Oswald stood
With raiment red as his who treads alone
The wine-vat when the grapes are all pressed out,
Yet scathless and untouched. His mother's smile
Was radiant on his pure and youthful face,
Joyous, but not exulting. At his foot
Cadwallon lay, with four-score winters white,
A threatening corse: not death itself could shake
The mace from either rigid hand close-clenched,
Or smooth his brow. Above him Oswald bent,
Then spake: 'He also loved his native land:
Bear him with honour hence to hills of Wales,
And lay him with his Fathers.'
                              Thus was raised
In righteousness King Oswald's throne. But he,
Mindful in victory of Columba's word,
Thus mused, 'The Master is as he that serves:
How shall I serve this people?' O'er the waves
Then sent he of his Twelve the eldest three:
They to Iona sailed, and standing there
In full assembly of Iona's Saints
Addressed them: 'To Columba Oswald thus:
Let him that propped the King on Heaven-Field's
    height,

That held the battle-balance high that day,
Unite my realm to Christ!' The monks replied,
'Such mission should be Aidan's.' Aidan went.
With gladness Oswald met him, and with gifts:
But Aidan said, ' Entreat me not to dwell
There where Paulinus dwelt, the man of God,
In thy chief city, York. Thy race is fierce;
And meekness only can subdue the proud:
Thy people first I want; through them the great.
Grant me some island 'mid the raging main
Humble and low, not cheered by smiling meads,
Where with my brethren I may watch with God,
Henceforth my only aid.' Oswald replied
'Let Lindisfarne be thine. That rock-based keep
Built by my grandsire Ida o'er it peers:
I shall be near thee though I see thee not.'

Then Aidan on the Isle of Lindisfarne
Upreared that monastery which ruled in Christ
So long the Northern realm. A plain rock-girt
Level it lies and low: nor flower nor fruit
Gladdens its margin: thin its sod, and bleak:
Twice, day by day, the salt sea hems it round:
And twice a day the melancholy sands,
O'er-wailed by sea-bird, and with sea-weed strewn,
Replace the lonely ocean. Sacred Isles
That westward, eastward, guard the imperial realm,
Iona! Lindisfarne! With you compared
How poor that lilied Delos of old Greece
For all its laurel bowers and nightingales!
England's great hands were ye to God forth stretched
Through adverse climes, beneath the Boreal star,
That took His Stigmata. In sanctity
Were her foundations laid. Her later crowns

Of Freedom first, of Science, and of Song
She owes them all to you!
                        In Lindisfarne
Aidan, and his, rejoicing dwelt with God:
Amid the winter storm their anthems rose;
And from their sanctuary lamp the gleam
Far shone from wave to wave. On starless nights
From Bamborough's turret Oswald watched it long,
Before his casement kneeling—first alone,
Companioned later. Kineburga there
Beside him knelt ere long, his tender bride,
Young, beauteous, modest, noble. 'Not for them,'
Thus spake the newly wedded, 'not for them,
For man's sake severed from the world of men,
In ceaseless vigil warring upon sin,
Ah, not for them the flower of life, the harp,
High feast, or bridal torch!' Purer perchance
Their bridal torch burned on because from far
That sacred lamp had met its earliest beam!

There Aidan lived, and wafted issuing thence
O'er wilds Bernician and fierce battle-fields
The strength majestic of his still retreat,
The puissance of a soul whose home was God.
'What man is this,' the warriors asked, 'that moves
Unarmed among us; lifts his crucifix,
And says, "Ye swords, lie prone"?' The revelling crew
Rose from their cups: 'He preaches abstinence:
Behold, the man is mortified himself:
The moonlight of his watchings and his fasts
He carries on his face.' When Princes forced
Largess upon him, he replied, 'I want
Not yours but you;' and with their gifts redeemed

The orphan slave. The poor were as his children:
He to the beggar stinted not his hand
Nor, giving, said 'Be brief.' Such seed bare fruit:
God in the dark, primeval woods had reared
A race whose fierceness had its touch of ruth
Brave, cordial, chaste, and simple. Reverence
That race preserved: Reverence advanced to Love:
The ties of life it honoured: lit from heaven
They wore a meaning new. The Faith of Christ
Banished the bestial from the heart of man;
Restored the Hope divine.
      In all his toils
Oswald with Aidan walked. Impartial law
Not licence, not despotic favour, stands
To Truth auxiliar true. Such laws were his:
Yet not through such alone he worked for Truth;
Function he claimed more high. When Aidan
 preached;
In forest depths when thousands girt him round;
When countless eyes, a clinging weight, were bent
Upon his lips—all knew they spake from God,—
The King, with monks from Ireland knit of old
Beside the Bishop stood; each word he spake
Changed to the Saxon tongue.
      Earth were not earth,
If reign like Oswald's lasted. Penda lived;
Nor e'er from Oswald turned for eight long years
An eye like some swart planet feared of man,
Omen of wars or plague. Cadwallon's fate,
Ally ill-starred, that fought without his aid
O'er-flushed old hatred with a fiery shame:
Cadwallon nightly frowned above his dreams.
The tyrant watched his time. At Maserfield
The armies met. There on Northumbria's day

Settled what seemed, yet was not, endless night;
There Faith and Virtue, deathless seemed to die:
There holy Oswald fell.   For God he fought,
Fought for his country.   Walled with lances round,
A sheaf of arrows quivering in his breast,
One moment yet he stood.   ' Preserve,' he cried,
' My country, God ! ' then added, gazing round,
' And these my soldiers : make their spirits Thine ! '
   Thus perished good King Oswald, King and Saint ;
Saint by acclaim of nations canonised
Ere yet the Church had spoken.   Year by year
The Hexham monks to Heaven-Field, where of old
Had stood that ' Cross which conquered,' made repair,
With chanted psalm ; and pilgrims daily prayed
Where died the just and true.   Not vain their vows :
In righteousness foundations had been laid :
The earthquake reached them not.   The Dane passed
    by ;
High up the Norman glittered : but beneath,
On Faith profounder based and gentler Law
The Saxon realm lived on.
                      But never more
From Heaven-Field's wreck the Briton raised his head;
Britain thenceforth was England.   His the right ;
The land was his of old ; and in God's House
His of the island races stood first-born :
Not less he sinned through hate, esteeming more
Memories of wrong than forward-looking hopes
And triumphs of the Truth.   For that cause God
His face in blessing to the younger turned,
More honouring Pagans who in ignorance erred
Than those who, taught of God, concealed their gift
Divorcing Faith from Love.   Natheless they clung,
That remnant spared, to rocky hills of Wales

With eagle clutch, whoe'er in England ruled
From Horsa's day to Edward's. Centuries eight
In gorge or vale sea-lulled they held their own,
By native monarchs swayed, while native harps
Rang out from native cliffs defiant song
Wild as their singing pines. Heroic Land!
Freedom was thine; the torrent's plunge; the peak;
The pale mist past it borne! Heroic Race!
Caractacus was thine, and Galgacus,
And Boadicea greater by her wrongs
Than by her lineage. Battle-axe of thine
Rang loud and long on Roman helms ere yet
Hengist had trod the island. Thine that King
World-famed, who led to fifty war-fields forth
'Gainst Saxon hosts his sinewy, long-haired race
Unmailed, yet victory-crowned; that King who left
Tintagel, Camelot, and Lyonnesse,
Immortal names, though wild as elfin notes
From phantom rocks echoed in fairy land—
Great Arthur! Year by year his deeds were sung
While he in Glastonbury's cloister slept,
First by the race he died for, next by those
Their children, exiles in Armoric Gaul,
By Europe's minstrels then, from age to age;
But ne'er by ampler voice, or richlier toned
Than England lists to-day. Race once of Saints!
Thine were they, Ninian thine and Kentigern,
Iltud and Beino, yea and David's self,
Thy crown of Saints, and Winifred, their flower
Who fills her well with healing virtue still.
Cadoc was thine, who to his Cambrian throne
Preferred that western convent at Lismore,
Yet taught the British Princes thus to sing:
'None loveth Song that loves not Light and Truth:

None loveth Light and Truth that loves not Justice:
None loveth Justice if he loves not God:
None loveth God that lives not blest and great.'

CEADMON THE COWHERD, THE FIRST ENGLISH POET.

Ceadmon, a cowherd, being at a feast, declares when the harp reaches him, that he cannot sing. As he sleeps, a divine Voice commands him to sing. He obeys, and the gift of song is imparted to him. Hilda, Abbess of Whitby, enrolls him among her monks; and in later years he sings the revolt of the Fallen Angels, and many Christian mysteries, thus becoming the first English poet.

ALONE upon the pleasant bank of Esk
Ceadmon the Cowherd stood. The sinking sun
Reddened the bay, and fired the river-bank,
And flamed upon the ruddy herds that strayed
Along the marge, clear-imaged. None was nigh:
For that cause spake the Cowherd, 'Praise to God!
He made the worlds; and now, by Hilda's hand
Planteth a crown on Whitby's holy crest:
Daily her convent towers more high aspire:
Daily ascend her Vespers. Hark that strain!'
He stood and listened. Soon the flame-touched herds
Sent forth their lowings, and the cliffs replied,
And Ceadmon thus resumed: 'The music note
Rings through their lowings dull, though heard by few!
Poor kine, ye do your best! Ye know not God,
Yet man, His likeness, unto you is God,

And him ye worship with obedience sage,
A grateful, sober, much-enduring race
That o'er the vernal clover sigh for joy,
With winter snows contend not. Patient kine,
What thought is yours, deep-musing? Haply this,
" God's help! how narrow are our thoughts, and few
Not so the thoughts of that slight human child
Who daily drives us with her blossomed rod
From lowland valleys to the pails long-ranged!"
Take comfort, kine! God also made your race!
If praise from man surceased, from your broad chests
That God would perfect praise, and, when ye died
Resound it from yon rocks that gird the bay:
God knoweth all things. Let that thought suffice!'

 Thus spake the ruler of the deep-mouthed kine:
They were not his; the man and they alike
A neighbour's wealth. He was contented thus:
Humble he was in station, meek of soul,
Unlettered, yet heart-wise. His face was pale;
Stately his frame, though slightly bent by age:
Slow were his eyes, and slow his speech, and slow
His musing step; and slow his hand to wrath;
A massive hand, but soft, that many a time
Had succoured man and woman, child and beast
And yet could fiercely grasp the sword. At times
As mightily it clutched his ashen goad
When like an eagle on him swooped some thought:
Then stood he as in dream, his pallid front
Brightening like eastern sea-cliffs when a moon
Unrisen is near its rising.
     Round the bay
Meantime, as twilight deepened, many a fire
Up-sprang, and horns were heard. Around the steep

With bannered pomp and many a tossing plume
Advancing slow a cavalcade made way.
Oswy, Northumbria's king, the foremost rode,
Oswy triumphant o'er the Mercian host,
Invoking favour on his sceptre new;
With him an Anglian prince, student long time
In Bangor of the Irish, and a monk
Of Frankish race far wandering from the Marne:
They came to look on Hilda, hear her words
Of far-famed wisdom on the Interior Life;
For Hilda thus discoursed: 'True life of man
Is life within: inward immeasurably
The being winds of all who walk the earth;
But he whom sense hath blinded nothing knows
Of that wide greatness: like a boy is he,
A boy that clambers round some castle's wall
In search of nests, the outward wall of seven,
Yet nothing knows of those great courts within,
The hall where princes banquet, or the bower
Where royal maids discourse with lyre and lute,
Much less its central church, and sacred shrine
Wherein God dwells alone.' Thus Hilda spake;
And they that gazed upon her widening eyes
Low whispered, each to each, 'She speaks of things
Which she hath seen and known.'
       On Whitby's height
The royal feast was holden: far below,
A noisier revel dinned the shore; therein
The humbler guests made banquet. Many a tent
Gleamed on the yellow sands by ripples kissed;
And many a savoury dish sent up its steam;
The farmer from the field had brought his calf;
Fishers that increase scaled which green-gulfed seas
From womb crystalline, teeming, yield to man;

And Jock, the woodsman, from his oaken glades
The tall stag, arrow-pierced. In gay attire
Now green, now crimson, matron sat and maid:
Each had her due: the elder, reverence most,
The lovelier that and love. Beside the board
The beggar lacked not place.
                              When hunger's rage,
Sharpened by fresh sea-air, was quelled, the jest
Succeeded, and the tale of foreign lands;
Yet, boast who might of distant chief renowned,
His battle-axe, or fist that felled an ox,
The Anglian's answer was 'our Hilda' still:
'Is not her prayer trenchant as sworded hosts?
Her insight more than wisdom of the seers?
What birth like hers illustrious? Edwin's self,
Deira's exile, next Northumbria's king,
Her kinsman was. Together bowed they not
When he of holy hand, missioned from Rome,
Paulinus, o'er them poured the absolving wave
And joined to Christ? Kingliest was she, that maid
Who spurned earth-crowns!' More late the miller
    rose—
He ruled the feast, the miller old, yet blithe—
And cried, 'A song!' So song succeeded song,
For each man knew that time to chant his stave,
But no man yet sang nobly. Last the harp
Made way to Ceadmon, lowest at the board:
He pushed it back, answering, 'I cannot sing:'
The rest around him flocked with clamour, 'Sing!'
And one among them, voluble and small,
Shot out a splenetic speech: 'This lord of kine,
Our herdsman, grows to ox! Behold, his eyes
Move slow, like eyes of oxen!'
                              Slowly rose

Ceadmon, and spake: 'I note full oft young men
Quick-eyed, but small-eyed, darting glances round
Now here, now there, like glance of some poor bird,
That light on all things and can rest on none:
As ready are they with their tongues as eyes;
But all their songs are chirpings backward blown
On winds that sing God's song by them unheard:
My oxen wait my service: I depart.'
Then strode he to his cow-house in the mead,
Displeased though meek, and muttered, 'Slow of eye!
My kine are slow: if rapid I, my hand
Might tend them worse.' Hearing his step, the kine
Turned round their hornèd fronts; and angry thoughts
Went from him as a vapour. Straw he brought,
And strewed their beds; and they, contented well
Laid down ere long their great bulks, breathing
　　deep
Amid the glimmering moonlight. He, with head
Propped on a favourite heifer's snowy flank,
Rested, his deer-skin o'er him drawn. Hard days
Bring slumber soon. His latest thought was this:
'Though witless things we are, my kine and I,
Yet God it was who made us.'
　　　　　　　　　　　　As he slept
Beside him stood a Man Divine, and spake:
'Ceadmon, arise, and sing.' Ceadmon replied,
'My Lord, I cannot sing, and for that cause
Forth from the revel came I. Once, in youth,
I willed to sing the bright face of a maid,
And failed, and once a gold-faced harvest-field,
And failed, and once the flame-eyed face of war,
And failed again.' To him the Man Divine,
'Those themes were earthly. Sing!' And Ceadmon
　　said,

'What shall I sing, my Lord?' Then answer came,
'Ceadmon, stand up, and sing thy song of God.'

At once obedient, Ceadmon rose, and sang;
And help was with him from great thoughts of old
Yearly within his silent nature stored,
That swelled, collecting like a flood which bursts
In spring its icy bar. The Lord of all
He sang; that God beneath whose hand eterne,
Then when He willed forth-stretched athwart the abyss,
Creation like a fiery chariot ran,
Forth-borne on wheels of ever-living stars:
Him first he sang. The builder, here below,
From fair foundations rears at last the roof;
But Song, a child of heaven, begins with heaven,
The archetype divine, and end of all;
More late descends to earth. He sang that hymn
'Let there be light, and there was light;' and lo!
On the void deep came down the seal of God
And stamped immortal form. Clear laughed the skies;
From circumambient deeps the strong earth brake,
Both continent and isle; while downward rolled
The sea-surge summoned to his home remote.
Then came a second vision to the man
There standing 'mid his oxen. Darkness sweet,
He sang, of pleasant frondage clothed the vales,
And purple glooms ambrosial cast from hills
Now by the sun deserted, which the moon,
A glory new-created in her place,
Silvered with virgin beam, while sang the bird
Her first of love-songs on the branch first-flower'd—
Not yet the lion stalked. And Ceadmon sang

O'er-awed, the Father of all humankind
Standing in garden planted by God's hand,
And girt by murmurs of the rivers four,
Between the trees of Knowledge and of Life,
With eastward face.   In worship mute of God
Eden's Contemplative he stood that hour,
Not her Ascetic, since, where sin is none,
No need for spirit severe. .
                         And Ceadmon sang
God's Daughter, Adam's Sister, Child, and Bride,
Our Mother Eve.   Lit by the matin star
That nearer drew to earth and brighter flashed
To meet her gaze, that snowy Innocence
Stood up with queenly port : she turned ; she saw
Earth's King, mankind's great Father : taught by
     God,
Immaculate, unastonished, undismayed,
In love and reverence to her Lord she drew
And, kneeling, kissed his hand : and Adam laid
That hand, made holier, on that kneeler's head,
And spake ; 'For this shall man his parents leave
And to his wife cleave fast.'
                         When Ceadmon ceased
Thus spake the Man Divine : 'At break of day
Seek out some prudent man, and say that God
Hath loosed thy tongue ; nor hide henceforth thy
     gift.'
Then Ceadmon turned, and slept among his kine
Dreamless.   Ere dawn he stood upon the shore
In doubt : but when at last o'er eastern seas
The sun, long wished for, like a god upsprang
Once more he found God's song upon his mouth
Murmuring high joy ; and sought an ancient friend,
And told him all the vision.   At the word

He to the Abbess with the tidings sped,
And she made answer, 'Bring me Ceadmon here.'

Then clomb the pair that sea-beat mount of God
Fanned by sea-gale nor trod, as others used,
The curving way, but faced the abrupt ascent
And halted not, so worked in both her will,
Till now between the unfinished towers they stood
Panting and spent. The portals open stood :
Ceadmon passed in alone. Nor ivory decked,
Nor gold, the walls. That convent was a keep
Strong 'gainst invading storm or demon hosts,
And naked as the rock whereon it stood,
Yet, as a church, august. Dark, high-arched roofs
Slowly let go the distant hymn. Each cell
Cinctured its statued saint, the peace of God
On every stony face. Like caverned grot
Far off the western window frowned : beyond,
Close by, there shook an autumn-blazoned tree :
No need for gems beside of storied glass.

He entered last that hall where Hilda sat
Begirt with a great company, the chiefs
Far ranged from end to end. Three stalls cross-
    crowned
Stood side by side, the midmost hers. The years
Had laid upon her brows a hand serene :
There left alone a blessing. Levelled eyes
Sable, and keen, with meditative might
Conjoined the instinct and the claim to rule :
Firm were her lips and rigid. At her right
Sat Finan, Aidan's successor, with head
Snow-white, and beard that rolled adown a breast
Never by mortal passion heaved in storm,

A cloister of majestic thoughts that walked
Humbly with God.   High in the left-hand stall
Oswy was throned, a man in prime, with brow
Less youthful than his years.   Exile long past,
Or deepening thought of one disastrous deed,
Had left a shadow in his eyes.   The strength
Of passion held in check looked lordly forth
From head and hand : tawny his beard ; his hair
Thick-curled and dense.   Alert the monarch sat
Half turned, like one on horseback set that hears,
And he alone, the advancing trump of war.
Down the long gallery strangers thronged in mass,
Dane or Norwegian, huge of arm through weight
Of billows oar-subdued, with stormy looks
Wild as their waves and crags ; Southerns keen-
    browed ;
Pure Saxon youths, fair-fronted, with mild eyes,
These less than others strove for nobler place,
And Pilgrim travel-worn.   Behind the rest
And higher-ranged in marble-arched arcade,
Sat Hilda's sisterhood.   Clustering they shone,
White-veiled, and pale of face, and still and meek,
An inly-bending curve, like some young moon
Whose crescent glitters o'er a dusky strait.
In front were monks dark-stoled : for Hilda ruled
Though feminine, two houses, one of men :
Upon two chasm-divided rocks they stood,
To various service vowed though single Faith :
Not ever, save at rarest festival,
Their holy inmates met.
                      'Is this the man
Favoured, though late, with gift of song?' thus spake
Hilda with gracious smile.   Severer then
She added : 'Son, the commonest gifts of God

He counts His best, and oft temptation blends
With ampler boon. Yet sing! That God who lifts
The violet from the grass could draw not less
Song from the stone hard by. That strain thou sang'st,
Once more rehearse it.'
                      Ceadmon from his knees
Arose and stood. With princely instinct first
The strong man to the Abbess bowed, and next
To that great twain the bishop and the king
Last to that stately concourse each side ranged
Down the long hall; then, dubious, answered thus:
'Great Mother, if that God who sent the song
Vouchsafe me to recall it, I will sing;
But I misdoubt it lost.' Slowly his face
Down-drooped, and all his body forward bent
While brooding memory, step by step, retraced
Its backward way. Vainly long time it sought
The starting-point. Then Ceadmon's large, soft hands
Opening and closing worked; for wont were they,
In musings when he stood, to clasp his goad,
And plant its point far from him, thereupon
Propping his stalwart weight. Customed support
Now finding not, unwittingly those hands
Reached forth, and on Saint Finan's crosier-staff
Settling, withdrew it from the old bishop's grasp;
And Ceadmon leant thereon, while passed a smile
From chief to chief to see earth's meekest man
The spiritual sceptre claim of Lindisfarne.
They smiled; he triumphed: soon the Cowherd found
That first fair corner-stone of all his song;
Thence rose the fabric heavenward. Lifting hands,
Once more his lordly music he rehearsed,

The void abyss at God's command forth-flinging
Creation like a Thought: where night had reigned,
The universe of God.
                    The singing stars
Which with the Angels sang when earth was made
Sang in his song. From highest shrill of lark
To ocean's moaning under cliffs low-browed,
And roar of pine-woods on the storm-swept hills,
No tone was wanting; while to them that heard
Strange images looked forth of worlds new-born,
Fair, phantom mountains, and, with forests plumed
Heaven-topping headlands, for the first time glassed
In waters ever calm. O'er sapphire seas
Green islands laughed. Fairer, the wide earth's flower
Eden, on airs unshaken yet by sighs
From bosom still inviolate forth poured
Immortal sweets that sense to spirit turned
In part those noble listeners *made* that song!
Their flashing eyes, their hands, their heaving breasts,
Tumult self-stilled, and mute, expectant trance,
'Twas these that gave their bard his twofold might—
That might denied to poets later born
Who, singing to soft brains and hearts ice-hard,
Applauded or contemned, alike roll round
A vainly-seeking eye, and, famished, drop
A hand clay-cold upon the unechoing shell
Missing their inspiration's human half.

  Thus Ceadmon sang, and ceased. Silent awhile
The concourse stood, for all had risen, as though
Waiting from heaven its echo. Each on each
Gazed hard and caught his hands. Fiercely ere long
Their gratulating shout aloft had leaped
But Hilda laid her finger on her lip

Or provident lest praise might stain the pure,
Or deeming song a gift too high for praise.
She spake: 'Through help of God thy song is sound:
Now hear His Holy Word, and shape therefrom
A second hymn, and worthier than the first.'

She spake, and Finan standing bent his head
Above the sacred tome in reverence stayed
Upon his kneeling deacon's hands and brow,
And sweetly sang five verses, thus beginning,
'*Cum esset desponsata,*' and was still
And next rehearsed them in the Anglian tongue:
Then Ceadmon took God's Word into his heart
And ruminating stood, as when the kine
Their flowery pasture ended, ruminate;
And was a man in thought. At last the light
Shone from his dubious countenance and he spake:
'Great Mother, lo! I saw a second Song!
T'wards me it sailed; but with averted face
And borne on shifting winds. A man am I
Sluggish and slow that needs must muse and brood;
Therefore those verses till the sun goes down
Will I revolve. If song from God be mine
Expect me here at morn.'
                      The morrow morn
In that high presence Ceadmon stood and sang
A second song, and worthier than his first;
And Hilda said, 'From God it came, not man;
Thou therefore live a monk among my monks,
And sing to God.' Doubtful he stood—'From youth
My place hath been with kine; their ways I know,
And how to cure their griefs.' Smiling she spake,
'Our convent hath its meads, and kine; with these
Consort each morn: at noon to us return.'

Then Ceadmon knelt, and bowed, and said, 'So be it:'
And aged Finan, and Northumbria's king
Oswy, approved; and all that host had joy.

   Thus in that convent Ceadmon lived, a monk,
Humblest of all the monks, save him that knelt
In cell close by, who once had been a prince.
Seven times a day he sang God's praises, first
When earliest dawn drew back night's sable veil
With trembling hand, revisiting the earth
Like some pale maid that through the curtain peers
Round her sick mother's bed, misdoubting half
If sleep lie there, or death; latest when eve
Through nave and chancel stole from arch to arch,
And laid upon the snowy altar-step
At last a brow all gold. In later years
By ancient yearnings driven through wood and vale
He tracked Dëiran or Bernician glades
To holy Ripon, or late-sceptred York,
Not yet great Wilfred's seat, or Beverley:
The children gathered round him, crying, 'Sing!'
They gave him inspiration with their eyes,
And with his conquering music he returned it.
Oftener he roamed that strenuous eastern coast
To Jarrow and to Wearmouth, sacred sites
The well-beloved of Bede, or northward more
To Bamborough, Oswald's keep. At Coldingham
His feet had rest; there where St. Ebba's Cape
That ends the lonely range of Lammermoor,
Sustained for centuries o'er the wild sea-surge
In region of dim mist and flying bird,
Fronting the Forth, those convent piles far-kenned
The worn-out sailor's hope.
                       Fair English shores,

Despite those blinding storms of north and east,
Despite rough ages blind with stormier strife,
Or froz'n by doubt, or sad with worldly care,
A fragrance as of Carmel haunts you still
Bequeathed by feet of that forgotten Saint
Who trod you once sowing the seed divine!
Fierce tribes that kenned him distant round him
    flocked;
On sobbing sands the fisher left his net
His lamb the shepherd on the hills of March
Suing for song. With wrinkled face all smiles,
Like that blind Scian circling Grecian coasts
If God the song accorded, Ceadmon sang;
If God denied it, after musings deep
He answered, 'I am of the kine and dumb;'
The man revered his art and fraudful song
Esteemed as fraudful coin.
                  Music denied,
He solaced them with tales wherein, so seemed it,
Nature and Grace, inwoven, like children played
Or like two sisters o'er one sampler bent,
Braided one text. Ever the sorrowful chance
Ending in joy, the human craving still,
Like creeper circling up the Tree of Life,
Lifted by hand unseen, witnessed that He,
Man's Maker, is the Healer too of man,
And life His school parental. Parables
He showed in all things. 'Mark,' one day he cried,
'Yon silver-breasted swan that stems the lake
Taking nor chill nor moisture! Such the soul
That floats o'er waters of a world corrupt,
Itself immaculate still.'
                    Better than tale
They loved their minstrel's harp. The songs he sang

Were songs to brighten gentle hearts ; to fire
Strong hearts with holier courage ; hope to breathe
Through spirits despondent, o'er the childless floor
Or widowed bed, flashing from highest heaven
A beam half faith, half vision. Many a tear,
His own, and tears of those that listened, fell
Oft as he sang that hand, lovely as light,
Forth stretched, and gathering from forbidden boughs
That fruit fatal to man. He sang the Flood
Sin's doom that quelled the impure, yet raised to height
Else inaccessible, the just. He sang
That patriarch facing at divine command
The illimitable waste—then, harder proof,
Lifting his knife o'er him, the Seed foretold :
He sang of Israel loosed, the ten black seals
Down pressed on Egypt's testament of woe,
Covenant of pride with penance ; sang the face
Of Moses glittering from red Sinai's rocks,
The Tables twain and Mandements of God.
On Christian nights he sang that jubilant star
Which led the Magians to the Bethlehem crib
By Joseph watched, and Mary. Pale, in Lent,
Tremulous and pale, he told of Calvary,
Nor added word, but, as in trance rehearsed
That Passion fourfold of the Evangelists
Which, terrible and swift—not like a tale—
With speed of things which must be done, not said,
A river of bale from guilty age to age
Along the astonied shores of common life
Annual makes way, the history of the world,
Not of one day, one People. To its fount
That stream he tracked, that primal mystery sang
Which, chanted later by a thousand years
Music celestial, though with note that jarred,

Some wandering orb troubling its starry chime,
Amazed the nations. 'There was war in heaven:
Michael and they, his angels warfare waged
With Satan and his angels.' Brief that war,
That ruin total. Brief was Ceadmon's song:
Therein the Eternal Face was undivulged:
Therein the Apostate's form no grandeur wore:
The grandeur was elsewhere. Who hate their God
Change not alone to vanquished but to vile.
On Easter morn he sang the Saviour Risen,
Eden Regained. Since then on England's shores
Though many sang, yet no man sang like him.

O holy House of Whitby! on thy steep
Rejoice howe'er the tempest night or day
Afflict thee, or the hand of Time to earth
Drag down thine airy arches long suspense;
Rejoice, for Ceadmon in thy cloisters knelt,
And singing paced beside thy sounding sea!
Long years he lived; and with the whitening hair
More youthful grew in spirit and more meek;
Yea, those that saw him said he sang within
Then when the golden mouth but seldom breathed
Sonorous strain, and when—that fulgent eye
No longer bright—still on his forehead shone
Not flame but purer light like that last beam
Which, when the sunset woods no longer burn
Maintains high place on Alpine throne remote,
Or utmost beak of promontoried cloud
And heavenward dies in smiles. Esteem of men
Daily he less esteemed, through single heart
More knit with God. To please a sickly child
He sang his latest song, and, ending, said,
'Song is but body, though 'tis body winged:

The soul of song is love: the body dead,
The soul should thrive the more.' That Patmian Sage
Whose head had lain upon the Saviour's breast,
Who in high vision saw the First and Last,
Who heard the harpings of the Elders crowned,
Who o'er the ruins of the Imperial House
And ashes of the twelve great Cæsars dead
Witnessed the endless triumph of the Just,
To humbler life restored, and, weak through age,
But seldom spake, and gave but one command,
The great '*Mandatum Novum*' of his Lord,
'My children, love each other!' Like to his
Was Ceadmon's age. Weakness with happy stealth
Increased upon him: he was cheerful still:
He still could pace, though slowly, in the sun,
Still gladsomely converse with friends who wept,
Still lay a broad hand on his well-loved kine.

The legend of the last of Ceadmon's days :—
That hospital wherein the old monks died
Stood but a stone's throw from the monastery:
'Make there my couch to-night,' he said, and smiled:
They marvelled, yet obeyed. There, hour by hour,
The man, low-seated on his pallet bed,
In silence watched the courses of the stars,
Or casual spake at times of common things,
And three times played with childhood's days, and
    twice
His father named. At last, like one that, long
Compassed with good, is smit by sudden thought
Of greater good, thus spake he: 'Have ye, sons,
Here in this house the Blessed Sacrament?'
They answered, wrathful, 'Father, thou art strong;
Shake not thy children! Thou hast many days!'

'Yet bring me here the Blessed Sacrament,'
Once more he said.   The brethren issued forth
Save four that silent sat waiting the close.
Ere long in grave procession they returned,
Two deacons first, gold-vested; after these
That priest who bare the Blessed Sacrament,
And acolytes behind him lifting lights.
Then from his pallet Ceadmon slowly rose
And worshipped Christ, his God, and reaching forth
His right hand, cradled in his left, behold!
Therein was laid God's Mystery.   He spake:
'Stand ye in flawless charity of God
T'ward me, my sons; or lives there in your hearts
Memory the least of wrong?'   The monks replied:
'Father, within us lives nor wrong, nor wrath,
But love, and love alone.'   And he: 'Not less
Am I in charity with you, my sons,
And all my sins of pride, and other sins,
Humbly I mourn.'   Then bending the old head
O'er the old hand, Ceadmon received his Lord
To be his soul's viaticum, in might
Leading from life that seems to life that is;
And long, unpropped by any, kneeling hung
And made thanksgiving prayer.   Thanksgiving made,
He sat upon his bed, and spake: 'How long
Ere yet the monks begin their matin psalms?'
'That hour is nigh,' they answered; he replied,
'Then let us wait that hour,' and laid him down
With those kine-tending and harp-mastering hands
Crossed on his breast, and slept.
                              Meanwhile the monks,
The lights removed in reverence of his sleep,
Sat mute nor stirred such time as in the Mass
Between '*Orate Fratres*' glides away,

And '*Hoc est Corpus Meum.*' Northward far
The great deep, seldom heard so distant, roared
Round those wild rocks half way to Bamborough
    Head ;
For now the mightiest spring-tide of the year
Following the magic of a maiden moon
Approached its height. Nearer, that sea which sobbed
In many a cave by Whitby's winding coast
Or died in peace on many a sandy bar
From river-mouth to river-mouth outspread,
They heard, and mused upon eternity
That circles human life. Gradual arose
A softer strain and sweeter making way
O'er that sea-murmur hoarse ; and they were ware
That in the black far-shadowing church whose bulk
Up-towered between them and the moon, the monks
Their matins had begun. A little sigh
That moment reached them from the central gloom
Guarding the sleeper's bed ; a second sigh
Succeeded: neither seemed the sigh of pain :
And some one said, 'He wakens.' Large and bright
Over the church-roof sudden rushed the moon
And smote the cross above that sleeper's couch,
And smote that sleeper's face. The smile thereon
Was calmer than the smile of life. Thus died
Ceadmon, the earliest bard of English song.

KING OSWY OF NORTHUMBRIA, OR THE WIFE'S VICTORY.

Oswy, King of Bernicia, being at war with his kinsman Oswin, slays him unarmed. He refuses to repent of this sin; yet at last, subdued by the penitence, humility, and charity of Eanfleda, his wife, repents likewise, and builds a monastery over the grave of Oswin. Afterwards he becomes a great warrior and dies a saint.

Young, beauteous, brave—the bravest of the brave—
Who loved not Oswin? All that saw him loved:
Aidan loved most, monk of Iona's Isle,
Northumbria's bishop next from Lindisfarne
Ruling in things divine. One morn it chanced
That Oswin, noting how with staff in hand
Old Aidan roamed his spiritual realm, footbare,
Wading deep stream and piercing thorny brake,
Sent him a horse, his best. The Saint was pleased;
But, onward while he rode, and, musing, smiled
To think of these his honours in old age,
A beggar claimed his alms. 'Gold have I none,'
Aidan replied; 'this horse be thine!' The King,
Hearing the tale, was grieved. 'Keep I, my lord,
No meaner horses fit for beggar's use
That thus my best should seem a thing of naught?'
The Saint made answer: 'Beggar's use, my King!
What was that horse? The foal of some poor mare!
The least of men—the sinner—is God's child!'
Then dropped the King on both his knees, and cried:
'Father, forgive me!' As they sat at meat

Oswin was mirthful, and at jest and tale
His hungry thanes laughed loud. But great, slow tears
In silence trickled down old Aidan's face:
These all men marked; yet no man question made.
At last to one beside him Aidan spake
In Erin's tongue unknown to all save them
' God will not leave such meekness long on earth.'

Who loved not Oswin? Not alone his realm,
Dëira, loved him, but Bernician lords
Whose monarch, Oswy, was a man of storms,
Fierce King albeit in youth baptized to Christ;
At heart half pagan. Swift as northern cloud
Through summer skies he swept with all his host
Down on the rival kingdom. Face to face
The armies stood. But Oswin, when he marked
His own a little flock 'mid countless wolves,
Addressed them thus: ' Why perish, friends, for me?
From exile came I : for my people's sake
To exile I return, or gladlier die:
Depart in peace.' He rode to Gilling Tower;
And waited there his fate. Thither next day
King Oswy marched, and slew him.
                         Twelve days passed;
Then Aidan, while through green Northumbria's woods
Pensive he paced, steadying his doubtful steps,
Felt death approaching. Giving thanks to God,
The old man laid him by a church half raised
Amid great oaks and yews, and leaning there
His head against the buttress passed to God.
They made their bishop's grave at Lindisfarne;
But Oswin rested at the mouth of Tyne
Within a wave-girt, granite promontory
Where sea and river meet. For many an age

The pilgrim from far countries came in faith
To that still shrine—they called it 'Oswin's Peace,'—
Thither the outcast fled for sanctuary:
The sick man there found health. Thus Oswin lived
Though dead, a benediction in the land.

What tenderest form kneels on the rain-washed
    ground
From Gilling's keep a stone's-throw? Whose those
    hands
Now pressed in anguish on a bursting heart
Now o'er a tearful countenance spread in shame?
What purest mouth, but roseless for great woe,
With zeal to youthful lovers never known
Presses a new-made grave, and through the blades
Of grass wind-shaken breathes her piteous prayer?
Save from remorse came ever grief like hers?
Yet how could ever sin, or sin's remorse,
Find such fair mansion? Oswin's grave it is;
And she that o'er it kneels is Eanfleda
Kinswoman of the noble dead, and wife
To Oswin's murderer, Oswy.
                      Saddest one
And sweetest! Lo, that cloud which overhung
Her cradle swathes once more in deeper gloom
Her throne late won, and new-decked bridal bed.
This was King Edwin's babe, whose natal star
Shone on her father's pathway doubtful long
Shone there a line of light, from pagan snares
Leading to Christian baptism. Penda heard—
Penda, that drew his stock from Odin's stock,
Penda, that drank his wine from skulls of foes,
Penda, fierce Mercia's king. He heard, and fell
In ruin on the region. Edwin dead,

Paulinus led the widow and her babe
Back to that Kentish shore whereon had reigned
Its grandsire Ethelbert.
     The infant's feet
Pattered above the pavement of that church
In Canterbury by Augustine raised;
The child grew paler when Gregorian chants
Shook the dim roofs. Gladly the growing girl
Hearkened to stories of her ancestress
Clotilda, boast of France, but weeping turned
From legends whispered by her Saxon nurse
Of Loke, the Spirit accursed that slanders gods,
And Sinna, Queen of Hell. The years went by;
The last had brought King Oswy's embassage
With suit obsequious, 'Let the princess share
With me her father's crown.' To simple hearts
Changes come gently. Soon, all trust, she stood
Before God's altar with her destined lord:
Adown her finger while the bride-ring ran
So slid into her heart a true wife's love:
Rooted in faith, it ripened day by day;
And now the end was this!
     There as she knelt
A strong foot clanged behind her. 'Weeping still!
Up, wife of mine! If Oswin had not died
His gracious ways had filched from me my realm,
The base so loved his meekness!' Turning not
She answered low: 'He died an unarmed man:'
And Oswy: 'Fool that fought not when he might;
At least his slaughtered troop had decked his grave!
I scorned him for his grief that men should die;
And, scorning him, I hated; yea, for that
His blood is on my sword!'
     The priests of God

Had faced the monarch and denounced his crime:
They might as well have preached to ocean waves:
He felt no anger: he but deemed them mad
And smiling went his way. Thus autumn passed:
The queen, he knew it, when alone wept on;
Near him the pale face smiled; the voice was sweet;
Loving the service; the obedience full:
Neither by words, by silence, nor by looks
She chid him. Like some penitent she walked
That mourns her own great sin.
      Yet Oswy's heart,
Remorseless thus, had moods of passionate love:
A warrior of his host, Tosti by name,
Lay low, plague-stricken: kith and kin had fled;
Whole days the king sustained upon his knees
The sufferer's head, and cheered his heart with songs
Of Odin, strangely blent with Christian hymns
While ofttimes stormy bursts of tears descended
Upon that face upturned. Ministering he sat
Till death the vigil closed.
     One winter night
From distant chase belated he returned,
And passed by Oswin's grave. The snow, new-fallen,
Whitened the precinct. In the blast she knelt,
While coldly glared the broad and bitter moon
Upon those flying flakes that on her hair
Settled, or on her thin light raiment clung.
She heard him not draw nigh. She only beat
Her breast, and, praying, wept: 'Our sin, our sin!'
There as the monarch stood a change came o'er him:
Old, exiled days in Alba as a dream
Redawned upon his spirit, and that look
In Aidan's eyes when, binding first that cross
Long by his pupil craved around his neck

He whispered: 'He who serveth Christ, his Lord,
Must love his fellow-man.' As when a stream
The ice dissolved, grows audible once more
So came to him those words. They dragged him
   down :
He knelt beside his wife, and beat his breast,
And said, 'My sin, my sin !' Till earliest morn
Glimmered through sleet that twain wept on, prayed
   on :
Was it the rising sun that lit at last
The fair face upward lifted;—kindled there
A lovelier dawn than o'er it blushed when first
Dropped on her bridegroom's breast? Aloud she cried :
'Our prayer is heard : our penitence finds grace :'
Then added : 'Let it deepen till we die !
A monastery build we on this grave :
So from this grave while fleet the years, that prayer
Shall rise both day and night, till Christ returns
To judge the world, a prayer for him who died,
A prayer for one who sinned, but sins no more.'

   Where Gilling's long and lofty hill o'erlooks
For leagues the forest-girdled plain, ere long
A monastery stood. That self-same day
In tears the penitential work began ;
In tears the sod was turned. The rugged brows
Of March relaxed 'neath April's flying kiss :
Again the violet rose, the thrush was loud ;
Mayday had come. Around that hallowed spot
Full many a warrior met ; some Christians vowed ;
Some muttering low of Odin. Near to these
Stood one of lesser stature, keener eye,
More fiery gesture. Splenetic, he marked,
Christian albeit himself, those Christian walls

By Saxon converts raised :—he was a Briton.
Invisibly that morn a dusky crape
O'erstretched the sky; and slowly swayed the bough
Heavy with midnight rains. Through mist the woods
Let out the witchery of their young fresh green
Backed by the dusk of ruddy oaks that still
Reserved at heart the old year's stubbornness,
Yet blent it with that purple distance glimpsed
Beyond the forest alleys.
               In a tent
Finan sang Mass: his altar was that stone
Which told where Oswin died. Before it knelt
The king, the queen: alone their angels know
Their thoughts that hour! The sacred rite complete,
They raised their brows, and, hand-in-hand, made way
To where, beyond the portal, shone blue skies
Nature's long-struggling smile at last divulged.
The throng—with passion it had prayed for each—
Divided as they passed. In either face
They saw the light of that conceded prayer,
The peace of souls forgiven.
                    From that day forth
Hourly in Oswy's spirit soared more high
The one true greatness. Flaming heats of soul,
Through faith subjected to a law divine,
Like fire, man's vassal, mastering iron ore
Learned their true work. The immeasurable strength
Had found at once its master and its end,
And, balanced thus while weighted, soared to God.
In all his ways he prospered, work and work
Yoked to one end. Till then the Kingdoms Seven,
Opposed in interests as diverse in name
Had looked on nothing like him. Now, despite
Mercia that frowned, they named him king of kings,

Bretwalda ; and the standard of the Seven
In peace foreran his feet. The Spirits of might
Before his vanguard winged their way in war,
Scattering the foe ; and in his peacefuller years
Upon the aerial hillside high and higher
The golden harvest clomb, waving delight
On eyes upraised from winding rivers clear
That shone with milky sails. His feet stood firm,
For with his growing greatness ever grew
His penitence. Still sang the cloistered choir,
Year after year pleading o'er Oswin's tomb,
'To him who perished grant thy Vision, Lord ;
To him the slayer, penitence and peace ;
Let Oswin pray for Oswy :' Oswin prayed.

What answered Penda when the tidings came
Of Oswy glorying in the yoke of Christ,
Of Oswy's victories next ? Grinding his teeth,
He spake what no man heard. Then rumour rose
Of demon-magic making Oswy's tongue
Fell as his sword. 'Within the sorcerer's court,'
It babbled, 'stood the brave East Saxon king :
Upon his shoulder Oswy laid a hand
Accursed and whispered in his ear. The king,
Down sank, perforce, a Christian !' Lightning flashed
From under Penda's grey and shaggy brows ;
'Forth to Northumbria, son,' he cried, 'and back ;
And learn if this be true.'
      That son obeyed,
Peada, to whose heart another's heart,
Alcfrid's, King Oswy's son, was knit long since
As David's unto Jonathan's. One time
A tenderer heart had leaned, or seemed to lean,

Motioning that way, Alfleda's Alcfrid's sister,
Younger than he six years. 'Twas so no more:
No longer on Peada's eyes her eyes
Rested well-pleased: not now the fearless hand
Tarried in his contented. 'Sir and king,'
Peada thus to Oswy spake, 'of old
Thy child, then child indeed, would mount my
 knee;
Now, when I seek her, like a swan she fleets
That arches back its neck 'twixt snowy wings
And, swerving, sideway drifts. My lord and king,
The child is maiden: give her me for wife!'
Oswy made answer: 'He that serves not Christ
Can wed no child of mine.' Alfleda then
Dropping her broidery lifted on her sire
Gently the dewy light of childlike eyes
And spake, 'But he in time will worship Christ!'
Then, without blush or tremor, to her work
Softly returned. Silent her mother smiled.
That moment, warned of God, from Lindisfarne
Finan, unlooked for, entered. Week by week
Reverend and mild he preached the Saviour-Lord:
Grave-eyed, with listening face and forehead bowed
The prince gave ear, not like that trivial race
Who catch the sense ere spoken, smile assent,
And in a moment lose it. On his brow
At times the apprehension dawned, at times
Faded. Oft turned he to his Mercian lords:
'How trow ye, friends? He speaks of what he
 knows!
Good tidings these! Each evening while I muse
Distinct they shine like yonder mountain range;
Each morning, mists conceal them.' Passed a month;
Then suddenly, as one that wakes from dream,

Peada rose : 'Far rather would I serve
Thy Christ,' he said, 'and thus Alfleda lose,
Than win Alfleda, and reject thy Christ.'
He spake: old Finan first gave thanks to God,
Who grants the true heart valour to believe,
Then took his hand and led him to that Cross
On Heaven-Field raised beneath the Roman Wall,
That Cross King Oswald's standard in the fight,
That Cross Cadwallon's sentence as he fell,
'That Cross which conquered;'—there to God baptized;
Likewise his thanes and earls.
       Meantime, far off
In Penda's palace-keep the revel raged,
High feast of rites impure. At banquet sat
The monarch and his chiefs; chant followed chant
Bleeding with wars foregone. The day went by,
And, setting ere its time, a sanguine sun
Dipped into tumult vast of gathering storm
That soon incumbent leant from tower to tower
And shook them to their base. As high within
The gladness mounted, meeting storm with storm,
Till cried that sacrificial priest whose knife
Had pierced the warrior victim's willing throat
That morn, 'Already with the gods we feast!
Hark! round Valhalla swell the phantom wars!'
Ere ceased the shout applausive, from his seat
Uprose the warrior Saxo, in his hand
The goblet, in the other Alp, his sword,
Pointing to heaven. 'To Odin health!' he cried;
'Would that this hour he rode into this hall!
He should not hence depart till blood of his
Had reddened Sleipner's flank, his snow-white steed:
This sword would shed that blood!' Warriors sixteen
Leaped up in wrath, and for a moment rage

Rocked the huge hall. But Saxo waved his sword,
And, laughing, shouted, 'Odin's sons, be still!
Count it no sin to battle with high gods!
Great-hearted they! They give the blow and take!
To Odin who was ever leal as I?'
As sudden as it rose the tumult fell:
So ceased the storm without: but with it ceased
The rapture and the madness, and the shout:
The wine-cup still made circuit; but the song
Froze in mid-air. Strange shadow hung o'er all:
Neighbour to neighbour whispered: courtiers slid
Through doors scarce open. Rumour had arrived,
If true or false none knew.
      The morrow morn
From Penda's court the bravest fled in fear,
Questioning with white lips, 'Will he slay his son?'
Or skulked at distance. Penda by the throat
Catching a white-cheeked courtier, cried: 'The truth!
What whisper they in corners?' On his knees
That courtier made confession. Penda then,
'Live, since my son is yet a living man!
A Christian, say'st thou? Let him serve his Christ!
That man whom ever most I scorned is he
Who vows him to the service of some god,
Yet breaks his laws; for that man walks, a lie.
My son shall live, and after me shall reign:
Northumbria's realm shall die!'
       Thus Penda spake
And sent command from tower and town to blow
Instant the trumpet of his last of wars,
Fanning from Odin's hall with airs ice-cold
Of doom the foes of Odin. 'Man nor child,'
He sware, 'henceforth shall tread Northumbrian soil,
Nor hart nor hind: I spare the creeping worm:

My scavenger is he.' The Mercian realm
Rose at his call, innumerable mass
Of warriors iron-armed. East Anglia sent
Her hosts in aid. Apostate Ethelwald,
Through Oswy's nephew, joined the hostile league,
And thirty chiefs besides that ruled by right
Princedom or province. Mightier far than these
Old Cambria, brooding o'er ancestral wrong,
The Saxon's sin original, met his call,
And vowed her to the vengeance.
       Bravest hearts
Hate most the needless slaughter. Oswy mused:
'Long since too much of blood is on this hand:
Shall I for pride or passion risk once more
Northumbria, my mother;—rudely stain
Her pretty babes with blood?' To Penda then,
Camped on the confines of the adverse realms,
He sent an embassage of reverend men,
Warriors and priests. Before them, staff in hand,
Peaceful, with hoary brows and measured tread,
Twelve heralds paced. Twelve caskets bare they
  heaped
With gems and gold, and thus addressed the King:
'Lord of the Mercian realm, renowned in arms!
Our lord, Northumbria's monarch, bids thee hail:
He never yet in little thing or great
Hath wronged thy kingdom; yet thy peace he woos:
Accept the gifts he sends thee, and, thus crowned,
Depart content.' Penda with backward hand
Waved them far from him, and vouchsafed no word.
In sadness they returned: but Oswy smiled
Hearing their tale, and said: 'My part is done:
Let God decide the event.' He spake, and took
The caskets twelve, and placed them, side by side,

Before the altar of his chiefest church
And vowed to raise to God twelve monasteries,
In honour of our Lord's Apostles Twelve,
On greenest upland, or in sylvan glade
Where purest stream kisses the richest mead.
His vow recorded, sudden through the church
Ran with fleet foot a lady mazed with joy,
Crying, 'A maiden babe! and lo, the queen
Late dying lives and thrives!' That eve the king
Bestowed on God the new-born maiden babe,
Laying her cradled 'mid those caskets twelve,
Six at each side; and said: 'For her nor throne
Nor marriage bower! She in some holy house
Shall dwell the Bride of Christ. But thou, just God,
This day avenge my people!'
      Windwaed field
Heard, distant still, that multitudinous foe
Trampling the darksome ways. With pallid face
Morning beheld their standards, raven-black—
Penda had thus decreed, before him sending
Northumbria's sentence. On a hill, thick-set
Stood Oswy's army, small, yet strong in faith,
A wedge-like phalanx, fenced by rocks and woods;
A river in its front. His standards white
Sustained the Mother Maid and Babe Divine:
From many a crag his altars rose, choir-girt
And crowned by incense wreath.
      An hour ere noon,
That river passed, in thunder met the hosts;
But Penda, straitened by that hilly tract,
Could wield not half his force. Sequent as waves
On rushed they: Oswy's phalanx like a cliff
Successively down dashed them. Day went by:
At last the clouds dispersed: the westering sun

Glared on the spent eyes of those Mercian ranks
Which in their blindness each the other smote,
Or, trapped by hidden pitfalls, fell on stakes
And died blaspheming. Little help that day
Gat they from Cambria. She on Heaven-Field height
Had felt her death-wound, slow albeit to die.
The apostate Ethelwald in panic fled :
The East Anglians followed. Swollen by recent rains,
And choked with dead, the river burst its bound,
And raced along the devastated plain
Till cry of drowning horse and shriek of man
Rang far and farther o'er that sea of death,
A battle-field but late. This way and that
Briton or Mercian where he might escaped
Through flood or forest. Penda scorned to fly :
Thrice with extended arms he met and cursed
The fugitives on rushing. As they passed
He flung his crownèd helm into the wave
And bit his brazen shield, above its rim
Levelling a look that smote with chill like death
Their hearts that saw it. Yet one moment more
He sat like statue on some sculptured horse
With uppraised hand, close-clenched, denouncing Heaven :
Then burst his mighty heart. As stone he fell
Dead on the plain. Not less in after times
Mercian to Mercian said, 'Without a wound
King Penda died, although on battle-field,
Therefore with Odin Penda shares not feast.'
Thus pagan died old Penda as he lived :
Yet Penda's sons were Christian, kindlier none ;
His daughters nuns ; and lamb-like Mercia's House,
Lion one while, made end. King Oswy raised
His monasteries twelve : benigner life

Around them spread: wild waste, and robber bands
Vanished: the poor were housed, the hungry fed:
And Oswy sent his little new-born babe
Dewed with her mother's tear-drops, Eanfleda,
Like some young lamb with fillet decked and flower
Yet dedicated not to death, but life,
To Hilda sent on Whitby's sea-washed hill,
Who made her Bride of Christ. The years went by,
And Oswy, now an old king, glory-crowned,
His country from the Mercian thraldom loosed
And free from north to south, in heart resolved
A pilgrim, Romeward faring with bare feet,
To make his rest by Peter's tomb and Paul's.
God willed not thus: within his native realm
The sickness unto death clasped him with hold
Gentle but firm. Long sleepless, t'ward the close
Amid his wanderings smiling, from the couch
He stretched a shrivelled hand, and pointing said,
'Who was it fabled she had died in age?
In all her youthful beauty holy and pure,
Lo, where she kneels upon the wintry ground,
The snow-flakes circling round her, yet with face
Bright as a star!' so spake the king, and taking
Into his heart that vision, slept in peace.
His daughter, abbess then on Whitby's height,
Within her church interred her father's bones
Beside her grandsire's, Edwin. Side by side
They rested, one Bernicia's king, and one
Dëira's—great Northumbria's sister realms;
Long foes, yet blended by that mingling dust.

THE VENGEANCE OF THE MONKS
OF BARDENEY

> Osthryda, Queen of Mercia, translates the relics of her uncle, Oswald of Northumberland, to the Abbey of Bardeney. The monks refuse them admittance because King Oswald had conquered and kept for one year Lindsay, a province of Mercia. Though hourly expecting the destruction of their Abbey, they will yield neither to threats nor to supplications, nor even to celestial signs and wonders. At last, being convinced by the reasoning of a devout man, they repent of their anger.

SILENT, with gloomy brows in conclave sat
The monks of Bardeney, nigh the eastern sea;
Rumour, that still outruns the steps of ill
Smote on their gates with news: 'Osthryda comes
To bury here her royal uncle's bones,
Northumbrian Oswald.' Oswald was a Saint;
Had loosed from Pagan bonds that Christian land
His own by right. But Oswald had subdued
Lindsay, a Mercian province; and the monks
Were sons of Mercia leal and true. Osthryda,
Northumbrian born, had wedded Mercia's King;
Therefore the monks of Bardeney pondered thus:
'This Mercian Queen spurns her adopted country!
Must Mercia therefore build her conqueror's tomb?
Though earth and hell cried "Ay," it should not be!'
  Thus mused the brethren till the sun went down:
Then lo! beyond a vista in the woods
Drew nigh a Bier, black-plumed, with funeral train:
Thereon the stern monks gazed, and gave command
To close the Abbey's gate. Beside that gate

Tent-roofed that Bier remained.
                          Before them soon
Stood up the royal herald. Thus he spake:
'Ye sacred monks of Bardeney's Abbey, hail!
Osthryda, wife of Ethelred our King,
Prays that God's peace may keep this House forever.
The Queen has hither brought, by help of God
King Oswald's bones, and sues for them a grave
Within this hallowed precinct.' Answer came:
'King Oswald, living, was Northumbria's King;
King Oswald, by the pride of life seduced
Wrested from Mercia's sceptre Lindsay's soil;
Therefore in Lindsay's soil King Oswald, dead,
May never find repose.'
                       Before them next
Three earls advanced full-armed, and spake loud-voiced:
'Our Queen is consort of the Mercian King;
Ye, monks, are Mercian subjects! Sirs, beware!
Our King and Queen have loved you well till now,
And ranked your abbey highest in their realm:
But hearts ingrate can sour the mood of love;
And Ethelred, though mild as summer skies
When mildly used, once angered'——Answer came:
'We know it, and await our doom, content:
If Mercia's King contemns his realm, more need
That Mercia's priests her confessors should die:
In Bardeney's church King Oswald ne'er shall rest:
Ye have your answer, Earls!'
                            Through that dim hall
Ere long a gentler embassage made way,
Three priests; arrived, they knelt, and, reverent,
    spake:
'Fathers and brethren, Oswald was a Saint!
He loosed his native land from pagan thrall:

Churches and convents everywhere he built :
His relics, year by year, grow glorious more
Through miracles and signs. Fathers revered,
Within this sanctuary beloved of God
Vouchsafe his dust interment!' They replied :
'We know that Oswald is a Saint with God :
We know he freed his realm from pagan thrall ;
We know that churches everywhere he built ;
We know that from his relics Grace proceeds
As light from sun and moon. In heaven a crown
Rests on Saint Oswald's head : yet here on earth
King Oswald's foot profaned our Mercian bound :
Therefore in Mercian earth he finds not grave.'

  Silent those priests withdrew. An hour well-nigh
Went by in silence. Then with forehead crowned
And mourner's veil, and step of one that mourns,
The Queen advanced, a lady at each side,
And 'mid the circle stood, and thus implored :
'Not as your Sovereign come I, holy Sirs,
Since all are equal in the House of God ;
Nor stand I here a stranger. Many a day
In this your church, I knelt, while yet a child ;
Then too, as now, within my breast there lived
The tenderest of its ardours and the best,
Zeal for my kinsman's fame. That time how oft
I heard my Father, Oswy, cry aloud,
"O Brother, had I walked but in thy ways
My foot had never erred!" In maiden youth
I met with one who shared my loyal zeal,
Mercian himself : 'twas thus he won my heart :
My royal husband shared it ; shares this hour
My trust that 'mid the altars reared by us
To grace this chiefest Minster of our realm
May rest the relics of our household Saint—

To spurn them from your threshold were to shame.'
  She spake: benign and soft the answering voice:
'Entreat us not, thou mourner true and kind,
Lest we, by pity from the straight path drawn,
Sin more than thou. Thou know'st what thing love is,
Thus loving one who died before thy birth!
Up to the measure of high love and fit
Thou lov'st him for this cause, because thy heart
Hath never rested on base love and bad:
Lady, a sterner severance monks have made:
Not base and bad alone do they reject,
But lesser good for better and for best:
Therefore what yet remains they love indeed:
A single earthly love is theirs unblamed,
Their Country! Lo, the wild-bird loves her nest,
Lions their caves:—to us God gave a Country.
What heart of man but loves that mother-land
Whose omnipresent arms are round him still
In vale and plain; whose voice in every stream;
Whose breath his forehead cools; whose eyes with joy
Regard her offspring issuing forth each morn
On duteous tasks; to rest each eve returning?
And who that loves her but must hate her foes?
Lady, accept God's Will, nor strive by prayer
To change it. In our guest-house rest this night,
Thou, and thy train.'
              Severe the Queen replied:
'Yea in thy guest-house I will lodge this night,
Unvanquished, undiscouraged, not to cease
From prayer: of that be sure. I make henceforth
My prayer to God, not man. To Him I pray,
That Lord of all, Who changes at His will
The stony heart to flesh.'
              She spake: then turned

On those old faces, keenlier than before,
Her large slow eyes; and instant in her face
The sadness deepened: but the wrath was gone.
That sadness said, 'Love then as deep as mine,
And grief like mine, in other breasts may spring
From source how different!' Long she gazed, like
    child
That knows not she is seen to gaze, with looks
As though she took that hoary-headed band
Into her sorrowing heart. Silent she sighed;
Then passed into the guest-house with her train:
There prayed all night for him, that Saint in heaven
Ill-honoured upon earth.
                      Within their church
Meantime the monks the 'Dies Iræ' sang,
The yellow tapers ranged as round a corse,
And Penitential Psalms in order due.
Their rite was for the living: ere the time
They sang the obsequies of sentenced men,
Foreboding wrath to come. Sad Fancy heard
The flames up-rushing o'er their convent home,
The ruin of their church late-built, the wreck
It might be of their Order. Fierce they knew
That Mercian royal House! Against their King
They hurled no ban: venial they deemed his crime:
'He moves within the limits of his right,
Though wrongly measuring right. He sees but this,
His subjects break his laws. Some sin of youth
It may be hides from him a right more high:'
Thus spake they in their hearts.
                          While rival thus
The brethren and the Queen sent up their prayer,
And sacred night hung midway in her course,
Behold, there fell from God tempest and storm

Buffeting that abbey's walls. The woods around
Devastated by stress of blast on blast,
Howled like the howling of wild beasts when fire
Invests their ambush, and their cubs late-born
Blaze in red flame. Trembling, the strong-built towers
Echoed the woodland moans. All night the Queen,
Propped by those two fair Seraphs, Faith and Love,
Prayed on in hope, or hearing not that storm,
Or mindful that where danger most abounds
There God is nearest still. Meantime the Tent
Covering that royal Bier, unshaken stood
Beside the unyielding abbey-gates close-barred,
Like something shielded by a heavenly charm:
When morning came, shattered all round it lay
Both trunk and bough; but in the rising sun
The storm-drop shook not on that snowy shrine.

Things wondrous more that Legend old records:
An hour past sunrise from the meads and moors
Came wide-eyed herdsmen thronging, with demand,
'What means this marvel? All the long still night,
While heaven and earth were dark, and peaceful sleep
Closed in her arms the wearied race of men,
Keeping our herds on meads and moorlands chill,
We saw a glittering Tent beside your gates:
Above it, and not far, a pillar stood,
All light, and high as heaven!' The abbot answered,
'Fair Sirs, ye dreamed a dream; and sound your sleep
Untroubled by the terror of the storm
Whereof those woodland fragments witness still,
And many a forest patriarch prostrate laid:
There rose no pillar by our gates: yon Tent
Stood there, and stood alone.' In two hours' space
Shepherds arrived, from hills remoter sped,

Making the same demand. With eye ill pleased
Thus answered brief the prior: 'Friends, ye jest!'
And they in wrath departed. Once again
Came foresters from Lindsay's utmost bound,
On horses blown, and spake: 'O'er yonder Tent,
Through all the courses of the long still night,
Behold, a shining pillar hovering stood:
It rained a glory on your convent walls:
It flung a trail of splendour o'er your woods:
We watched it hour by hour. Like Oswald's Cross
On Heaven-Field planted in the days of old,
It waxed in height:—the stars were quenched.'
    Replied
With reddening brows the youngest of those monks,
'Sirs, ye have had your bribe, and told your tale:
Depart!' and they departed great in scorn.

    Long time the brethren sat; discoursed long time
Each with his neighbour. 'Craft of man would force
Dishonest deed on this our holy House,
By miracles suborned;' thus spake the first:
The second answered, 'Ay, confederates they!
The good Queen knew not of it:' then the third,
'Not so! these men are simple folks, I ween:
Nor time for fraud had they. What sail is yon
So weather-worn that nears the headland?' Soon
A pilot stood before them; at his side
A priest, long years an inmate of their House,
But late a pilgrim in the Holy Land.
Their greetings over, greetings warm and kind,
Thus spake the Pilgrim: 'Brothers mine, rejoice;
Our God is with us! For our House I prayed
Three times with forehead on the Tomb of Christ;
Last night there came to me, in visible form,

An answer to that prayer. All day our ship,
Before a great wind rushed t'ward Mercian shores:
To them I turned not: on the East I gazed:
"O happy East," I mused, "O Land, true home
Of every Christian heart! The Saviour's feet
Thy streets, thy cornfields trod! With these compared
Our country's self seems nothing!" In my heart
Imaged successive, rose once more those sites
Capernaum, Nain, Bethsaida, Bethlehem—
Where'er my feet had strayed. At midnight, cries
Of wonder rang around me, and I turned:
I saw once more our convent on its hill:
I saw beside its gate a Tent snow-white;
I saw a glittering pillar o'er that Tent
'Twixt heaven and earth suspense! Serene it shone,
Such pillar as led forth the Chosen Race
By night from Egypt's coasts. From wave to wave
Moon-like it paved a path! I cried, "Thank God!
For who shall stay yon splendour till it reach
That Syrian shore? England," I said, "my country,
Shall lay upon Christ's Tomb a hand all light,
Whatever tempest shakes the world of men,
Thenceforth His servant vowed!"'

                                  When ceased that voice
There fell upon the monks a crisis strange;
And where that Pilgrim looked for joy, behold,
Doubt, wrath, and anguish! Faces old long since
Grew older, stricken as by hectic spasm,
So fierce a pang had clutched them by the throat;
While drops of sweat on many a wrinkled brow
Hung large like dewy beads condensed from mist
On cliffs by torrents shaken. Mute they sat;
Then sudden rose, uplifting helpless hands,
As when from distant rock sore-wounded men,

Who all day long have watched some dreadful fight,
Behold it lost, or else foresee it lost,
And with it lost their country's hearths and homes,
And yet can bring no succour. Thus with them:
They knew themselves defeated; deemed the stars
Of heaven had fought against them in their course;
Yet still believed, and could not but believe
Their cause the cause of Justice, and its wreck
The wreck of priestly honour, patriot faith:
At last the youngest of the brethren spake;
' Come what come may, God's monks must guard the
    Right.'
Death-like a silence on that conclave fell.
Then rose a monk white-headed, well-nigh blind,
Esteemed a Saint, who had not uttered speech
Since came the tidings of the Queen's resolve:
Low-voiced he spake, with eyes upon the ground
And inward smile that dimly reached his lips:
' Brethren, be wary lest ye strive with God
Through wrath, that blind incontinence of age,
For what He wills He works. By passion warped
Ye deem this trial strange, this conflict new,
Yourselves doomed men that stand between two Fates,
On one side right, on one side miracles!
Brethren, the chief of miracles is this,
That knowing what ye know ye know no more:
Ye know long since that Oswald is a Saint:
Ye know the sins of Saints are sins forgiven:
What then? Shall man revenge where God forgives?
Be wroth with those He loves? Ye, seeing much,
See not the sun at noontide! God last night
Sent you in love a miracle of love
To quell in you a miracle of wrath:—
Discern its import true!

　　　　　　Sum up the past!
Thus much is sure: we heard those thunder peals
Unheard by hind or shepherd, near or far:
'Tis sure not less that light the shepherds saw
We saw not; neither we nor yet the Queen.
What then? Is God not potent to divulge
The thing He wills, or hide it? Brethren, God
Shrouding from us that beam far dwellers saw
Admonished us perchance that far is near;
That ofttimes distance makes intelligible
What, nigh at hand, is veiled. This too He taught,
That when Northumbrian foot our Mercia spurned
The men who saw that ruin saw not all:
The light of Christ drew near us in that hour;
His pillar o'er us stood, and in our midst:
The pang, the shame, were transient. See the whole!'

　　The old man paused a space, and then resumed:
'Brethren, that day our country suffered wrong:
One day she may inflict it. Years may bring
The aggressor of past time a penitent grief;
The wronged may meet her penitence with scorn
Guiltier through malice than her foe's worst rage:
Were it not well to leave that time unborn
Magnanimous ensample? Hard it were
To lay in Mercian earth the unforgiven:
Wholly to pardon—that I deem not hard.
My voice is this: forgive we Oswald's sin,
And lay his relics in our costliest shrine!'

　　Thus spake the aged man. That self-same eve,
The western sun descending, while the church,
Grey shaft transfigured by the glow divine,
Grey wall in flame of light pacific washed,
Shone out all golden like that flower all gold
Which shoots through sunset airs an arrowy beam,

In charity perfected moved the monks,
No longer sad, a long procession forth,
With foreheads smoothed as by the kiss of death
And eyes like eyes of Saints from death new risen,
Bearing the relics of Northumbria's King,
Oswald, the man of God. Behind them paced
Warriors and chiefs; Osthryda last, the Queen,
With face whereon that great miraculous light,
By her all night unseen, appeared to rest,
And foot that might have trod the ocean waves
Unwetted save its palm. A shrine gem-wrought
Received the royal relics. O'er them drooped
Northumbria's standard, guest of Mercian airs
Through which it once had sailed, a portent dire :
And whosoe'er in after centuries knelt
On Oswald's grave, and, praying, wooed his prayer,
Departed, in his heart the peace of God,
Passions corrupt expelled, and demon snares,
Irreverent love, and anger past its bound.

HOW SAINT CUTHBERT KEPT HIS PENTECOST AT CARLISLE.

Saint Cuthbert while a boy wanders among the woods of Northumbria, bringing solace to all. Later he lives alone in the island of Farne. Being made bishop, many predict that he will be able neither to teach his people nor to rule his diocese. His people flock to him gladly, but require that he should teach them by parable and tale. This he does, and likewise rules his diocese with might. He discourses concerning common life. Keeping his Pentecost at Carlisle, he preaches on that Feast and the Resurrection from the Dead. Herbert, an eremite, beseeching him that the two may die the same day, he prays accordingly, and they die the same hour.

SAINT CUTHBERT, yet a youth, for many a year
Walked up and down the green Northumbrian vales
Well loving God and man. The rockiest glens
And promontories shadowing loneliest seas,
Where lived the men least cared for, most forlorn,
He sought, and brought to each the words of peace.
Where'er he went he preached that God all Love:
For, as the sun in heaven, so flamed in him
That love which later fired Assisi's Saint:
Yea, rumour ran that every mountain beast
Obeyed his loving call ; that when all night
He knelt upon the frosty hills in prayer
The hare would couch her by his naked feet
And warm them with her fur. To manhood grown
He dwelt in Lindisfarne ; there, year by year
Prospering yet more in vigil and in fast ;
And paced its shores by night, and blent his hymns
With din of waves. Yet ofttimes o'er the strait

He passed, once more in search of suffering men
Wafting them solace still.   Where'er he went
Those loved as children first, again he loved
As youth and maid, and in them nursed that Faith
Through which pure youth passes o'er passion's waves
Like Him Who trod that Galilean sea:
He clasped the grey-grown sinner in his arms
And won from him repentance long delayed,
Then with him shared the penance he enjoined.
O heart both strong and tender! offering Mass
Awe-struck he stood as though on Calvary's height:
The men who marked him shook.

      Twelve winters passed:
Then mandate fell upon the Saint from God,
Or breathed upon him from the heavenly height,
Or haply from within.   It drave him forth
A hermit into solitudes more stern.
'Farewell,' he said, 'my brethren and my friends!
No holier life than yours, pure Cœnobites
Pacing one cloister, sharing one spare meal,
Chanting to God one hymn! yet I must forth—
Farewell, my friends, farewell!'   On him they gazed
And knew that God had spoken to his soul
And silent stood though sorrowing.

      Long that eve
The brethren grieved noting his vacant stall,
Yet thus excused their sadness: 'Well for him,
And high his place in heaven; but woe to those
Henceforth of services like his amerced!
Here lived he in the world; here many throng;
To him in time some lesser bishopric
Might well have fallen, behoof of countless souls!
Such dream is past forever.'

      Forth he fared

To Farne, a little rocky islet nigh,
Where man till then had never dared to dwell
By dreadful rumours scared. In narrow cave
Worn from the rock, and roughly walled around,
The anchoret made abode, with lonely hands
Raising from one poor strip his daily food
Barley thin-grown, and coarse. He saw by day
The clouds on-sailing, and by night the stars;
And heard the eternal waters. Thus recluse
The man lived on in vision still of God
Through contemplation known: and as the shades
Each other chase all day o'er steadfast hills,
Even so, athwart that Vision unremoved
Forever rushed the tumults of this world,
Man's fleeting life, the rise and fall of states,
While changeless measured change; the spirit of prayer
Fanning that wondrous picture oft to flame
Until the glory grew insufferable.
Long years thus lived he. As the Apostle Paul
Though raised in raptures to the heaven of heavens,
Not therefore loved his brethren less, but longed
To give his life—his all—for Israel's sake
So Cuthbert, loving God, loved man the more,
His wont of old. To him the mourners came,
And sinners bound by Satan. At his touch
Their chains fell from them light as summer dust:
Each word he spake was as a Sacrament
Clothed with God's grace; beside his feet they sat,
And in their perfect mind; thence through the world
Bare their deliverer's name.
     So passed his life:
There old he grew, and older yet appeared,
By fasts outworn, though ever young at heart;
When lo! before that isle a barge there drew

Bearing the royal banner. Egfrid there
With regal sceptre sat, and many an earl,
And many a mitred bishop at his side.
Northumbria's see was void: a council's voice
Joined with a monarch's called him to its throne:
In vain he wept, and knelt, and sued for grace:
Six months' reprieve alone he won; then ruled
In Lindisfarne, chief bishop of the North.

   But certain spake who deemed that they were wise,
Fools all beside: 'Shall Cuthbert crosier lift?
A child, 'tis known he herded flocks for hire,
Housed in old Renspid's hut, his Irish nurse,
Who told him tales of Leinster Kings, his sires
And how her hands, their palace wrecked in war
Had snatched him from its embers. Yet a boy
He rode to Melrose and its wondering monks,
A mimic warrior, in his hand a lance,
With shepherd youth for page, and spake: " 'Tis known
Christ's kingdom is a kingdom militant:
A son of Kings I come to guard His right
And battle 'gainst his foes!" For lance and sword
A book they gave him; and they made him monk:
Savage since then he couches on a rock
As fame reports, with birds' nests in his beard!
Can dreamers change to Bishops? Vision-dazed
Move where he may that slowly wandering eye
Will see in man no more than kites or hawks;
Men, if they note, will flee him.' Thus they buzzed,
Self-praised, and knowing not that simpleness
Is sacred soil, and sown with royal seed
The heroic seed and saintly.
                        Mitred once
Such gibes no more assailed him: one short month

Sufficed the petty cavil to confute;
One month well chronicled in book which verse
Late born, alas, in vain would emulate.
At once he called to mind the days that were;
His wanderings in Northumbrian glens; the hearths
That welcomed him so joyously; at once
Within his breast the heart parental yearned;
He longed to see his children, scattered wide
From Humber's bank to Tweed, from sea to sea,
And cried to those around him: 'Let us forth,
And visit all my charge: and since Carlisle
Remotest sits upon its western bound,
Keep there this year our Pentecost!' Next day
He passed the sands left hard by ebbing tide
His cross-bearer and brethren six in front
And trod the mainland. Reverent, first he sought
His childhood's nurse, and 'neath her humble roof
Abode one night. To Melrose next he fared
Honouring his master old. Southward once more
Returning, scarce a bow-shot from the woods
There rode to him a mighty thane, one-eyed,
With warriors circled, on a jet-black horse,
Barbaric shape and huge, yet frank as fierce
Who thus made boast: 'A Jute devout am I!
What raised that convent-pile on yonder rock?
This hand! I wrenched the hillside from a foe
By force, and gave it to thy Christian monks
To spite yet more those Angles! Island Saint,
Unprofitable have I found thy Faith!
Behold, those priests, thy thralls, are savage men,
Unrighteous, ruthless! For a sin of mine
They laid on me a hundred days of fast!
A man am I keen-witted: friend and liege

I summoned, shewed my wrong, and ended thus :
"Sirs, ye are ninety-nine, the hundredth I ;
I counsel that we share this fast among us !
To-morrow from the dawn to evening's star
No food as bulky as a spider's tongue
Shall pass our lips; and thus in one day's time
My hundred days of fast shall stand fulfilled."
Wrathful they rose, and sware by Peter's keys
That fight they would, albeit 'gainst Peter's self ;
But fast they would not save for personal sins.
Signal I made : then backward rolled the gates,
And, captured thus, they fasted without thanks,
Cancelling my debt—a hundred days in one !
Beseech you, Father, chide your priests who breed
Contention thus 'mid friends !' The Saint replied
' Penance is irksome, Thane : to 'scape its scourge
Ways are there various ; and the easiest this,
Keep far from mortal sin.'
                    Where'er he faced
The people round him pressed—the sick, the blind,
Young mothers sad because a babe was pale ;
Likewise the wives of fishers praying loud
Their husbands' safe return. Rejoiced he was
To see them, hear them, touch them ; wearied never :
Whate'er they said delighted still he heard :
The rise and fall of empires touched him less,
The book rich-blazoned, or the high-towered church :
' We have,' he said ' God's children, and their God :
The rest is fancy's work.' Him too they loved ;
Loved him the more because, so great and wise
He stumbled oft in trifles. Once he said,
' How well those pine-trees shield the lamb from
    wind !'
A smile ran round ; at last the boldest spake

'Father, these are not pine-trees—these are oaks.'
And Cuthbert answered, 'Oaks, good sooth, they are!
In youth I knew the twain apart: the pine
Wears on his head the Cross.' Instruction next
He gave them, how the Cross had vanquished sin:
Then first abstruse to some appeared his words.
'Father,' they answered, 'speak in parables!
For pleasant is the tale, and, onward passed,
Keeps in our heart thy lesson.'
                                    While they spake
A youth rich-vested tossed his head and cried:
'Father, why thus converse with untaught hinds?
Their life is but the life of gnats and flies:
They think but of the hour. Behold yon church!
I reared it both for reverence of thy Christ
And likewise that through ages yet to come
My name might live in honour!' At that word
Cuthbert made answer: 'Hear the parable!
My people craved for such.
                              A monk there lived
Holiest of men reputed. He was first
On winter mornings in the freezing stall;
Meekest when chidden; fervent most in prayer:
And, late in life, when heresies arose,
That book he wrote, like tempest winged from God,
Drave them to darkness back. Grey-haired he died;
With honour was interred. The years went by;
His grave they opened. Peacefully he slept,
Unchanged, the smile of death upon his lips:
O'er the right hand alone, for so it seemed,
Had Death retained his power: five little lines,
White ashes, showed where once the fingers lay.
All saw it—simple, learned, rich and poor:
None might divine the cause. That night, behold!

A Saintly Shape beside the abbot stood,
Bright like the sun except one lifted palm:
Thereon there lay a stain. "Behold that hand!"
The Spirit spake, "that, toiling twenty years
Sent forth that book which pacified the world;
For it the world would canonise me Saint!
See that ye do it not! Inferior tasks
I wrought for God alone. Building that book
Too oft I mused, 'Far years will give thee praise.'
I expiate that offence."'
      Another day
A sweet-faced woman raised her voice, and cried,
'Father! those sins denounced by God I flee;
Yet tasks imposed by God too oft neglect:
Stands thus a soul imperilled?' Cuthbert spake:
'Ye sued for parables; I speak in such
Though ill, a language strange to me, and new.
There lived a man who shunned committed sin,
Yet daily by omission sinned and knew it:
In his own way, not God's, he served his God;
And there was with him peace; yet not God's peace.
So passed his youth. In age he dreamed a dream:
He dreamed that, being dead, he raised his eyes,
And saw a mountain range of frozen snows,
And heard "Committed sins innumerable
Though each one small, so small thou knew'st them
  not,
Uplifted, flake by flake as sin by sin,
Yon barrier 'twixt thy God and thee! Arise,
Remembering that of sins despair is worst:
Be strong, and scale it!" Fifty years he scaled
Those hills; so long it seemed. A cavern next
Entering, with mole-like hands he scooped his way,
And reached at last the gates of morn. Ah me!

A stone's cast from him rose the tree of Life:
He heard its sighs ecstatic: Full in view
The Beatific River rolled; beyond
All-glorious shone the City of the Saints
Clothed with God's light! And yet from him that realm
Was severed by a gulf! Not wide that strait;
It seemed a strong man's leap twice told—no more;
But, as insuperably soared that cliff,
Unfathomably thus its sheer descent
Walled the abyss. Again he heard that Voice:
"Henceforth no place remains for active toils,
Penance for acts perverse. Inactive sloth
Through passive suffering meets its due. On earth
That sloth a nothing seemed; a nothing now
That chasm whose hollow bars thee from the Blest,
Poor slender film of insubstantial air.
Self-help is there denied thee: for that cause
A twofold term thou need'st of pain love-taught
To expiate Love that lacked." That term complete
An angel caught him o'er that severing gulf:
Thenceforth he saw his God.'
                              With such discourse
Progress, though slow and interrupted oft,
The Saint of God, by no delay perturbed,
Made daily through his sacred charge. One eve
He walked by pastures arched along the sea,
With many companied. The on-flowing breeze
Glazed the green hill-tops, bending still one way
The glossy grasses; limitless below
The ocean mirror, clipped by cape or point
With low trees inland leaning, lay like lakes
Flooding rich lowlands. Southward far, a rock
Touched by a rainy beam, emerged from mist,

And shone, half green, half gold. That rock was
    Farne:
Though strangers, those that kenned it guessed its
    name :
'Doubtless 'twas there,' they said, 'our Saint abode!'
Then pressed around him, questioning: 'Rumour goes,
Father beloved, that in thine island home
Thou sat'st all day with hammer small in hand,
Shaping, from pebbles veined, miraculous beads
That save their wearers still from sword and lance:—
Are these things true?' Smiling the Saint replied:
'True, and not true! That isle in part is spread
With pebbles divers-fashioned, some like beads:
I gathered such, and gave to many a guest,
Adding, "Such beads shall count thy nightly prayers;
Pray well; then fear no peril!"'
                              Others came
And thus demanded: 'Rumour fills the world,
Father, that birds miraculous crowned thine isle,
And awe-struck let thee lift them in thy hand,
Though scared by all beside.' Smiling once more
The Saint made answer, 'True, and yet not true!
Sea-birds elsewhere beheld not throng that isle;
A breed so loving and so firm in trust
That, yet unharmed by man, they flee not man;
Wondering they gaze; who wills may close upon them!
I signed a league betwixt that race and man:
Pledging the mariners who sought my cell
To reverence still that trust.' He ended thus:
'My friends, ye seek me still for parables;
Seek them from Nature rather:—here are two!
Those pebble-beads are words from Nature's lips
Exhorting man to pray; those fearless birds
Teach him that trust to innocence belongs

By right divine, and more avails than craft
To shield us from the aggressor.' Some were glad
Hearing that doctrine; others cried, 'Not so!
Our Saint—all know it—makes miraculous beads;
But, being humble, he conceals his might:'
And many an age, when slept that Saint in death,
Passing his isle by night the sailor heard
Saint Cuthbert's hammer clinking on the rock;
And age by age men cried, 'Our Cuthbert's birds
Revere the Saint's command.'
       While thus they spake
A horseman over moorlands near the Tweed
Made hasty way, and thus addressed the Saint:
'Father, Queen Ermenburga greets thee well,
And this her message:—"Queen am I forlorn,
Long buffeted by many a storm of State,
And worn at heart besides; for in our house
Peace lived not inmate, but a summer guest;
And now, my lord, the King is slain in fight;
And changed the aspect now things wore of old:
Thou therefore, man of God, approach my gates
With counsel sage. This further I require;
Thy counsel must be worthy of a Queen,
Nor aught contain displeasing."' Cuthbert spake:
'My charge requires my presence at Carlisle;
Beseech the Queen to meet me near its wall
On this day fortnight.'
      Thitherwards thenceforth
Swiftlier he passed, while daily from the woods
The woodmen flocked, and shepherds from the hills,
Concourse still widening. These among there moved
A hermit meek as childhood, calm as eld,
Long years Saint Cuthbert's friend. Recluse he lived
Within a woody isle of that fair lake

By Derwent lulled and Greta. Others thronged
Round Cuthbert's steps; that hermit stood apart
With large dark eyes upon his countenance fixed
And pale cheek dewed with tears. The name he bore
Was 'Herbert of the Lake.'
        Two weeks went by,
And Cuthbert reached his journey's end. Next day
God sent once more His Feast of Pentecost
To gladden men; and all His Church on earth
Shone out, irradiate as by silver gleams
Flashed from her whiter Sister in the skies;
And every altar laughed, and every hearth;
And many a simple hind in spirit heard
The wind which through that 'upper chamber' swept
Careering through the universe of God,
New life through all things poured. Cuthbert that day,
Borne on by wingèd winds of rapturous thought,
Forth from Carlisle had fared alone, and reached
Ere long a mead tree-girdled;—in its midst
Swift-flowing Eden raced from fall to fall,
Showering at times her spray on flowers as fair
As graced that earlier Eden; flowers so light
Each feeblest breath impalpable to man
Now shook them and now swayed. Delighted eye
The Saint upon them fixed. Ere long he gazed
As glad on crowds thronging the river's marge,
For now the high-walled city poured abroad
Her children rich and poor. At last he spake:
'Glory to Him Who made both flowers and souls!
He doeth all things well! A few weeks past
Yon river rushed by wintry banks forlorn;
What decks it thus to-day? The voice of Spring!
She called those flowers from darkness forth; she flashed

Her life into the snowy breast of each :
This day she sits enthroned on each and all :
The thrones are myriad ; but the Enthroned is One ! '
He paused ; then, kindling, added thus : ' O friends !
'Tis thus with human souls through faith re-born :
One Spirit calls them forth from darkness ; shapes
One Christ, in each conceived, its life of life ;
One God finds rest enthroned on all. Once more
The thrones are many ; but the Enthroned is One ! '
Again he paused, and mused ; again he spake :
' Yea, and in heaven itself, a hierarchy
There is that glories in the name of " Thrones : "
The high cherubic knowledge is not theirs :
Not theirs the fiery flight of Seraph's love,
But all their restful beings they dilate
To make a single, myriad throne for God—
Children, abide in unity and love !
So shall your lives be one long Pentecost,
Your hearts one throne for God ! '
       As thus he spake
A breeze, wide-wandering through the woodlands near,
Illumed their golden roofs, while louder sang
The birds on every bough. Then horns were heard
Resonant from stem to stem, from rock to rock,
While moved in sight a stately cavalcade
Flushing the river's crystal. Of that host
Foremost and saddest Ermenburga rode,
A Queen sad-eyed, with large imperial front
By sorrow seamed : a lady rode close by ;
Behind her earls and priests. Though proud to man
Her inborn greatness made her meek to God :
She signed the Saint to stay not his discourse,
And placed her at his feet.
      His words were great

He spake of Pentecost; no transient grace,
No fugitive act, consummated, then gone,
But God's perpetual presence in that Church
O'er-shadowed still, like Mary, by His Spirit,
Fecundated in splendour by His Truth,
Made loving through His Love. The reign of Love
He showed, though perfected in Christ alone,
Not less co-eval with the race of man:
For what is man? Not mind: the beasts can think:
Not passions; appetites: the beasts have these:
Nay, but Affections ruled by Laws Divine:
These make the life of man. Of these he spake;
Proclaimed of these the glory. These to man
Are countless loves revealing Love Supreme:
These and the Virtues, warp and woof, enweave
A single robe—that sacrificial garb
Worn from the first by man, whose every act
Of love in spirit was self-sacrifice,
And prophesied the Sacrifice Eterne:
Through these the world becomes one household vast;
Through these each hut swells to a universe
Traversed by stateliest energies wind-swift,
And planet-crowned, beneath their Maker's eye.
All hail, Affections, angels of the earth!
Woe to that man who boasts of love to God,
And yet his neighbour scorns! While Cuthbert spake
A young man whispered to a priest, 'Is yon
That Anchoret of the rock? Where learned he then
This loving reverence for the hearth and home?
Mark too that glittering brow!' The priest replied:
'What! shall a bridegroom's face alone be bright?
He knows a better mystery! This he knows,
That, come what may, all o'er the earth forever
God keeps His blissful Bridal-feast with man:

Each true heart there is guest!'
                            Once more the Saint
Arose and spake: 'O loving friends, my children,
Christ's sons, His flock committed to my charge!
I spake to you but now of humbler ties,
Not highest, with intent that ye might know
How pierced are earthly bonds by heavenly beam;
Yet, speaking with lame tongue in parables,
I showed you but similitudes of things—
Twilight, not day. Make question then who will;
So shall I mend my teaching.'
                            Prompt and bright
As children issuing forth to holyday,
Then flocked to Cuthbert's school full many a man
Successive: each with simpleness of heart
His doubt propounded; each his question asked,
Or, careless who might hear, confessed his sins,
And absolution won. Among the rest,
A little seven years' boy, with sweet, still face,
Yet strong not less, and sage, drew softly near,
His great calm eyes upon the patriarch fixed
And silent stood. From Wessex came that boy:
By chance Northumbria's guest. Meantime a chief
Demanded thus: 'Of all the works of might,
What task is worthiest?' Cuthbert made reply:
'His who to land barbaric fearless fares,
And open flings God's palace gate to all,
And cries "Come in!"' That concourse thrilled for
    joy:
Alone that seven years' child retained the word:
The rest forgat it. 'Winifrede' that day
Men called him; later centuries, 'Boniface,'
Because he shunned the ill, and wrought the good:
In time the Teuton warriors knew that brow,

Their great Apostle he: they knew that voice:
And happy Fulda venerates this day
Her martyr's gravestone.
                          Next, to Cuthbert drew
Three maidens hand in hand, lovely as Truth,
Trustful, though shy: their thoughts, when hidden
    most,
Wore but a semilucid veil, as when
Through gold-touched crystal of the lime new-leaved
On April morns the symmetry looks forth
Of branch and bough distinct. Smiling, they put
At last their question: 'Tell us, man of God,
What life, of lives that women lead, is best;
Then show us forth in parables that life!'

  He answered: 'Three; for each of these is best:
First comes the Maiden's: she who lives it well
Serves God in marble chapel white as snow,
His priestess—His alone. Cold flowers each morn
She culls ere sunrise by the stainless stream,
And lays them on that chapel's altar-stone
And sings her matins there. Her feet are swift
All day in labours 'mid the vales below,
Cheering sad hearts: each evening she returns
To that high fane, and there her vespers sings;
Then sleeps, and dreams of heaven.'
                                   With witching smile
The youngest of that beauteous triad cried:
'That life is sweetest! I would be that maid!'
Cuthbert resumed: 'The Christian Wife comes next:
She drinks a deeper draught of life: round her
In ampler sweep its sympathies extend:
An infant's cry has knocked against her heart,
Evoking thence that human love wherein
Self-love hath least. Through infant eyes a spirit

Hath looked upon her, crying, "I am thine!
Creature from God; dependent yet on thee!"
Thenceforth she knows how greatness blends with
 weakness;
Reverence, thenceforth, with pity linked, reveals
To her the pathos of the life of man
A thing divine, and yet at every pore
Bleeding from crownèd brows. A heart thus large
Hath room for many sorrows. What of that?
Its sorrow is its dowry's noblest part.
She bears it not alone. Such griefs, so shared
Sickness, and fear, and vigils lone and long
Waken her heart to love sublimer far
Than ecstasies of youth could comprehend;
Lift her perchance to heights serene as those
The Ascetic treadeth.'
                            'I would be that wife;'
Thus cried the second of those maidens three:
Yet who that gazed upon her could have guessed
Creature so soft could bear a heart so brave?
She seemed that goodness which was beauteous too;
Virtue at once and Virtue's bright reward;
Delight that lifts, not lowers us; made for heaven;
Made too to change to heaven some brave man's hearth.
She added thus: 'Of lives that women lead
Tell us the third!'
                        Gently the Saint replied:
'The third is Widowhood—a wintry sound;
And yet, for her who widow is indeed
That winter something keeps of autumn's gold,
Something regains of Spring's first flower snow-white,
Snow-cold, and colder for its rim of green.
She feels no more the warmly-greeting hand;
The eyes she brightened rest on her no more;

Her full-orbed being now is cleft in twain :
Her past is dead : daily from memory's self
Dear things depart ; yet still she is a wife,
A wife the more because of bridal bonds
Lives but their essence, waiting wings in heaven ;
More wife ; and yet, in that great loneliness,
More maiden too than when first maidenhood
Lacked what it missed not.   Like that other maid
She too a lonely Priestess serves her God ;
Yea, though her chapel be a funeral vault,
Its altar black like Death ; the flowers thereon,
Tinct with the Blood Divine.   Above that vault
She hears the anthems of the Spouse of Christ,
Widowed like her, though Bride.'

        'O fair, O sweet,
O beauteous lives all three ; fair lot of woman !'
Thus cried again the youngest of those Three,
Too young to know the touch of grief or cause it,
A plant too lightly leaved to cast a shade.
The eldest with pale cheek, and lids tear-wet,
Made answer sad : 'I would not be a widow.'

 Then Cuthbert spake once more with smile benign :
'I said that each of these three lives is best :—
There are who live those three conjoined in one :
The nun thus lives !   What maid is maid like her
Who, free to choose, has vowed a maidenhood
Secure 'gainst chance or choice ? What bride like her
Whose Bridegroom is the spouse of vestal souls ?
What widow lives in such austere retreat,
Such hourly thought of him she ne'er can join
Save through the gate of death ?   If those three lives
In separation lived are fair and sweet,
How show they, blent in one ?'

        Of those who heard

The most part gladdened; those who knew how high
Virtue, renouncing all besides for God,
Hath leave to soar on earth.   Yet many sighed,
Jealous for happy homesteads.   Cuthbert marked
That shame-faced sadness, and continued thus:
'To praise the nun reproaches not, O friends,
But praises best that life of hearth and home
At Cana blessed by Him who shared it not.
The uncloistered life is holy too, and oft
Through changeful years in soft succession links
Those three fair types of woman; holds, diffused,
That excellence severe which life detached
Sustains in concentration.'   Long he mused;
Then added thus: 'When last I roved these vales
There lived, not distant far, a blessed one
Revered by all: her name was Ethelreda:
I knew her long, and much from her I learned.
Beneath her Pagan father's roof there sat
Ofttimes a Christian youth.   With him the child
Walked, calling him "her friend."   He loved the
    maid:
Still young, he drew her to the fold of Christ;
Espoused her three years later; died in war
Ere three months passed.   For her he never died!
Immortalised by faith that bond lived on;
And now close by, and now 'mid Saints of heaven
She saw her husband walk.   She never wept;
That fire which lit her eye and flushed her cheek
Dried up, it seemed, her tears: the neighbours round
Called her "the lady of the happy marriage."
She died long since, I doubt not.'   Forward stepped
A slight, pale maid, the daughter of a bard,
And answered thus: 'Two months ago she died.'
Then Cuthbert: 'Tell me, maiden, of her death;

And see you be not chary of your words,
For well I loved that woman.' Tears unfelt
Fast streaming down her pallid cheek, the maid
Replied, yet often paused : 'A sad, sweet end!
A long night's pain had left her living still :
I found her on the threshold of her door :
Her cheek was white ; but, trembling round her lips
And dimly o'er her countenance spread, there lay
Something that, held in check by feebleness,
Yet tended to a smile. A cloak tight-drawn
From the cold March wind screened her, save one hand
Stretched on her knee, that reached to where a beam
Thin slip of watery sunshine, sunset's last,
Slid through the branches. On that beam, methought,
Rested her eyes half-closed. It was not so :
For when I knelt, and kissed that hand ill-warmed,
Smiling she said : "The small, unwedded maid
Has missed her mark! You should have kissed the
  ring!
Full forty years upon a widowed hand
It holds its own. It takes its latest sunshine."
She lived through all that night and died while dawned
Through snows Saint Joseph's morn.'
      The Queen, with hand
Sudden and swift, brushed from her cheek a tear ;
And many a sob from that thick-crowding host
Confessed what tenderest love can live in hearts
Defamed by fools as barbarous. Cuthbert sat
In silence long. Before his eyes she passed
The maid, the wife, the widow, all in one ;
With these, through these, he saw once more the
  child,
Yea, saw the child's smile on the lips of death,
That magic, mystic smile! O heart of man,

What strange capacities of grief and joy
Are thine! How vain, how ruthless such, if given
For transient things alone! O life of man!
What wert thou but some laughing demon's scoff
If prelude only to the eternal grave!
'Deep cries to deep'; ay, but the deepest deep
Crying to summits of the Mount of God
Drags forth for echo, 'Immortality.'
It was the Death Divine that vanquished death!
Shorn of that Death Divine the Life Divine,
Albeit its feeblest tear had cleansed all worlds
Cancelled all guilt, had failed to reach and sound
The deepest in man's nature, Love and Grief,
Profoundest each when joined in penitent woe;
Failed thence to wake man's hope. The loftiest light
Flashed from God's Face on Reason's orient verge
Answers that bird-cry from the *Heart* of man—
Poor Heart that, darkling, kept so long its watch
The auspice of the dawn.
      Like one inspired
The Saint arose, and raised his hands to God;
Then to his people turned with such discourse
As mocks the hand of scribe. No more he spake
In parables; adumbrated no more
'Dimly as in a glass' his doctrine high,
But placed it face to face before men's eyes,
Essential Truth, God's image, meet for man
Himself God's image. Worlds he showed them new,
Worlds countless as the stars that roof our night,
Fair fruitage of illimitable boughs
Pushed from that Tree of life from Calvary sprung
That over-tops and crowns the earth and man,
Preached the Resurgent, the Ascended God
Dispensing 'gifts to men.' The tongue he spake

Seemed Pentecostal—grace of that high Feast—
For all who heard, the simple and the sage,
Heard still a single language sounding forth
To all one Promise. From that careworn Queen
Who doffed her crown, and placed it on the rock
Murmuring, 'Farewell forever, foolish gaud,'
To him the humblest hearer, all made vow
To live thenceforth for God. The form itself
Of each was changed to saintly and to sweet;
Each countenance beamed as though with rays cast
    down
From fiery tongues, or angel choirs unseen.

  Thus like high gods on mountain-tops of joy
Those happy listeners sat. The body quelled—
With all that body's might usurped to cramp
Through ceaseless, yet unconscious weight of sense
Conceptions spiritual, might more subtly skilled
Than lusts avowed, to sap the spirit's life—
In every soul its nobler Powers released
Stood up, no more a jarring crowd confused
Each trampling each and oft the worst supreme,
Not thus, but grade o'er grade, in order due,
And pomp hierarchical. Yet hand in hand,
Not severed, stood those Powers. To every Mind
That Truth new learned was palpable and dear,
Not abstract nor remote, with cordial strength
Enclasped as by a heart; through every Heart
Serene affections swam 'mid seas of light
Reason's translucent empire without bound,
Fountained from God. Silent those listeners sat
Parleying in wordless thought. For them the world
Was lost—and won; its sensuous aspects quenched;
Its heavenly import grasped. The erroneous Past
Lay like a shrivelled scroll before their feet;

And sweet as some immeasurable rose,
Expanding leaf on leaf, varying yet one,
An Everlasting Present round them glowed.
Dead was desire, and dead not less was fear—
The fear of change—of death.
                              An hour went by;
The sun declined: then rising from his seat
Herbert, the anchoret of the lonely lake,
Made humble way to Cuthbert's feet with suit:
'O Father, and O friend, thou saw'st me not;
Yet day by day thus far I tracked thy steps
At distance, for my betters leaving place,
The great and wise that round thee thronged; the
    young
Who ne'er till then had seen thy face; the old
Who saw it then yet scarce again may see it.
Father, a happier lot was mine, though late,
Or had been save for sin of mine: each year
I sought thy cell, thy words of wisdom heard;
Yet still, alas! lived on like sensual men
Who yield their hearts to creatures—fixing long
A foolish eye on gold-touched leaf, or flower—
Not Him, the great Creator. Father and Friend,
The years run past. I crave one latest boon:
Grant that we two may die the self-same day!'
Then Cuthbert knelt, and prayed. At last he spake:
'Thy prayer is heard; the self-same day and hour
We two shall die.'
                 That promise was fulfilled;
For two years only on exterior tasks
God set His servant's hands, the man who 'sought
In all things rest,' nor e'er had ceased from rest
Then when his task was heaviest. Two brief years
He roamed on foot his spiritual realm;

The simple still he taught: the sad he cheered:
Where'er he went he founded churches still
And convents; yea, and, effort costlier far,
Spared not to scan defect with vigilant eye:
That eye the boldest called not 'vision-dazed';
That Saint he found no 'dreamer': sloth or greed
'Scaped not his vengeance: scandals hid he not,
But dragged them into day, and smote them down:
Before his face he drave the hireling priest
The bandit thane: unceasing cried, 'Ye kings,
Cease from your wars! Ye masters, loose your slaves!'
Two years sufficed; for all his earlier years
Had trained the Ascetic for those works of might
Beyond the attempt of all but boundless love,
And in him kept unspent the fire divine.
Never such Bishop walked till then the North,
Nor ever since, nor ever, centuries fled,
So lived in hearts of men. Two years gone by,
His strength decayed. He sought once more his cell
Sea-lulled; and lived alone with God; and saw
Once more, like lights that sweep the unmoving hills,
God's Providences girdling all the world,
With glory following glory. Tenderer-souled
Herbert meantime within his isle abode,
At midnight listening Derwent's gladsome voice
Mingling with deep-toned Greta's, 'Mourner' named;
Pacing, each day, the shore; now gazing glad
On gold-touched leaf, or bird that cut the mere,
Now grieved at wandering thoughts. For men he
    prayed;
And ever strove to raise his soul to God;
And God, Who venerates still the pure intent,
Forgat not his; and since his spirit and heart
Holy albeit, were in the eyes Divine

Less ripe than Cuthbert's for the Vision Blest,
Least faults perforce swelling where gifts are vast,
That God vouchsafed His servant sickness-pains
Virtue to perfect in a little space,
That both might pass to heaven the self-same hour.

    It came: that sun which flushed the spray up-hurled
In cloud round Cuthbert's eastern rock, while he
Within it dying chanted psalm on psalm,
Ere long enkindled Herbert's western lake:
The splendour waxed; mountain to mountain laughed,
And, brightening nearer drew, and, nearing, clasped
That heaven-dropp'd beauty in more strict embrace:
The cliffs successive caught their crowns of fire;
Blencathara last. Slowly that splendour waned;
And from the glooming gorge of Borrodale,
Her purple cowl shadowing her holy head
O'er the dim lake twilight with silent foot
Stepped like a spirit. Herbert from his bed
Of shingles watched that sunset till it died;
And at one moment from their distant isles
Those friends, by death united, passed to God.

SAINT FRIDESWIDA, OR THE FOUNDATIONS OF OXFORD.

Frideswida flies from the pursuit of a wicked king, invoking the Divine aid and the prayers of St. Catherine and St. Cecilia. She escapes; and at the hour of her death those Saints reveal to her that in that place, near the Isis, where she had successively opened a blind man's eyes and healed a leper, God will one day raise up a seat of Learning, the light and the health of the realm.

'ONE love I; One: within His bridal bower
My feet shall tread: One love I, One alone:
His Mother is a Virgin, and His Sire
The unfathomed fount of pureness undefiled:
Him love I Whom to love is to be chaste:
Him love I touched by Whom my forehead shines:
Whom she that clasps grows spotless more and more:
Behold, to mine His spirit He hath joined:
And His the blood that mantles in my cheek:
His ring is on my finger.'
       Thus she sang;
Then walked and plucked a flower: she sang again:
'That which I longed for, lo, the same I see:
That which I hoped for, lo, my hand doth hold:
At last in heaven I walk with Him conjoined
Whom, yet on earth, I loved with heart entire.'
 Thus carolled Frideswida all alone,
Treading the opens of a wood far spread
Around the upper waters of the Thames.
Christian almost by instinct, earth to her
Was shaped but to sustain the Cross of Christ.

Her mother lived a saint: she taught her child,
From reason's dawn, to note in all things fair
Their sacred undermeanings. 'Mark, my child,
In lamb and dove, not fleshly shapes,' she said,
'But heavenly types: upon the robin's breast
Revere that red which bathed her from the Cross
With slender bill striving to loose those Nails!'
Dying, that mother placed within her hand
A book of saintly legends. Thus the maid
Grew up with mysteries clothed, with marvels fed,
A fearless creature swift as wind or fire:
But fires of hers were spirit-fires alone,
All else like winter moon. The Wessex King
Had gazed upon the glory of her face
And deemed that face a spirit's. He had heard
Her voice; it sounded like an angel's song;
But wonder by degrees declined to love
Such love as Pagans know. The unworthy suit
She scorned, from childhood spoused in heart to Christ:
She fled: upon the river lay a boat:
She rowed it on through forests many a mile;
A month had passed since then.
       Midsummer blazed
On all things round: the vast, unmoving groves
Stretched silent forth their immemorial arms
Arching a sultry gloom. Within it buzzed
Feebly the insect swarm: the dragon-fly
Stayed soon his flight: the streamlet scarce made way:
In shrunken pools, panting, the cattle stood,
Languidly browsing on the dried-up sprays:
No bird-song shook the bower. Alone that maid
Glided light-limbed, as though some Eden breeze
Hers only, charioted the songstress on,
Like those that serve the May. Beneath a tree

Low-roofed at last she sank, with eyes up-raised
On boughs that, ivy-twined and creeper-trailed
Darkened the shining splendour of the sky:
Between their interspaces, here and there,
It flashed in purple stars.
                          Enraptured long,
For admiration was to her as love,
The maiden raised at last her mother's book,
And lit upon her childhood's favourite tale,
Catherine in vision wed to Bethlehem's Babe
Who from His Virgin-Mother leaning, dropped
His ring adown her finger.   Princely pride
And pride not less of soaring intellect
At once in her were changed to pride of love:
In vain her country's princes sued her grace;
Kingdoms of earth she spurned.   Around her seat
The far-famed Alexandrian Sages thronged,
Branding her Faith as novel.   Slight and tall,
'Mid them, keen-eyed the wingless creature stood
Like daughter of the sun on earth new-lit :—
That Faith she shewed to be of all things greatest,
All lesser truths its prophets.   Swift as beams
Forth flashed such shafts of high intelligence
That straight their lore sophistic shrivelled up,
And Christians they arose.   The martyr's wheel
Was pictured in the margin, dyed with red,
And likewise, azure-tinct on golden ground,
Her queenly throne in heaven.   'Ah shining Saint!'
Half weeping, smiling half, the virgin cried;
'Yet dear not less thy sister of the West;
For never gaze I on that lifted face,
Or mark that sailing angel near her stayed,
But straight her solemn organs round me swell;
All discords cease.'   Then with low voice she read

Of Rome's Cecilia, her who won to Christ
(That earlier troth inviolably preserved)
Her Roman bridegroom wondering at that crown
Invisible itself that round her breathed
Rose-breath celestial; her that to the Church
Gave her ancestral house; and, happier gift,
Devotion's heavenliest instrument of praise;
Her that, unfearing, dared that Roman sword;
And when its work was done, for centuries lay
Like marble, 'mid the catacombs unchanged
In sleep-resembling death.
      From earliest dawn
That maiden's eyes had watched: wearied at noon
Their silver curtains closed. Huge mossy roots
Pillowed her head, that slender book wide-leaved
In stillness, like some brooding white-winged dove
Spread on her bosom: 'gainst its golden edge
Rested, gold-tinged, the dimpled ivory chin—
Loud thunders broke that sleep; the tempest blast
Came up against the woods, while bolt on bolt
Ran through them sheer. She started up: she saw
That Pagan prince and many a sworded serf
Rushing towards her. Fleeter still she fled;
But, as some mountain beast tender and slight
That, pasturing spring-fed lilies of Cashmere,
Or slumbering where its rock-nursed torrents fall,
Sudden not distant hears the hunter's cry
And mocks pursuit at first, but slackens soon
Breathless and spent, so failed her limbs ere long;
A horror of great faintness o'er her crept;
More near she heard their shout. She staggered on;
To threat'ning phantoms all things round were
  changed;
About her towered in ruin hollow trunks

Of spiked and branchless trees, survivors sole
Of woods that, summer-scorched, then lightning-struck
A century past, for one short week had blazed
And blackened ever since. She knelt: she raised
Her hands to God: she sued for holier prayer
Saint Catherine, Saint Cecilia. At that word
Behind her close a cry of anguish rang:
Silence succeeded. As by angels' help
She reached a river's bank: sun-hardened clay
Retained the hoof-prints of the drinking herd;
And, shallower for long heats, the oxen's ford
Challenged her bleeding feet. She crossed unharmed,
And soon in green-gold pastures girt by woods
Stood up secure. Then forth she stretched her hands,
Like Agnes praising God amid the flame:
'Omnipotent, Eternal, Worshipful,
One God, Immense, and All-compassionate,
Thou from the sinner's snare hast snatched the feet
Of her that loved Thee. Glory to Thy name.'
    Thenceforth secure she roamed those woods and
        meads;
The dwellers in that region brought her bread,
Upon that countenance gazing, some with awe
But all with love. To her the maidens came:
'Tell us,' they said, 'what mystery hast thou learned
So sweet and good;—thy Teacher, who was he;
Grey-haired, or warrior young?' To them in turn
Ceaseless she sang the praises of her Christ,
His Virgin Mother and His heavenly court,
Warriors on earth for justice. They for her
Renounced all else, the banquet and the dance,
And nuptial rites revered. A low-roofed house
Inwoven of branches 'mid the woods they raised;
There dwelt, and sang her hymn, and prayed her prayer,

And loved her Saviour-Sovereign.   Year by year
More high her bright feet scaled the heavenly mount
Of lore divine and knowledge of her God,
And with sublimer chant she hymned His praise;
While oft some bishop, tracking those great woods
In progress to his charge, beneath their roof
Baptizing or confirming made abode,
And all that lacked supplied, nor discipline
Withheld, nor doctrine high.   The outward world
To them a nothing, made of them its boast:
A Saint, it said, within that forest dwelt
A Saint that helped their people.   Saint she was
And therefore wrought for heaven her holy deeds;
Immortal stand they on the heavenly roll;
Yet fewest acts suffice for heavenly crown;
And two of hers had consequence on earth
Like water circles widening limitless,
For man still helpful.   Hourly acts of hers
Interior acts invisible to men,
Perchance were worthier.   Humblest faith and prayer
Are oft than miracle miraculous more:
To us the exterior marks the interior might:
These two alone record we.
       Years had passed:
One day when all the streams were dried by heat
And rainless fields had changed from green to brown,
T'wards her there drew, by others led, a man
Old, worn, and blind.   He knelt, and wept his prayer:
'Help, Saint of God!   That impious King am I,
That King abhorred, his people's curse and bane,
Who chased thee through these woods with fell resolve,
Worst vengeance seeking for insulted pride:
Rememberest thou that, near thee as I closed
Kneeling thou mad'st thy prayer?   Instant from God

Blindness fell on me. Forward still I rushed,
Ere long amid those spiked and branded trunks
To lie as lie the dead. If hope remains
For me if any hope survives on earth
It rests with thee; thee only!' On her knees
She sank in prayer; her fingers in the fount
She dipped; then o'er him signed the Saviour's cross,
And thrice invoked that Saviour. At her word
Behold, that sightless King arose, and saw,
And rendered thanks to God.
       The legend saith
Saint Catherine by her stood that night, and spake:
'Once more I greet thee on thy dying day.'

 Again the years went by. That sylvan lodge
Had changed to convent. Beautiful it stood
Not far from Isis, though on loftier ground:
Sad outcasts knew it well: whate'er their need
There found they solace. One day toward it moved,
Dread apparition and till then unknown,
Like one constrained, with self-abhorrent steps,
A leper long in forest caverns hid.
Back to their cells the nuns had shrunk, o'erawed:
Remained but Frideswida. Thus that wretch
With scarce organic voice, and aiding sign,
Wailed out the supplication of despair:
'Fly not, O saintly virgin! Yet, ah me!
What help though thou remainest? Warned from
  heaven,
I know that not thy fountain's healing wave
Could heal my sorrow: not those spotless hands:
Not even thy prayer. To me the one sole aid
Were aid impossible—a kiss of thine.'
A moment stood she: not in doubt she stood:

First slowly, swiftly then to where he knelt
She moved: with steadfast hand she raised that cloth
Which veiled what once had been a human face:
O'er it she signed in faith the cross of Christ;
She wept aloud, 'My brother!' Folding then
Stainless to stained, with arms about him wound
In sacred silence mouth to mouth she pressed
A long, long sister's kiss. Like infant's flesh
The blighted and the blasted back returned:
That leper rose restored.
      The legend saith
That Saint Cecilia by her stood that night:
'Once more I greet thee on thy dying day.'

 It came at last, that day. Her convent grew
In grace with God and man: the pilgrim old
Sought it from far; the gifts of kings enlarged it:
It came at last, that day. There are who vouch
The splendour of that countenance never waned:
Thus much is sure; it waxed to angels' eyes:—
Welcomed it came, that day desired, not feared.
By humbleness like hers those two fair deeds
Were long forgotten: each day had its task:
Not hardest that of dying. Why should sobs
Trouble the quiet of a holy house
Because its holiest passes? Others wept;
The sufferer smiled: 'Ah, little novices,
How little of the everlasting lore
Your foolish mother taught you if ye shrink
From trial light as this!' She spake; then sank
In what to those around her seemed but sleep,
The midnoon August sunshine on her hair
In ampler radiance lying than that hour
When, danger near her yet to her unknown,

Beneath that forest tree her eyelids closed—
Her book upon her bosom.
                              Near her bed
Not danger now but heralds ever young,
Saint Catherine, Saint Cecilia, stood once more,
Linked hand in hand, with aureoles interwreathed:
One gazing stood as though on radiance far
With widening eyes: a listener's look intent
The other's, soft with pathos more profound.
The Roman sister spake: 'Rejoice, my child,
Rejoice, thus near the immeasurable embrace
And breast expectant of the unnumbered Blest
That swells to meet thee! Yea, and on the earth
For thee reward remaineth. Happy thou
Through prayer his sight restoring to thy foe,
Sole foe that e'er thou knew'st though more his own!
Child! darkness is there worse than blindness far
Wherein erroneous wanders human Pride;
That prayer of thine from age to age shall guard
A realm against such darkness. Where yon kine
Stand in mid ford, quenching their noontide thirst,
Thy footsteps crossed of old the waters. God
In the unerasing current sees them still!
Close by, a nation from a purer flood
Shall quench a thirst more holy, quaffing streams
Of Knowledge loved as Truth. Majestic piles
Shall rise by yonder Isis, honouring, each,
My clear-eyed sister of the sacred East
That won to Christ the Alexandrian seers,
Winning, herself, from chastity her lore:
High on their fronts in statued grandeur ranged
With face to East, and cincture never loosed,
All Sciences shall stand, daughters divine
Of Him that Truth eterne and boon to man

Holding in reverent hand, not lamp alone,
But lamp and censer both, and both alike
From God's great Altar lighted.'
                              Spake in turn
That Alexandrian with the sunlike eyes:
'Beside those Sciences shall stand a choir
As fair as they; as tall; those sister Arts,
High daughters of celestial Harmony,
Diverse yet one, that bind the hearts of men
To steadfast Truth by Beauty's sinuous cords;
She that to marble changes mortal thought;
She that with rainbow girds the cloud of life;
She that above the morning mist exalts
Rock-rooted domes of prayer; and she that rears
With words auguster temples. Happy thou
Healing that leper with thy virgin kiss!
A leprosy there is more direful, child!—
Therein the nations rot when flesh is lord
And spirit dies. Such ruin Arts debased
Gender, or, gendered long, exasperate more.
But thou, rejoice! From this pure centre Arts
Unfallen shall breathe their freshness through the land,
With kiss like thine healing a nation's wound
Year after year successive; listening, each,
My sister's organ music in the skies,
Prime Art that, challenging not eye but ear,
To Faith is nearest, and of Arts on earth
For that cause, living soul.'
                              That prophecy
Found its accomplishment. In later years,
There where of old the Oxen had their Ford,
The goodliest city England boasts arose,
Mirrored in sacred Isis; like that flood
Its youth for aye renewing. Convents first

Through stately groves levelled their placid gleam,
With cloisters opening dim on garden gay
Or moonlit lawn dappled by shadowing deer ;
Above them earliest soared the chapel's bulk
With storied window whence, in hues of heaven,
Martyrs looked down, or Confessor, or Saint
On tomb of Founder with its legend meek
'Pro animâ orate.' Night and day
Mounted the Church's ever-varying song
Sustained on organ harmonies that well
Might draw once more to earth, with wings outspread
And heavenly face made heavenlier by that strain
Cecilia's Angel. Of those convents first
Was Frideswida's, ruled in later years
By Canons Regular, later yet rebuilt
By him of York, that dying wept, alas,
'Had I but served my Maker as my king!'
To colleges those convents turned ; yet still
The earlier inspiration knew not change :
The great tradition died not: near the bridge
From Magdalen's tower still rang the lark-like hymn
On May-day morn : high ranged in airy cells,
Facing the East, all Sciences, all Arts,
And greater far than these all Virtues stood,
Best imaged there in no ideal forms,
Craft unhistoric of some dreamer's brain,
But life-like shapes of plain heroic men
Who in their day had fought the fight of Faith,
Warriors and sages, poets, saints, and kings,
And earned their rest : the long Procession paced,
Up winding slow the college-girded street
To where in high cathedral slept the Saint,
Singing its 'Alma Redemptoris Mater,'
On August noons, what time the Assumption Feast

From purple zenith of the Christian heaven
Brightened the earth. That hour not bells alone
Chiming from countless steeples made reply:
Laughed out that hour high-gabled roof and spire;
Kindling shone out those Sciences, those Arts
Pagan one time, now confessors white-robed;
And all the holy City gave response,
'Deus illuminatio mea est.' *

THE BANQUET HALL OF WESSEX, OR THE KING WHO COULD SEE.

Kenwalk, King of Wessex, is a Pagan, but refuses to persecute Christians. He is dethroned by the Mercian King, and lives an exile in a Christian land. There he boasts that he never accords faith to what he hears, and believes only what he sees; yet, his eye being single, he sees daily more of the Truth. Wessex is delivered, and a great feast held at which the Pagan nobles, priests, and bards all conspire for the destruction of the Faith. Birinus, the bishop, having withstood them valiantly, Kenwalk declares himself a Christian. Birinus prophesies of England's greatest King.

King Cynegils lay dead, who long and well
Had judged the realm of Essex. By his bier
The Christians standing smote their breasts, and said,
'Ill day for us:' but all about the house
Clustering in smiling knots of twos and threes
The sons of Odin whispered, or with nods
Gave glad assent. Christ's bishop sent from Rome
Birinus, to the king had preached for years
The Joyous Tidings. Cynegils believed

* The motto of the University of Oxford.

And with him many; but the most refrained:
With these was Kenwalk; and, his father dead,
Kenwalk was king.
                    A valiant man was he
A man of stubborn will, but yet at heart
Magnanimous and just.   To one who said
'Strike, for thine hour is come!' the king new-crowned
Made answer, 'Never!   Each man choose his path!
My father chose the Christian, Odin's I.
I crossed my father oft a living man;
I war not on him dead.'
                    That giant hand
Which spared Religion ruled in all beside:
He harried forth the robbers from the woods
And wrecked the pirates' ships. He burned with fire
A judge unjust, and thrice o'er Severn drave
The invading Briton. Lastly, when he found
That woman in his house intolerable,
From bed and realm he hurled her forth though
    crowned,
Ensuing thence great peace.
                    Not long that peace:
The Mercian king, her brother, heard her tale
With blackening brow. The shrill voice stayed at last,
Doubly incensed the monarch made reply:
'Sister, I never loved you;—who could love?
But him who spurned you from his realm I hate:
Fear nought! your feast of vengeance shall be full!'
He spake; then cried, 'To arms!'
                    In either land,
Like thunders low and far, or windless plunge
Of waves on coasts long silent that proclaim,
Though calm the sea for leagues, tempest far off
That shoreward swells, thus day by day was heard

The direful preparation for a war
Destined no gladsome tournament to prove
But battle meet for ancient foes resolved
To clear old debts; make needless wars to come.
Not long that strife endured; on either side
Valour was equal; but on one, conjoined,
The skill most practised and the heavier bones:
The many fought the few. On that last field
'Twas but the fury of a fell despair
Not hope, that held the balance straight so long:
Ere sunset all was over. From the field
A bleeding remnant dragged their king half dead:
The Mercian host pursued not.
      Many a week
Low lay the broken giant nigh to death:
At last, like creeping plant down-dragged, not crushed,
That, washed by rains, and sunshine-warmed, once more
Its length uplifting feels along the air,
And gradual finds its 'customed prop, so he,
Strengthening each day, with dubious eyes at first
Around him peered, but raised at length his head,
And, later, question made. His health restored
He sought East Anglia, where King Anna reigned,
His chief of friends in boyhood. Day by day
A spirit more buoyant to the exile came
And winged him on his way: his country's bound
Once passed, his darker memories with it sank:
Through Essex hastening stronger grew his step;
East Anglian breezes from the morning sea
Fanned him to livelier pulse: wild April growths
Gladdened his spirit with glittering green. More fresh
He walked because the sun outfaced him not,
Veiled, though not his. That shrouded sun had ta'en
Its passion from the wild bird's song, but left

Quiet felicities of notes low-toned
That kept in tune with streams too amply brimmed
To chatter o'er their pebbles.   Kenwalk's soul
Partook not with the poet's.   Loveliest sights
Like music brightening those it fails to charm,
Roused but his mirthful mood.   To each that passed
He tossed his jest : he scanned the labourer's task ;
Reviled the luckless boor that ploughed awry
And beat the smith that marred the horse's hoof :
At times his fortunes thus he moralised :
' Here walk I, crownless king, and exiled man :
My Mercian brother lists his sister's tongue :
Say, lark ! which lot is happiest ? '

          Festive streets
Tapestries from windows waving, banners borne
By white-clad children chanting anthems blithe ;
With these East Anglia's king received his friend
Entering the city gate.   In joyous sports
That day was passed.   At banquet Christian priests
Sat with his thanes commingled.   Anna's court
Was Christian, and, for many a league around,
His kingdom likewise.   As the earth in May
Glistens with vernal flowers, or as the face
Of one whose love at last has found return
Irradiate shines so shone King Anna's house
A home of Christian peace.   Fair sight it was—
Justice and Love, the only rivals there
O'er-ruled it, and attuned.   Majestic strength
Looked forth in every glance of Anna's eye
Too great for pride to dwell there.   Tender-souled
As that first streak the harbinger of dawn
Revealed through cloudless ether, such the queen
All charity, all humbleness, all grace
All womanhood.   Harmonious was her voice,

Dulcet her movements, undisguised her thoughts
As though they trod an Eden land unfallen
And needed raiment none.   Some heavenly birth
Their children seemed, blameless in word and act,
The sisters as their brothers frank, and they
Though bolder, not less modest.   Kenwalk marked,
And marking, mused in silence, 'Contrast strange
These Christians with the pagan races round !
Something those pagans see not these have seen :
Something those pagans hear not these have heard :
Doubtless there's much in common.   What of that ?
'Tis thus 'twixt man and dog ; yet knows the dog
His master walks in worlds by him not shared—
Perchance for me there may be worlds unknown !'

   Thus God to Kenwalk shewed the things that bear
Of God true witness, seeing in his soul
Justice and Judgment, and, with these conjoined,
Valour and Truth : for as the architect
On tower four-square and solid plants his spire
And not on meads below though gay with flowers
On those four virtues God the fabric rears
Of virtues loftier yet—those three, heaven-born,
And pointing heavenward.
                      To those worlds unknown
Kenwalk ere long stood nigh.   In three short months
The loveliest of those children, and last born,
Lay cold in death.   Old nurses round her wailed :
The mighty heart of Kenwalk shook for dread
Entering the dim death-chamber.   On a bier
The maiden lay, the cross upon her breast :
Close by, the mother sat, pale as the child,
Yet calm as pale.   When Kenwalk near her drew
She lifted from that bier a slender book

And read that record of the three days' dead
Raised by the Saviour from that death-cave sealed
A living man. Once more she read those words,
'I am the Resurrection and the Life,'
Then added, low, with eyes up cast to heaven,
'With Him my child awaits me.' Kenwalk saw;
And, what he saw believing, half believed—
Not more—the things he heard.
                              Yes, half believed;
Yet, call it obduracy, call it pride
Call it self-fear, or fear of priestly craft
He closed his ear against the Word Divine:
The thing he saw he trusted; nought beyond.
Three years went by. Once, when his friend had named
The Name all-blessed, Kenwalk frowned. Since then
That Name was named no more. In later days
They chased the wild deer; on the billow breathed
Inspiring airs; in hall of joyance trod
The mazes of the dance. Then war broke out:
Reluctant long King Anna sought the field;
Hurled back aggression. Kenwalk, near him still,
Watched him with insight keener than his wont
And, wondering, marked him least to pagans like
Inly, when like perforce in outward deed.
The battle frenzy took on him no hold:
Severe his countenance grew; austere and sad;
Fatal, not wrathful. Vicar stern he seemed
Of some dread, judgment-executing Power,
Against his yearnings; not despite his will.
Once, when above the faithless town far off
The retributive smoke leaped up to heaven,
He closed with iron hand on Kenwalk's arm
And slowly spake—a whisper heard afar—
'See you that town? Its judgment is upon it!

I gave it respite twice. This day its doom
Is irreversible.'
                        The invader quelled
Anna and Kenwalk on their homeward way
Rode by the grave of saintly Sigebert,
King Anna's predecessor. Kenwalk spake:
'Some say the people keep but memory scant
Of benefits: I trust the things I see:
I never passed that tomb but round it knelt
A throng of supplicants! King Sigebert
Conversed, men say, with prophet and with seer:
I never loved that sort:—who wills can dream—
Yet what I see I see.'
                        'They pray for him,'
Anna replied, 'who perished for their sake:
Long years he lived recluse at Edmondsbury,
A tonsured monk: around its walls one day
Arose that cry, "The Mercian, and his host!
Forth, holy King, and lead, as thou wert wont
Thy people to the battle, lest they die!"
Again I see him riding at their head
Lifting a cross, not sword. The battle lost
Again I see him fall.' With rein drawn tight
King Kenwalk mused; then smote his hands, and
    cried
'My father would have died like Sigebert!
He lacked but the occasion!' After pause,
Sad-faced, with bitter voice he spake once more:
'Such things as these I might have learned at home!
I shunned my father's house lest fools might say,
"He thinks not his own thoughts."'
                        Thus month by month,
Though Faith which 'comes by hearing' had not come
To Kenwalk yet, no less since sight he used

In honest sort and resolute to learn,
God shewed him memorable things and great
Which sight unblest discerns not, tutoring thus
A kingly spirit to a kingly part:
Before him near Faith lay.
                            The morrow morn
Great tidings came: in Wessex war was raised:
Kenwalk, departing thus to Anna spake,
To Anna, and his consort: 'Well I know
What thanks are those the sole your hearts could
    prize:'
With voice that shook he added: 'Man am I
That make not pledge: yet, if my father's God
Sets free my father's realm——' again he paused;
Then westward rode alone.
                            Well planned, fought well
For Kenwalk, of the few reverse makes wise,
From him had put his youth's precipitance,
That virtuous warfare triumphed. Swift as fire
The news from Sherburne and from Winbourne flashed
To Sarum, Chertsey, Malmsbury. That delight
On earth the nearest to religious joy,
The rapture of a trampled land set free,
Swelled every breast: the wounded in their wounds
Rejoiced, not grieved: the sick forgat their pains:
The mourner dashed away her tear and cried
'Wessex is free!' Remained a single doubt:
Christians crept forth from cave and hollow tree:
Once more the exiled monk was seen; and one
Who long in minstrel's garb with harp in hand
Old, poor, half blind, had sat beside a bridge
And, charming first the wayfarer with song,
Had won him next with legends of the Cross,
Stood up before his altar. Rumour ran

'Once more Birinus lifts his crosier-staff!'
Then muttered priests of Odin, 'Cynegils
We know was Christian. Kenwalk holds—or held
Ancestral Faith, yet warred not on the new:
Tolerance means still connivance.'
                                    Peace restored
Within King Kenwalk's echoing palace hall,
The hall alike of council and of feast,
The Great Ones of the Wessex realm were met:
Birinus sat among them, eyed from far
With anger and with hatred. Council o'er
Banquet succeeded, and to banquet song,
The Saxon's after-banquet. Many a harp
That day by flying hand entreated well
Divulged its secret, amorous, or of war;
And many a warrior sang his own great deeds
Or dirge of ancient friend Valhalla's guest;
Nor stinted foeman's praise. Silent meanwhile
Far down the board a son of Norway sat,
Ungenial guest with clouded brows and stern,
And eyes that flashed beneath them: bard was he,
Warrior and bard. Not his the song for gold!
He sang but of the war-fields and the gods;
He lays of love despised. 'Thy turn is come,
Son of the ice-bound North,' thus spake a thane:
'Sing thou! The man who sees that face, already
Half hears the tempest singing through the pines
That shade thy gulfs hill-girt.' The stranger guest
Answered, not rising: 'Yea, from lands of storm
And seas cut through by fiery lava floods
I come, a wanderer. Ye, meantime, in climes
Balm-breathing, gorge the fat, and smell the sweet:
Ye wed the maid whose sire ye never slew
And bask in unearned triumph. Feeble spirits!

Endless ye deem the splendours of this hour,
And call defeat opprobrious! Sirs, our life
Is trial. Victory and Defeat are Gods
That toss man's heart, their plaything, each to each:
Great Mercia knows that truth—of all your realms
Faithfullest to Odin far!'
       'Nay, minstrel, sing,'
Once more, not wroth, they clamoured. He replied:
'Hear then my song; but not those songs ye sing:
I have against you somewhat, Wessex men!
Ye are not as your fathers, when, in youth,
I trod your coasts. That time ye sang of Gods
Sole theme for manlike song. On Iceland's shores
We keep our music's virtue undefiled:
While summer lasts we fight: by winter hearths
Or ranged in sunny coves by winter seas,
Betwixt the snow-plains and the hills of fire,
Singing we feed on legends of the Gods:
Ye sing but triumphs of the hour that fleets;
Ye build you kingdoms: next ye dash them down:
Ye bow to idols! O that song of mine
Might heal this people's wound!'
       Then rose the bard
And took his harp, and smote it like a man;
And sang full-blooded songs of Gods who spurn
Their heaven to war against that giant race
Throned 'mid the mountains of old Jötunheim
That girdle still the unmeasured seas of ice
With horror and strange dread. Innumerable
In ever-winding labyrinths glacier-thronged
Those mountains raise their heads among the stars,
That palsied glimmer 'twixt their sunless bulks
O'er-shadowing seas and lands. O'er Jötunheim
The glittering car of day hath never shone:

There endless twilight broods.   Beneath it sit
The huge Frost-Giants, sons of Örgelmir,
Themselves like mountains, solitary now,
Now grouped, with knees drawn up and heads low
    bent
Plotting new wars.   Those wars the Northman sang ;
And thunder-like rang out the vast applause.
That hour Birinus whispered one close by :
'Not casual this !   Ill spirits, be sure, this day
And impious men will launch their fiercest bolts
To crush Christ's Faith for ever !'
                                             Jocund songs
That bard sang next : how Thor had roamed disguised
Through Jötunheim, and found the giant-brood
Feasting ; and how their king gave challenge thus :
'Sir, since you deign us visit, show us feats !
Behold yon drinking horn ! with us a child
Drains it at draught.'   The God inclined his head
And swelled his lips ; and three times drank : yet lo !
Nigh full that horn remained, the dusky mead
In mockery winking !   Spake once more the king :
'Behold my youngest daughter's chief delight,
Yon wild-cat grey !   She lifts it : lift it thou !'
The God beneath it slipped his arm and tugged,
And tugging, ever higher rose and higher ;
The wild cat arched her back and with him rose ;—
But one foot left the ground !   Last, forward stept
A haggard, lame, decrepid, toothless crone,
And cried, 'Canst wrestle, friend ?'   He closed upon
    her :
Firm stood she as a mountain : she in turn
Closed upon Thor, and brought him to one knee :
Lower she could not bend him.   Thor for rage
Clenched both his fists until his finger-joints

Grew white as snow late fallen!
                              Loud and long
The laughter rose: the minstrel frowned dislike:
'I have against you somewhat, Wessex men!
In laughter spasms ye reel, or shout applause
Music surceased. Like rocks your fathers sat;
In every song they knew some mystery lay,
Mystery of man or nature. Greater God
Is none than Thor, whom, clamouring, thus ye flout.
That Giant-King his greatness knew: at morn,
While vexed at failure through the gates he passed,
Addressed him reverent: "Lift thy head, great Thor!
Disguised thou cam'st: not less we knew thee well:
Brave battle fought'st thou, seeming still to fail:
Thy foes were phantoms! Phantasies I wove
To snare thine eyes because I feared thy hand,
And pledged thy strength to tasks impossible.
That horn thou could'st not empty was the sea!
At that third draught such ebb-tide stripp'd the shore
As left whole navies stranded! What to thee
Wild-cat appeared was Midgard's endless snake
Whose infinite circle clasps the ocean round:
Then when her foot thou liftedst, tremour went
From iron vale to vale of Jötunheim:
Hadst thou but higher raised it one short span,
The sea had drowned the land! That toothless crone
Was Age, that drags the loftiest head to earth:
She bent thy knee alone. Come here no more!
On equal ground thou fight'st us in the light:
In this, our native land, the stronger we,
And mock thee by Illusions!"'
                              After pause,
With haughty eye cast round, the minstrel spake:
'Now hear ye mysteries of the antique song,

Though few shall guess their import!' Then he sang
Legends primeval of that Northern race
And dread beginnings of the heavens and earth,
When, save the shapeless chaos, nothing was:
Of Ymer first, by some named Örgelmir,
The giant sire of all the giant brood:—
Him for his sins the sons of Bör destroyed;
Then fashioned of his blood the seas and streams
And of his bones the mountains; of his teeth
The cliffs firm set against the aggressive waves;
Last, of his skull the vast, o'er-hanging heaven
And of his brain the clouds.
                         'Sing on,' they cried :
Next sang he of that mystic shape, earth-born,
The wondrous cow, Auhumla. Herb that hour
Was none, nor forest growth; yet on and on
She wandered by the vapour-belted seas,
And, wandering, from the stones and icebergs cold
That creaked forlorn against the grey sea-crags
She licked salt spray, and hoary frost, and lived;
And ever where she licked sprang up, full-armed,
Men fair and strong!
                         Once more they cried 'Sing on!'
Last sang the minstrel of the Night and Day:
Car-borne they sweep successive through the heaven:
First rides the dusky maid by men called Night;
Sleep-bringing, pain-assuaging, kind to man;
With dream-like speed cleaving the starry sphere:
Hrimfaxi is her horse: his round complete
Foam from his silver bit bespangles earth,
And mortals call it 'Morn.' Day follows fast,
Her brother white: Skinfaxi is his horse:
When forth he flings the splendours from his mane
Both Gods and men rejoice.

                              Thus legends old
The Northman sang, till, fleeting from men's eyes
The present lived no longer.   In its place
He fixed that vision of the world new formed
Which on the childhood of the Northern mind
Like endless twilight lay;—spaces immense;
Unmeasured energies of fire and flood;
Great Nature's forces terrible yet blind
In ceaseless strife alternately supreme,
Or breast to breast with dreadful equipoise
In conflict pressed.   Once more o'er those that heard
He hung that old world's low, funereal sky:
Before their eyes he caused its cloud to stream
Shadowing infinitude.   He spake no word
Like Heida of that war 'twixt Good and Ill;
That peace which crowns the just; that God Unknown:
Enough to him his Faith without its soul!
With glorying eye he marked that panting throng;
Then, sudden, changed his note.   Again of war
He sang, but war no more of Gods on Gods;
He sang the honest wars of man on man;
Of Odin, king of men, ere yet, death past,
He flamed abroad in godhead.   Field on field
He sang his battles; traced from realm to realm
His conquering pilgrimage: then ended, fierce:
'What God was this—that God ye honoured once?
What man was this—your half-forgotten king?
Your law-giver he was; he framed your laws!
Your poet he: he shaped your earliest song!
Your teacher he: he taught you first your runes!
Your warrior—yours!   His warfare consummate,
For you he died!   Old age at last, sole foe
Unvanquished, found him throned in Gylfin's land:
Summoning his race around him thus he spake:

" My sons, I scorn that age should cumber youth !
Ye have your lesson—see ye keep it well !
I taught you how to conquer ; how to live ;
Now learn to die ! " His dagger high he raised ;
Nine times he plunged it through his bleeding breast,
Then sheathed it in his heart. Ere from his lips
The kingly smile had vanished he was dead !'

So sang the bard and rose : his work was done :
Abroad the tempest burst. 'Twas not his songs
Alone that raised it ! Memories which they waked
Memories of childhood, fainter year by year,
Tripled his might. Meantime a Saxon priest
Potential there, bent low, with eye-brow arched,
O'er Eardulf's ear, Eardulf old warrior famed,
And whispered long, and as he whispered glanced
Oft at Birinus. Keen of eye the King
The action noting well, the aim divined,
And thus to Offa near him spake, low-toned :
' The full-fed priest of Odin sends a sword
To slay that naked babe he hates so sore
The Faith of Christ !'
                    Rising with fiery face
And thundering hand that shook the banquet board
Eardulf began : "' Ye are not what ye were ! "
So saith our stranger kinsman from the North,
A man plain-tongued ; I would that all were such !
Lords, and my King, this stranger speaks the truth !
I tell you too, we are not what we were :
Nor lengthened trail he hunts who seeks the cause.
Lo, there the cause among us ! Man from Rome !
I ask who sent thee hither ? From the first
Rome and our native races stand at war ;
Her hope was this, to make our sons like hers

Liars and slaves, our daughters false and vile,
And, thus subverted, rule our land and us.
Frustrate in war, now sends she forth her priests
In peaceful gown to sap the manly hearts
Her sword but manlier made. Ho, Wessex men!
You see your foe! My counsel, Lords, is this:
The worm that stung us tread we to the earth
Then spurn it from our coasts!'
       Ere ceased the acclaim
Subdued and soft the Pagan pontiff rose,
And three times half retired, as one who yields
His betters place; and thrice, answering the call
Advanced, and leaning stood: at last he spake
Sweet-voiced, not loud; 'Ye Wessex Earls and
  Thanes,
I stand here but as witness not as judge;
Ye are the judges. Late ye heard—yea, twice—
Words strange and new; "Ye are not what ye were!"
I witness this; things are not what they were;
For round me as I roll these sorrowing eyes
Now old and dim—perchance the fault is theirs—
They find no longer, ranged along your walls
Amid the deep-dyed trophies of old time,
That chiefest of your Standards, lost, men say,
In that ill-omened battle lost which wrecked
But late our Wessex kingdom. Odin's wrath—
I spare to task your time and patience, Lords,
Enforcing truth which every urchin knows—
'Twas Odin shamed his foe! Ah Cynegils!
What made thee Odin's foe? Our friend was he!
Base tolerance first, connivance next, then worse,
Favoured that Faith perfidious! Stood and stands
A bow-shot hence that church the strangers built;
Their church, their font! The strangers, who are they?

Snake-like and supple, winding on and on
Through courtly chambers darkling still they creep,
Nor dare to face a people front to front;
Let them stand up in light and all is well !
And who their converts ?   Late, to please a king
They donned his novel worship like a robe;
When dead he lay they doffed it !   Earls and Thanes,
A nobler day is come ; a sager king ;
In him I trust ; in you ; in Odin most,
Our nation's strength, the bulwark of our throne.
I proffer nought of counsel.   Ye have eyes :
The opprobrium sits among you !'
        From the floor
The storm of iron feet rang loud, and swords
Leaped flashing from their sheaths.   In silence some
Waited the event : the larger part by far
Clamoured for vengeance on the outlandish Faith,
The loudest they, the apostates of past time.
Then stately from his seat Birinus rose,
And stood in calm marmorean.   Long he stood
Not eager though expectant.   By degrees
That tumult lessening, with a quiet smile
And hand extended, far commanding peace,
Thus he addressed that concourse.
       'Earls and Thanes,
Among so many here I stand alone,
Why peaceful ? why untroubled?   In your hands
I see a hundred swords against me bent :
Sirs, should they slay me, Truth remains unpierced.
A thousand wheat ears swayed by summer gust
Affront one oak ; it slights the mimic threat :
So slight I, strong in faith, whose swords that err—
Your ignorance, not your sin.   The Truth of God,
The Heart of man against you fight this day

And, with his heart, his hope. In every land
Through all the unnumbered centuries yet to come
The cry of women wailing for their babes
Restored through Christ alone, the cry of men
Who know that all is lost if earth is all,
The cry of children still unstained by sin,
The sinners' cry redeemed from yoke of sin,
Thunder against you. Pass to lesser themes.

'Eardulf, that raged against me, told you, Lords,
That Rome was still the hater of your race
And warred thereon. She warred much more on mine
Roman but Christian likewise! Ye were foes;
Warring on you she warred on hostile tribes:
In us she tore her proper flesh and blood:
Mailed men were you that gave her blow for blow;
We were her tender children; on her hearths
We dwelt, or delved her fields and dressed her vines:
What moved her hatred? This. We loved a God
All love to man. With every God beside
Rome made her traffic: fellowship with such
Unclean we deemed: thenceforth Rome saw in us
Her destined foe.
　　　　　　　'Three centuries, Earls and Thanes,
Her hand was red against us. Vengeance came:
Who wrought it? Who avenged our martyred Saints
That, resting 'neath God's altar, cried, "How long?"
Alaric, and his, the Goths! And who were they?
Your blood, your bone, your spirit and your soul!
They with your fathers roamed four hundred years
The Teuton waste; they swam the Teuton floods,
They pointed with the self-same hand of scorn
At Rome, their common foe! Great Odin's sons
Together came ye from the shining East:

True man was he: ye changed him to false god!
That Odin, when the destined hour had pealed
Beckoned to Alaric, marched by Alaric's side
Invisibly to Rome!
     'Ye know the tale:
Her senate-kings their portals barred; they deemed
That awe of Rome would drive him back amazed;
And sat secure at feast. But he that slew
Remus, his brother, on the unfinished wall,
A bitter expiation paid that night!
The wail went up: the Goths were lords of Rome!
Alaric alone in that dread hour was just
And with his mercy tempered justice. Why?
Alaric that day was Christian: of his host
The best and bravest Christian. Senators
In purple nursed lived on, thenceforth in rags;
To Asian galleys and Egyptian marts
The rich were driven! the mighty. Gold in streams
Ran molten from the Capitolian roofs:
The idol statues choked old Tyber's wave:
But life and household honour Alaric spared;
And round the fanes of Peter and of Paul
His soldiers stood on guard. Upon the grave
Of that bad Empire sentenced, nay of all
The Empires of this world absorbed in one
In one condemned, they throned the Church of Christ;
His Kingdom's seat established.
      'Since that hour
That kingdom spreads o'er earth. In Eastern Gaul
Long since your brave Burgundians kneel to Christ;
Pannonia gave Him to the Ostro-Goths
Barbaric named; and to the Suevi Spain:
The Vandals o'er the Mauritanian shores
Exalt His Cross with joy. Your pardon, sirs:

Those lands to you are names ; but Odin knew them ;
A living man he trod them in his youth ;
Hated their vices ; bound his race to spurn
Their bait, their bond ! That day he saw hath dawned ;
O'er half a world the vivifying airs
Launched from your northern forests chaste and cold
Have blown, and blow this hour ! The Saxon race
Alone its destiny knows not.   Ye have won
Here in this Isle the old Roman heritage :
Perfect your victory o'er that Pagan Rome
With Christian Rome partaking !

         ' Earls and Thanes,
But one word more.   Your pontiff late averred
That kings to us are gods ; through them we conquer :
I answer thus : That Kingdom God hath raised
Is sovereign and is one ; kingdoms of earth,
How great soe'er, to it are provinces
In spiritual things.   If princes turn to God
They save their souls.   If kingdoms war on God
Their choice is narrow, and their choice is this :
To break, like that which falleth on a stone ;
Or else, like that whereon that stone doth fall,
To crumble into dust.'

        The Pagan priest
Whispered again to Eardulf, ' Praise to Thor !
He flouts our king !   The boaster's chance is gone ! '
Then rose that king and spake in careless sort :
' Earls and my Thanes, I came from exile late :
It may be that to exile I return :
Not less my arm is long ; my sword is sharp :
Let him that hates me fear me !

         ' Earls and Thanes,
I passed that exile in a Christian realm :
There of the Christian greatness, Christian right,

I somewhat heard, and hearing, disbelieved;
Saw likewise somewhat, and believed in part:
Saw more, till nigh that part had grown to whole:
I saw that war itself might be a thing
Though stern, yet stern in mercy; saw that peace
Might wear a shape dearest to manliest heart,
Peace based on fearless justice militant
'Gainst wrong alone and riot. Earls and Thanes
Returned this day and in this regal hall
A spectacle I saw, if grateful less,
Not therefore less note-worthy—countless swords
In judgment drawn against a man unarmed;
Yea, and a man unarmed with brow unmoved
Confronting countless swords. These things I saw;
Fair sight that tells me how to act, and when;
For I was minded to protract the time
Which strangles oft best purpose. At the font
Of Christ—it stands a bow-shot from this spot
As late we learned—at daybreak I and mine
Become henceforth Christ's lieges.
                              'Earls and Thanes
I heard but late a railer who affirmed
That kings were tyrants o'er the faiths of men
Flexile to please them: thus I made reply;
The meanest of my subjects, like his king,
Shall serve his God in freedom: if the chief
Questions the equal freedom of his king
That man shall die the death! Through Christian
    Faith—
I hide not this—one danger threats the land:
It threats as much, nay more my royal House:
That danger must be dared since truth is truth:
That danger ye shall learn to-morrow noon:
Till comes that hour, farewell!'

                              The matin beam,
God's wingèd messenger from loftier worlds,
Through the deep window of the baptistery
Glittered on eddies of the bath-like font
Not yet quiescent since its latest guest
Had thence arisen; beside its marge the king
In snowy raiment stood; upon his right,
Alfred, his first-born, boy of seven years old,
And, close beside, in wonder not in dread,
Mildrede, his sister, younger by one year,
Holding her brother's hand. From either waist
Flowed a white kirtle to the small snow feet
With roses tinged. Above it all was bare,
And with the fontal dew-drops sparkling still;
While from each head with sacred unction sealed
Floated the chrismal veil. That eye is blind
Which sees not beauty save on female brows:
On either face that hour the lustre lay;
But hers was lustre passive, lustre pale;
The boy's was active, daring, penetrating—
Keen as the Morning Star's. With dewy eyes
The strong king on them gazed, and inly mused,
'To God I gave them up: yet ne'er till now
Seemed they so wholly mine!'

                              Birinus spake:
'Ye have been washed in baptism, though no sin
Hath yet been yours save Adam's, and confirmed;
And houselled ye shall be at Mass seven days
Since Christ in infant bosoms loves to dwell.
Pray, day by day, that Christ would keep you pure:
Pray for your Father: likewise pray for me
Old sinner soon to die.' Then raised those babes
Their baptism tapers high, and fixing eyes

That moved not on their backward-fluttering flames,
Led the procession to their palace home,
Their father pacing last.
                    That day at noon
The monarch sat upon his royal throne
Birinus near him standing : at his feet
His children played ; while round him silent thronged
Warriors and chiefs. The king addressed them thus ;
' Birinus and the rest, I hold it meet
A king should hide a secret from his foes
But with his friends be open.   Yestereve
I, Christian now, unfalteringly avouched
That in the victory of the Christian Faith,
True though it be, one danger I discerned :
That danger, and its root, I now divulge.
Saw ye the scorn within that Northman's eye
Last eve, when, praising Thor, in balance stern
He weighed what now we are with what we were
When first he trod our shores !   He spake the truth :
His race and ours are kin ; but his retain
Stronglier their manly virtue, frost and snow
Like whetstones sharpening still that virtue's edge ;
We soften with the years.   Beggars this day
Sue us for bread !   Sirs, in a famine once
I saw, then young, a hundred at a time
That, linking hand in hand, loud singing rushed,
Like hunters chasing hart to sea-beat cliffs
And o'er them plunged !   Now comes this Faith of
    Christ !
That Faith to which, because that Faith is true,
I pledged this morn my word, my seal, my soul,
The fate and fortunes of our native land
And all my royal House well knowing this
The king who loves his kingdom more than God

Better than both loves self—no king at heart.
Now comes this Christian Faith! That Faith, be sure,
Is not a hardening faith: gentle it makes:
I told you, Lords, we soften day by day;
I might have added that with growing years
Hardness we doubly need. When Rome was great
Our race, however far diffused, was one,
Made one by hate of Rome. When Rome declined
That bond dissolved. A second bond remained
In Odin's Faith:—Northmen alone retain it.
In them a new Rome rises! Earls and Thanes!
The truth be ours though for that truth we die!
Hold fast that truth; yet hide not what it costs.
Through fog and sea-mist of the days to come
I see huge navies with the raven flag
Steering to milder borders Christian half,
Brother 'gainst brother ranging. Kingdoms Seven
Of this still fair and once heroic land
I say, beware that hour! If come it must
Then fall the thunder while I walk this earth
Not when I skulk in crypts!'
       The others mute
From joy malicious some, some vexed with doubt,
Birinus made reply: 'My Lord and King
Inly this day I gladden, certain now
That neither fancy-drawn nor anger-spurred,
Nor seeking crowns for others or thyself,
Nor shunning woes the worst that earth can know
For others or thyself, but urged by faith,
God's greatest gift to man, thou mad'st this day
Submission true to Christ. So be it, King!
So rest content! God with a finger's touch
Could melt that cloud which threats thy realm well-
  loved;

That threat I deem nor trivial nor obscure
Not thus He wills. Danger, distress, reverse,
Are heralds sent from God like peace and joy
To nations as to men. Happy that land
Which worketh darkling; worketh without wage;
And worketh still for God! If God desired
A people for His sacrificial lamb
Happiest of nations should that nation be
Which died His willing victim!

       'King and Son,'
With voice a moment troubled he resumed,
'Thy future rests with God! Yet shake, oh shake
One boding brief, 'tis causeless, from thy breast,
Deeming thy race less valiant than the North:
Faithfuller they stand and nearer to their sires!
Remorseless less to others and to self
I grant them; that implies not valiant less:
The brave are still in spirit the merciful;
Far down within their being stirs a sense
Of more than race or realm. Some claim world-wide,
Whereof the prophet is the wailing babe
Smites on their hearts, a cradle decks therein
For Him they know not yet, the Bethlehem Babe.
That claim thy fathers felt! Through Teuton woods
Dead Rome's historian saw what he records,*
Moved forth of old in cyclic pilgrimage
Thick-veiled, the sacred image of the Earth,
All reverend Mother, crowned Humanity!
Not war-steeds haled her car but oxen meek;
And, as it passed oppugnant bounds, the trump
Ceased from its blare; the lance, the war-axe fell:
Grey foes shook hands; their children played together.
Beyond the limit line of dateless wars

    * Tacitus.

Looked forth the vision thus of endless peace.
Think'st thou that here was lack of manly heart?
King, this was manhood's self!'
                              While thus he spake,
Alfred, and Mildrede, children of the king,
That long time, by that voice majestic charmed,
Had turned from distant sports, upon their knees
Softly and slowly to Birinus crept,
Their wide eyes from his countenance moving not
And so knelt on; Alfred, the star-eyed boy
Supported by his father's sceptre-staff
His plaything late, now clasped in hands high-held.
Him with a casual eye Birinus marked
At first; then stood with upward brow in trance—
Sudden, as though with Pentecostal flame
His whole face brightened; on him fell from God
Spirit Divine; and thus the prophet cried:

'Who speaks of danger when the Lord of all
Decrees high triumph? Victory's chariot winged
Up-climbs the frowning mountains of Dismay,
As when above the sea's nocturnal verge
Twin beams, divergent horns of orient light
Announce the ascending sun. Whatever cloud
Protracts the conflict victory comes at last.

'What ho! ye sons of Odin and the North!
Far off your galleys tarry! English air
Reafen, your raven standard, darkened long,
Woven of enchantments in the moon's eclipse:
It rains its plague no more! The Kingdoms Seven
Ye came to set a ravening each on each:
Lo, ye have pressed and soldered them in one!

'Behold, a Sceptre rises—not o'er Kent
The first-born of the Faith; nor o'er those vales
Northumbrian, trod so long by crownèd Saints;
Nor Mercia's plains invincible in war:
O'er Wessex, barbarous late, and waste, and small
The Hand that made the worlds that Sceptre lifts;
Hail tribe elect, the Judah of the Seven!

'Piercing the darkness of an age unborn
I see a King that hides his royal robe
Assumes the minstrel's garb. Where meet the floods
That King abides his time. I see him sweep
Disguised, his harp within the Northmen's camp;
In fifty fights I see him victory-crowned;
I see the mighty and the proud laid low
The humble lifted. God is over all.

'The ruined cities 'mid their embers thrill:
A voice went forth: they heard it. They shall rise,
Their penance done, and cities worthier far
With Roman vices ne'er contaminate.
These shall not boast mosaic floor gem-wrought
And trod by sinners. In the face of heaven
Their minster turrets these shall lift on high
Inviting God's great angels to descend
And chaunt with them God's City here on earth.

'Who through the lethal forest cleaves a road
Healthful and fresh? Who bridges stream high-
  swollen?
Who spreads the harvest round the poor man's cot;
Sets free the slave? On justice realms are built:
Who makes his kingdom great through equal laws
Not based on Pagan right, but rights in Christ,

First just, then free? Who from her starry gates
Beckons to Heavenly Wisdom—her who played
Ere worlds were shaped, before the eyes of God?
Who bids her walk the peopled fields of men
The reverend street with college graced and church?
Who sings the latest of the Saxon songs?
Who tunes to Saxon speech the Tome Divine?

'Sing, happy land! The Isle that, prescient long
Long waiting, hid her monarch in her heart,
Shall look on him and cry, "My flesh, my bone,
My son, my king!" To him shall Cambria bow,
And Alba's self. His strength is in his God;
The third part of his time he gives to prayer,
And God shall hear his vows. Hail, mighty King!
For aye thine England's glory! As I gaze,
Methinks I see a likeness on thy brow,
A likeness not to Warrior, Priest, or Chief,
But Him, that child who kneels beside my feet!
The sceptre comes to him who sceptre spurned;
Through him it comes who sceptre clasped in sport;
From Wessex's soil shall England's hope be born
Two centuries hence; and Alfred is his name!'

EPILOGUE.

BEDE'S LAST MAY.

Bede issues forth from Jarrow, and visiting certain villagers in a wood, expounds to them the Beatitudes of our Lord. Wherever he goes he seeks records of past times, and promises in return that he will bequeath to his fellow-countrymen translations from divers Sacred Scriptures, and likewise a history of God's Church in their land. Having returned to his monastery, he dies a most happy death on the feast of the Ascension, while finishing his translation of St. John's gospel.

THE ending of the Book of Saxon Saints.
With one lay-brother only blessed Bede
In after times 'The Venerable' named,
Passed from his convent, Jarrow. Where the Tyne
Blends with the sea all beautiful it stood
Bathed in the sunrise. At the mouth of Wear
A second convent, Wearmouth rose. That hour
The self-same matin splendour gilt them both;
And in some speech of mingling lights not words
Both sisters praised their God.
                    'Apart, yet joined'—
So mused the old man gazing on the twain:
Then onward paced with head above his book
Murmuring his office. Algar walked behind,
A youth of twenty years with tonsured head
And face, though young, forlorn. An hour had passed;
They reached a craggy height; and looking back
Beheld once more beyond the forest roof

Those two fair convents glittering—at their feet
Those two clear rivers winding! Bound by rule
Again the monk addressed him to his book;
Lection and psalm recited, thus he spake:

'Why placed our holy Founder thus so near
His convents? Why, albeit a single rule
At last a single hand had sway o'er both,
Placed them at distance? Hard it were to guess:
I know but this that severance here on earth
Is strangely linked with union of the heart,
Union with severance. Thou hast lost, young friend,
But lately lost thy boyhood's dearest mate
Thine earliest friend, a brother of thy heart
True Christian soul though dwelling in the world;
Fear not such severance can extinguish love
Here or hereafter! He whom most I loved
Was severed from me by the tract of years:
A child of nine years old was I when first
Jarrow received me: pestilence ere long
Swept from that house her monks save one alone
Ceolfrid, then its abbot. Man and child
We two the lonely cloisters paced; we two
Together chaunted in the desolate church:
I could not guess his thoughts; to him my ways
Were doubtless as the ways of some sick bird
Watched by a child. Not less I loved him well:
Me too he somewhat loved. Beneath one roof
We dwelt, and yet how severed! Save in God
What know men, one of other? Here on earth,
Perhaps 'tis wiser to be kind to all
In large goodwill of helpful love yet free
Than link to one our heart—
Poor youth! that love which walks in narrow ways

Is tragic love, be sure.'
                    With gentle face
The novice spake his gratitude. Once more,
His hand upon the shoulder of the youth,
For now they mounted slow a bosky dell
The old man spake—yet not to him—in voice
Scarce louder than the murmuring pines close by;
For, by his being's law he seemed, like them,
At times when pensive memories in him stirred,
Vocal not less than visible: 'How great
Was he, our Founder! In that ample brow
What brooding weight of genius! In his eye
How strangely was the pathos edged with light!
How oft, his churches roaming, flashed its beam
From pillar on to pillar resting long
On carven imagery of flower or fruit
Or deep-dyed window whence the heavenly choirs,
Gave joy to men below! With what a zeal
He drew the cunningest craftsmen from all climes
To express his thoughts in form; while yet his hand
Like meanest hand among us patient toiled
In garden and in bakehouse, threshed the corn
Or drave the calves to milk-pail! Earthly rule
Had proved to him a weight intolerable;
In spiritual beauty, there and there alone
Our Bennett Biscop found his native haunt,
The lucent planet of his soul's repose:
And yet—O wondrous might of human love—
One was there, one, to whom his heart was knit,
Siegfried, in all unlike him save in worth.
His was plain purpose, rectitude unwarped
Industry, foresight. On his friend's behalf
He ruled long years those beauteous convents twain,
Yet knew not they were beauteous! An abyss

Severed in spirit those in heart so near:
More late exterior severance came: three years
In cells remote they dwelt by sickness chained:
But once they met—to die. I see them still:
The monks had laid them on a single bed;
Weeping, they turned them later each to each:
I saw the snowy tresses softly mix;
I saw the faded lips draw near and meet;
Thus gently interwreathed I saw them die—
Strange strength of human love!'
                                            Still walked they on:
As high the sun ascended woodlands green
Shivered all golden; and the old man's heart
Brightened like them. His ever active mind
Inquisitive took note of all it saw;
And as some youth enamoured lifts a tress
Of her he loves, and wonders, so the monk,
Well loving Nature loved her in detail
Now pleased with nestling bird, anon with flower
Now noting how the beech from dewy sheath
Pushed forth its silken leaflets fringed with down,
Exulting next because from sprays of lime
The little fledgeling leaves, like creatures winged
Brake from their ruddy shells. Jesting, he cried:
'Algar! but hear those birds! Men say they sing
To fire their darkling young with gladsome news,
And bid them seek the sun!' Sadly the youth
With downward front replied: 'My friend is dead;
For me to gladden were to break a troth.'
Upon the brow of Bede a shadow fell;
Silent he paced, then stopped: 'Forgive me, Algar!
Old men grow hard. Yet boys and girls salute
The May: like them the old must have their "maying";
This is perchance my last.'

                    As thus he spake
They reached the summit of a grassy hill;
Beneath there wound a stream upon its marge
A hamlet nestling lonely in the woods:
Its inmates saw the Saint and t'wards him sped
Eager as birds that, when the grain is flung
In fountained cloister-court of Eastern church
From all sides flock with sudden rush of wings
Darkening the pavement.   Youths and maids came
    first;
Their elders followed: some his garments kissed
And some his hands.   The venerable man
Stretched forth his arms, as though to clasp them all:
Above them next he signed his Master's cross;
Then, while the tears ran down his aged face,
Brake forth in grateful joy; 'To God the praise!
When, forty years ago, I roamed this vale
A haunt it was of rapine and of wars;
Now see I pleasant pastures, peaceful homes
And faces peacefuller yet.   That God Who walked
With His disciples 'mid the sabbath fields
While they the wheat-ears bruised, His sabbath keeps
Within your hearts this day!   His harvest ye!
Once more a-hungered are His holy priests;
They hunger for your souls; with reverent palms
Daily the chaff they separate from the grain;
Daily His Church within her heart conceives you,
Yea, with her heavenly substance makes you one;
Ye grow to be her eyes that see His truth;
Her ears that hear His voice; her hands that pluck
His tree of life; her feet that walk His ways.
Honouring God's priests ye err not O my friends
Since thus ye honour God.   In Him rejoice!'

So spake he, and his gladness kindled theirs,
With it their courage. One her infant brought
And sued for him a blessing. One, bereaved,
Cried out: 'Your promised peace has come at last;
No more I wish him back to earth!' Again
Old foes shook hands; while now, their fears forgot,
Children that lately nestled at his feet
Clomb to his knee. Then called from out that crowd
A blind man; 'Read once more that Book of God!
For, after you had left us, many a month
I, who can neither see the sun nor moon
Saw oft the God-Man walking farms and fields
Of that fair Eastern land!' He spake, and lo!
All those around that heard him clamoured, 'Read!'

Then Bede, the Sacred Scriptures opening, lit
Upon the 'Sermon on the Mount,' and read:
'The Saviour lifted up His holy eyes
On His disciples, saying, Blessed they;'
Expounding next the sense. 'Why fixed the Lord
His eyes on them that listened? Friends, His eyes
Go down through all things, searching out the heart;
He sees if heart be sound to hold His Word
And bring forth fruit in season, or as rock
Naked to bird that plucks the random seed.
Friends, with the heart alone we understand;
Who doth His will shall of the doctrine know
If His it be indeed. When Jesus speaks
Fix first your eyes upon His eyes divine
There reading what He sees within your heart:
If sin He sees, repent!'
      With hands upheld
A woman raised her voice, and cried aloud,
'Could we but look into the eyes of Christ

Nought should we see but love!' And Bede replied:
'From babe and suckling God shall perfect praise!
Yea, from His eyes looks forth the Eternal Love,
Though oft through sin of ours in sadness veiled:
But when He rests them on disciples true
Not on the stranger, love is love alone!
O great, true hearts that love so well your Lord!
That heard so trustingly His tidings good
So long, by trial proved, have kept His Faith,
To you He cometh—cometh with reward
In heaven, and here on earth.'
       With brightening face
As one who flingeth largess far abroad,
Once more he raised the sacred tome, and read
Read loud the Eight Beatitudes of Christ;
Then ceased, but later spake: 'In ampler phrase
Those Blessings ye shall hear once more rehearsed
And deeplier understand them. Blessed they
The poor in spirit; for to humble hearts
Belongs the kingdom of their God in heaven;
Blessed the meek—nor gold they boast nor power
Yet theirs alone the sweetness of this earth;
Blessed are they who mourn, for on their hearts
The consolation of their God shall fall;
Blessed are they who hunger and who thirst
For righteousness; they shall be satisfied;
Blessed the merciful, for unto them
The God of mercy mercy shall accord;
Blessed are they, the pure in heart; their eyes
Shall see their God: Blessed the peacemakers;
This title man shall give them—Sons of God;
Blessed are they who suffer for the cause
Righteous and just: a throne is theirs on high:
Blessed are ye when sinners cast you forth,

And brand your name with falsehood for my sake;
Rejoice, for great is your reward in heaven.'

Once more the venerable man made pause,
Giving his Master's Blessings time to sink
Through hearts of those who heard. Anon with speech
Though fervent, grave, he shewed the glory and grace
Of those majestic Virtues crowned by Christ
While virtues praised by worldlings passed unnamed;
How wondrously consentient each with each
Like flowers well matched or music notes well joined:
Then changed the man to deeper theme; he shewed
How these high virtues, ere to man consigned,
Were warmed and moulded in the God-Man's heart;
Thence born, and in its sacred blood baptized.
'What are these virtues but the life of Christ?
The poor in spirit; must not they be lowly
Whose God is One that stooped to wear our flesh?
The meek; was He not meek Whom sinners mocked?
The mourners; sent not He the Comforter?
Zeal for the good; was He not militant?
The merciful; He came to bring us mercy;
The pure in heart; was He not virgin-born?
Peacemakers; is not He the Prince of Peace?
Sufferers for God; He suffered first for man.
O Virtues blest by Christ, high Doctrines ye!
Dread Mysteries; royal records; standards red
Wrapped by the warrior King His warfare past,
Around His soldiers' bosoms! Recognise,
O man, that majesty in lowness hid!
Put on Christ's garments. Fools shall call them
    rags—
Heed not their scoff! A prince's child is Man,
Born in the purple; but his royal robes

None other are than those the Saviour dyed,
Treading His Passion's wine-press all alone :
Of such alone be proud!'
      The old man paused ;
Then stretched his arms abroad, and said : 'This day
Like eight great angels making way from Heaven
Each following each, those Eight Beatitudes,
Missioned to earth by Him Who made the earth
Have sought you out! What welcome shall be theirs?'
In silence long he stood ; in silence watched,
With faded cheek now flushed and widening eyes,
The advance of those high tidings. As a man
Who, when the sluice is cut, with beaming gaze
Pursues the on-rolling flood from fall to fall,
Green branch adown it swept, and showery spray
Silvering the berried copse, so followed Bede
The progress of those high Beatitudes
Brightening, with visible beams of faith and love,
That host in ampler circles, speechless some
And some in passionate converse. Saddest brows
Most quickly caught, that hour, the glory-touch,
Reflected it the best.
    In such discourse
Peaceful and glad the hours went by, though Bede
Had sought that valley less to preach the Word
Than see once more his children. Evening nigh
He shared their feast ; and heard with joy like theirs
Their village harp ; and smote that harp himself.
In turn become their scholar, hour by hour
Forth dragged he records of their chiefs and kings,
Untangling ravelled evidence, and still
Tracking traditions upwards to their source,
Like him, that Halicarnassean sage,
Of antique history sire. 'I trust, my friends,

To leave your sons, for lore by you bestowed
Fair recompense, large measure well pressed down,
Recording still God's kingdom in this land
History which all may read, and gentle hearts
Loving, may grow in grace.   Long centuries passed
If wealth should make this nation's heart too fat
And things of earth obscure the things of heaven
Haply such chronicle may prompt high hearts
Wearied with shining nothings, back to cast
Remorseful gaze through mists of time, and note
That rock whence they were hewn.   From youth to age
Inmate of yonder convent on the Tyne,
I question every pilgrim, priest, or prince,
Or peasant grey, and glean from each his sheaf:
Likewise the Bishops here and Abbots there
Still send me deed of gift, or chronicle
Or missive from the Apostolic See:
Praise be to God Who fitteth for his place
Not only high but mean!   With wisdom's strength
He filled our mitred Wilfred, born to rule;
To saintly Cuthbert gave the spirit of prayer;
On me, as one late born, He lays a charge
Slender, yet helpful still.'
       Then spake a man
Burly and big, that last at banquet sat,
'Father, is history true?' and Bede replied;
'The man who seeks for Truth like hidden gold,
And shrinks from falsehood as a leper's touch
Shall write true history; not the truth unmixed
With fancies, base or high; not truth entire;
Yet truth beneficent to man below.
One Book there is that errs not: ye this day
Have learned therefrom your Lord's Beatitudes:
That book contains its histories—like them none

Since written none from standing point so high,
With insight so inspired, such measure just
Of good and ill; high fruit of aid divine.
The slothful spurn that Book; the erroneous warp:
But they who read its page, or hear it read
Their guide God's Spirit, and the Church of God
Shall hear the voice of Truth for ever nigh,
Shall see the Truth, now sunlike, and anon
Like dagger-point of light from dewy grass
Flashed up, a word that yet confutes a life,
Pierces, perchance a nation's heart: shall see
Far more—the Truth Himself in human form
Walking not farms and fields of Eastern lands
Alone, but these our English fields and farms;
Shall see Him on the dusky mount at prayer;
Shall see Him in the street and by the bier;
Shall see Him at the feast, and at the grave;
Now from the boat discoursing, and anon
Staying the storm, or walking on its waves;
Thus shall our land become a holy land
And holy those who tread her!' Lifting then
Heavenward that tome, he said, 'The Book of God!
As stands God's Church, 'mid kingdoms of this world
Holy alone, so stands, 'mid books, this Book!
Within the "Upper Chamber" once that Church
Lived in small space; to-day she fills the world:
This Book which seems so narrow is a world:
It is an Eden of mankind restored;
It is a heavenly City lit with God:
From it the Spirit and the Bride say "Come:"
Blessed who reads this Book!'
       Above the woods
Meantime the stars shone forth; and came that hour
When to the wanderer and the toiling man

Repose is sweet. Upon a leaf-strewn bed
The venerable man slept well that night:
Next morning young and old pursued his steps
As southward he departed. From a hill
O'er-looking far that sea-like forest tract
And many a church far-kenned through smokeless air,
He blessed that kneeling concourse, adding thus
'Pray still, O friends, for me, since spiritual foes
Threat most the priesthood:—pray that holy death,
Due warning given, may close a life too blest!
Pray well, since I for you have laboured well,
Yea, and will labour till my latest sigh;
Not only seeking you in wilds and woods
Year after year, but in my cell at night
Changing to accents of your native tongue
God's Book Divine. Farewell, my friends, farewell!'
He left them; in his heart this thought, 'How like
The great death-parting every parting seems!'
But deathless hopes were with him, and the May;
His grief went by.
     So passed a day of Bede's;
And many a studious year were stored with such;
Enough but one for sample. Two glad weeks
He and his comrade onward roved. At eve
Convent or hamlet, known long since and loved,
Gladly received them. Bede with heart as glad
Renewed with them the memory of old times,
Recounted benefits by him received
Then strong in youth, from just men passed away,
And preached his Master still with power so sweet
The listeners ne'er forgat him. Evermore,
Parting, he planted in the ground a cross,
And bade the neighbours till their church was built
Round it to pray. Meanwhile his youthful mate

Changed by degrees. The ever varying scene
The biting breath and balmy breast of spring
And most of all that old man's valiant heart
Triumphed above his sadness, fancies gay
Pushing beyond it like those sunnier shoots
That gild the dark vest of the vernal pine.
He took account of all things as they passed;
He laughed; he told his tale. With quiet joy
His friend remarked that change. The second week
They passed to Durham; next to Walsingham;
To Gilling then; to stately Richmond soon
High throned above her Ouse; to Ripon last:
Then Bede made pause, and spake; 'Not far is York;
Egbert who fills Paulinus' saintly seat
Would see me gladly: such was mine intent,
But something in my bosom whispers, "Nay,
Return to that fair river crossed by night,
The Tees, the fairest in this Northern land:
Beside its restless wave thine eye shall rest
On vision lovelier far and more benign
Than all it yet hath seen."' Northward once more
They faced, and, three days travelling, reached at eve
Again those ivied cliffs that guard the Tees:
There as they stood a homeward dove, with flight
Softer for contrast with that turbulent stream,
Sailed through the crimson eve. 'No sight like that!'
Thus murmured Bede; 'ever to me it seems
A Christian soul returning to its rest.'
A shade came o'er his countenance as he mused;
Algar remarked that shade, though what it meant
He knew not yet. The old man from that hour
Seemed mirthful less, less buoyant, beaming less,
Yet not less glad.
   At dead of night, while hung

The sacred stars upon their course half way,
He left his couch, and thus to Egbert wrote,
Meek man —too meek—the brother of the king,
With brow low bent, and onward sweeping hand,
Great words, world-famed: 'Remember thine account!
The Lord's Apostles are the salt of earth;
Let salt not lose its savour! Flail and fan
Are given thee. Purge thou well thy threshing floor!
Repel the tyrant; hurl the hireling forth;
That so from thy true priests true hearts may learn
True faith, true love, and nothing but the truth!'

Before the lark he rose the morrow morn,
And stood by Algar's bed, and spake: 'Arise!
Playtime is past; the great, good work returns;
To Jarrow speed we!' Homeward, day by day,
Thenceforth they sped with foot that lagged no more,
That youth, at first so mournful, joyous now,
That old man oft in thought. Next day, while eve
Descended dim, and clung to Hexham's groves,
He passed its abbey, silent. Wonder-struck
Algar demanded, 'Father, pass you thus
That church where holy John * ordained you priest?
Pass you its Bishop, Acca, long your friend?
Yearly he woos your visit; tells you tales
Of Hexham's saintly Wilfred; shows you still
Chalice or cross new-won from distant shores:
Nor these alone:—glancing from such last year
A page he read you of some Pagan bard
With smiles; yet ended with a sigh, and said:
"Where is he now?"' The man of God replied:
'Desire was mine to see mine ancient friend;
For that cause came I hither:—time runs short':—

* St. John of Beverley.

Then, Algar sighing, thus he added mild,
'Let go that theme; thy mourning time is past:
Thy gladsome time is now.' As on they walked,
Later he spake: 'It may be I was wrong;
Old friends should part in hope.'
        On Jarrow's towers,
Bright as that sunrise while that pair went forth
The sunset glittered when, their wanderings past,
Bede and his comrade by the bank of Tyne
Once more approached the gates. Six hundred monks
Flocked forth to meet them. 'They had grieved, I
 know,'
Thus spake, low-voiced, the venerable man,
'If I had died remote. To spare that grief
Before the time intended I returned.'
Sadly that comrade looked upon his face,
Yet saw there nought of sadness. Silent each
Advanced they till they met that cowlèd host:
But three weeks later on his bed the boy
Remembered well those words.
        Within a cell
To Algar's near that later night a youth
Wrote thus to one far off, his earliest friend:
'O blessed man! was e'er a death so sweet!
He sang that verse, "A dreadful thing it is
To fall into the hands of God, All-Just;"
Yet awe in him seemed swallowed up by love;
And ofttimes with the Prophets and the Psalms
He mixed glad minstrelsies of English speech,
Songs to his childhood dear!
        'O blessed man!
The Ascension Feast of Christ our Lord drew nigh;
He watched that splendour's advent; sang its hymn:
"All-glorious King, Who, triumphing this day,

Into the heaven of heavens didst make ascent,
Forsake us not, poor orphans! Send Thy Spirit,
The Spirit of Truth, the Father's promised Gift,
To comfort us, His children : Hallelujah."
And when he reached that word, "Forsake us not,"
He wept—not tears of grief. With him we wept;
Alternate wept; alternate read our rite;
Yea, while we wept we read. So passed that day,
The sufferer thanking God with labouring breath,
"God scourges still the son whom He receives."

'Undaunted, unamazed, daily he wrought
His daily task; instruction daily gave
To us his scholars round him ranged, and said,
"I will not have my pupils learn a lie,
Nor, fruitless, toil therein when I am gone."
Full well he kept an earlier promise, made
Ofttimes to humble folk, in English tongue
Rendering the Gospels of the Lord. On these,
The last of these, the Gospel of Saint John,
He laboured till the close. The days went by,
And still he toiled, and panted, and gave thanks
To God with hands uplifted; yea, in sleep
He made thanksgiving still. When Tuesday came
Suffering increased; he said, "My time is short;
How short it is I know not." Yet we deemed
He knew the time of his departure well.

'On Wednesday morn once more he bade us write:
We wrote till the third hour, and left him then
To pace, in reverence of that Feast all-blest,
Our cloister court with hymns. Meantime a youth,
Algar by name, there was who left him never;

The same that hour beside him sat and wrote:
More late he questioned: "Father well-beloved,
One chapter yet remaineth; have you strength
To dictate more?" He answered: "I have strength;
Make ready, son, thy pen, and swiftly write."
When noon had come he turned him round and
 said,
"I have some little gifts for those I love;
Call in the Brethren;" adding with a smile,
"The rich man makes bequests, and why not I?"
Then gifts he gave, incense or altar-cloth,
To each, commanding, "Pray ye for my soul;
Be strong in prayer and offering of the Mass,
For ye shall see my face no more on earth:
Blessed hath been my life; and time it is
That unto God God's creature should return;
Yea, I desire to die, and be with Christ."
Thus speaking, he rejoiced till evening's shades
Darkened around us. That disciple young
Once more addressed him, "Still one verse remains;"
The master answered, "Write, and write with speed;"
And dictated. The young man wrote; then said,
" 'Tis finished now." The man of God replied:
"Well say'st thou, son, ' 'tis finished.' In thy
 hands
Receive my head, and move it gently round,
For comfort great it is, and joy in death,
Thus, on this pavement of my little cell,
Facing that happy spot whereon so oft
In prayer I knelt, to sit once more in prayer,
Thanking my Father." "Glory," then he sang,
"To God, the Father, Son, and Holy Ghost;"
And with that latest Name upon his lips
Passed to the Heavenly Kingdom.'

                                    Thus with joy
Died holy Bede upon Ascension Day
In Jarrow Convent.   May he pray for us,
And all who read his annals of God's Church
In England housed, his great bequest to man!

NOTES.

Page 191. *The Irish Mission in England during the seventh century was one of the great things of history.*

The following expressions of Dr. von Döllinger respecting the Irish Church are more ardent than any I have ventured to use :—

'During the sixth and seventh centuries the Church of Ireland stood in the full beauty of its bloom. The spirit of the Gospel operated amongst the people with a vigorous and vivifying power: troops of holy men, from the highest to the lowest ranks of society, obeyed the counsel of Christ, and forsook all things that they might follow Him. There was not a country in the world, during this period, which could boast of pious foundations or of religious communities equal to those that adorned this far distant island. Among the Irish the doctrines of the Christian religion were preserved pure and entire ; the names of heresy or of schism were not known to them ; and in the Bishop of Rome they acknowledged and venerated the Supreme Head of the Church on earth, and continued with him, and through him with the whole Church, in a never interrupted communion. The schools in the Irish cloisters were at this time the most celebrated in the West . . . The strangers who visited the island, not only from the neighbouring shores of Britain, but also from the most remote nations of the Continent, received from the Irish people the most hospitable reception, a gratuitous entertainment, free instruction, and even the books that were necessary for the studies. . . . On the other hand, many holy and learned Irishmen left their own country to proclaim the Faith, to establish or to reform monasteries in distant lands, and thus to become the benefactors of almost every country in Europe . . . The foundation of many of the English Sees is due to Irishmen. . . . These holy men served God, and not the world ; they possessed neither gold nor silver, and all that they received from the rich passed through their hands into the hands of the poor. Kings and nobles visited them from time to time only to pray in their churches, or to listen to their sermons; and as long as they remained in the cloisters they were content with the humble food of the brethren. Wherever one of these ecclesiastics or monks came, he was received by all with joy; and whenever he was seen journeying across the country, the people streamed around him to implore his benediction, and to hearken to his words. The priests entered the villages only to preach or to administer the Sacraments: and so free were they from avarice, that it was only when compelled by the rich and noble that they would accept lands for the erection of monasteries.'

Page 196. *For both countries that early time was a period of wonderful spiritual greatness.*

I cannot deny myself the pleasure of quoting the following passage, illustrating the religious greatness both of the Irish and the English at the period referred to:

'The seventh and eighth centuries are the glory of the Anglo-Saxon Church, as the sixth and seventh are of the Irish. As the Irish missionaries travelled down through England, France, and Switzerland, to Lower Italy, and attempted Germany at the peril of their lives, converting the barbarian, restoring the lapsed, encouraging the desolate, collecting the scattered, and founding churches, schools, and monasteries as they went along; so amid the deep pagan woods of Germany, and round about, the English Benedictine plied his axe, and drove his plough, planted his rude dwelling, and raised his rustic altar upon the ruins of idolatry; and then, settling down as a colonist upon the soil, began to sing his chants and to copy his old volumes, and thus to lay the slow but sure foundations of the new civilisation. Distinct, nay antagonistic, in character and talents, the one nation and the other, Irish and English—the one more resembling the Greek, the other the Roman—open from the first perhaps to jealousies as well as rivalries, they consecrated their respective gifts to the Almighty Giver, and, labouring together for the same great end, they obliterated whatever there was of human infirmity in their mutual intercourse by the merit of their common achievements. Each by turn could claim pre-eminence in the contest of sanctity and learning. In the schools of science England has no name to rival Erigena in originality, or St. Virgil in freedom of thought; nor (among its canonised women) any saintly virgin to compare with St. Bridget; nor, although it has 150 saints in its calendar, can it pretend to equal that Irish multitude which the Book of Life alone is large enough to contain. Nor can Ireland, on the other hand, boast of a doctor such as St. Bede, or of an apostle equal to St. Boniface, or of a martyr like St. Thomas; or of so long a catalogue of royal devotees as that of the thirty male or female Saxons who, in the course of two centuries, resigned their crowns; or as the roll of twenty-three kings, and sixty queens and princes, who, between the seventh and the eleventh centuries, gained a place among the saints.'—Cardinal Newman, *Historic Sketches*, 'The Isles of the North,' pp. 128-9.

Page 215.

Instant each navy at the other dashed
Like wild beast, instinct-taught.

This image will be found in the description of a Scandinavian sea-fight in a remarkable book less known than it deserves to be, *The Invasion*, by Gerald Griffin, author of *The Collegians*.

The Saxons were, however, in early times as much pirates as the Danes were at a later.

Page 217. The achievement of Hastings had been rehearsed at a much earlier period by Harald.

Page 233. *At Ely, Elmham, and beside the Cam.*

In the reign of Sigebert, Felix, Bishop of East Anglia, founded schools respecting which Montalembert remarks: 'Plusieurs ont fait remonter à ces écoles monastiques l'origine de la célèbre université de Cambridge.'

Page 237. *How beautiful, O Sion, are thy courts!*

The following hymns are from the Office for the Consecration of a Church.

St. Fursey. Page 254.

How one with brow
Lordlier than man's, and visionary eyes.

'Whilst Sigebert still governed the kingdom there came out of Ireland a holy man named Fursey, renowned both for his words and actions, and remarkable for singular virtues, being desirous to live a stranger for Our Lord, wherever an opportunity should offer. . . . He built himself the monastery (Burghcastle in Suffolk) wherein he might with more freedom indulge his heavenly studies. There falling sick, as the book about his life informs us, he fell into a trance, and, quitting his body from the evening till the cockcrow, he was found worthy to behold the choirs of angels, and hear the praises which are sung in heaven. . . . He not only saw the greater joys of the Blessed, but also extraordinary combats of Evil Spirits.'—Bede, *Hist.*, book iii. cap. xix. 'C'était un moine irlandais nommé Fursey, de très-noble naissance et célèbre depuis sa jeunesse dans son pays par sa science et ses visions. . . . Dans la principale de ses visions Ampère et Ozanam se sont accordés à reconnaitre une des sources poétiques de la *Divine Comédie.*'—Montalembert, *Les Moines d'Occident*, tome iv. pp. 93-4.

Page 291. '*None loveth Song that loves not Light and Truth.*'

This is one of the poetic aphorisms of Cadoc, a Cambrian prince and saint, educated in the Irish monastery of Lismore, and afterwards the founder of the great Welsh monastery of Llancarvan, in which he gave religious instruction to the sons of the neighbouring princes and chiefs.

Page 294.
True life of man
Is life within.

This thought is taken from one of St. Teresa's beautiful works.

Page 310. *Ceadmon, the earliest bard of English song.*

'A part of one of Ceadmon's poems is preserved in King Alfred's Saxon version of Bede's *History.*' (Note to Bede's *Ecclesiastical History*, edited by Dr. Giles, p. 218.)

Page 340. *Who told him tales of Leinster Kings, his sires.*

'L'origine irlandaise de Cuthbert est affirmé sans réserve par Reeves dans ses *Notes sur Wattenbach*, p. 5. Lanigan (c. iii. p. 88) constate qu'Usher, Ware, Colgan, en ont eu la même opinion. . . . Beaucoup d'autres anciens auteurs irlandais et anglais en font un natif de l'Irlande.'—Montalembert, *Les Moines d'Occident*, tome ii. pp. 391-2.

Page 349. *The thrones are myriad, but the Enthroned is One.*

'Oft as Spring
Decks on thy sinuous banks her thousand thrones,
Seats of glad instinct, and love's carolling.'
Wordsworth (addressed to the river Greta).

Page 362. *Saint Frideswida, or the Foundations of Oxford.*

Saint Frideswida died in the same year as the Venerable Bede, viz. A.D. 735. Her story is related by Montalembert, *Les Moines d'Occident*, vol. v. pp. 298—302, with the following references, viz. Leland, *Collectanea*, ap. Dugdale, t. i. p. 173 ; cf. Bolland, t. viii. October, p. 535 à 568. I learn from a Catholic prayer-book published in 1720 that the Saint's Feast used to be kept on the 19th of October. Her remains, as is commonly believed, still exist in the Cathedral of Oxford.

Page 386. *Your teacher he: he taught you first your Runes.*

'The Icelandic chronicles point out Odin as the most persuasive of men. They tell us that nothing could resist the force of his words; that he sometimes enlivened his harangues with verses, which he composed extempore; and that he was not only a great poet, but that it was he who first taught the art of poesy to the Scandinavians. He was also the inventor of the Runic characters.'—*Northern Antiquities*, p. 83. Mallet asserts that it was to Christianity that the Scandinavians owed the practical use of those Runes which they had possessed for centuries:—'nor did they during so many years ever think of committing to writing those verses with which their memories were loaded; and it is probable that they only wrote down a small quantity of them at last. . . . Among the innumerable advantages which accrued to the Northern nations from the introduction of the Christian religion, that of teaching them to apply the knowledge of letters to useful purposes is not the least valuable. Nor could a motive less sacred have eradicated that habitual and barbarous prejudice which caused them to neglect so admirable a secret.'—P. 234. Mallet's statement respecting the Greek emigration of the Northern 'Barbarians' from the East is thus confirmed by Burke. 'There is an unquestioned tradition among the Northern nations of Europe importing that all that part of the world had suffered a great and general evolution by a migration from Asiatic Tartary of a people whom they call Asers. These everywhere expelled or subdued the ancient inhabitants of the Celtick or Cimbrick original. The leader of this Asiatic army was called Odin, or Wodin; first their general, afterwards their tutelar deity. . . . The Saxon nation believed themselves the descendants of those conquerors.'—Burke, *Abridgment of English History*, book ii. cap. i.

Page 395. *Like hunters chasing hart to sea-beat cliffs.*

This is recorded by Lingard and Burke.

Page 401. *Bede's Last May.*

This narrative of the death of Bede is closely taken from a letter written by Cuthbert, a pupil of his, then residing in Jarrow, to a fellow-pupil at a distance. An English version of that letter is prefixed to Dr. Giles's translation of Bede's *Ecclesiastical History*. (Henry G. Bohn.) The death of Bede took place on Wednesday, May 26, A.D. 735, being Ascension Day.

Page 405. *They hunger for your souls ; with reverent palms.*

'But in a mystical sense the disciples pass through the cornfields when the holy Doctors look with the care of a pious solicitude upon those whom they have initiated in the Faith, and who, it is implied, are hungering for the best of all things —the salvation of men. But to pluck the ears of corn means to snatch men away from the eager desire of earthly things. And to rub with the hands is, by examples of virtue, to put from the purity of their minds the concupiscence of the flesh, as men do husks. To eat the grains is when a man, cleansed from the filth of vice by the mouths of preachers, is incorporated amongst the members of the Church.'—Bede, quoted in the *Catena Aurea.—Commentary on St. Mark*, cap. ii. v. 23.

END OF VOL. IV.

www.ingramcontent.com/pod-product-compliance
Lightning Source LLC
Chambersburg PA
CBHW031954300426
44117CB00008B/753